an appreciation of r.a. lafferty

FEAST OF LAUGHTER
volume 2 / march 2015

JUST BECAUSE SOMETHING IS UNBEARABLE DOES NOT MAKE IT TRUE

Feast of Laughter: An Appreciation of R. A. Lafferty
Volume 2: March 2015

Published by the Ktistec Press

ISBN-13: 978-0692397466
ISBN-10: 0692397469

feastoflaughter.org

East of Laughter: An Appreciation of R. A. Lafferty on Facebook

The Toast

If you love R. A. Lafferty's wondrous and transpossible stories, you've come to that love by unmarked roads. You've made your own way into one of the densest and most crazily jigsawed mythworlds ever created—a body of work that nobody will ever see all the way into, and no two will ever see the same way. You've helped dig out a labyrinth, and it's a joyous thing, but the labyrinth is more than the digging. This volume is dedicated to the observation that the fog of obscurity is ever so slowly lifting from Lafferty's world, and every year it's a little easier to find your way in. It's dedicated to all the raw colts—the old ones and young—who are coming to these works for the first time.

> A matrix is the very opposite of a graveyard.
> *Arrive at Easterwine*

This volume is also dedicated to yon champions of Lafferty's literary heritage, the Locus Science Fiction Foundation, who we dearly love and will love even more after they decree the appearance of Lafferty stories at Ye Olde Feast of Laughter.

> *Can you hear us, folks at Locus?*
> *Can you bring us into focus?*
> *We have written often, sirs,*
> *even so with no answers.*

Introduction

How is this possible?

About five months ago, a group of Lafferty fans on Facebook decided to create a fanzine devoted to R. A. Lafferty. We put the first issue together in a month and published it on Amazon and free online. We had no idea what we were doing, yet out of the sheer devotion and ebullience of everyone involved, it grew into something magnificent.

Somewhere during that first hectic month we all agreed that this should be a twice-yearly production, published every year on Lafferty's birthday, November 7, and on the day he died, March 18.

This is the second Feast of Laughter, March 18, 2015. In the first issue, we threw everything in, holding nothing back to use for the second issue. Yet somehow, this issue is bigger, with more thoughtful writing, more professional writing, and more of just about everything from the first issue. It also strikes a better balance between new writing and unearthed and reprinted content.

This issue brings us an essay by Michael Swanwick and Howard Waldrop's attempt at writing a Lafferty story. It also brings us an exploration into international Lafferty fandom in the Netherlands, Japan, and Russia. "Nat!", the creator of the internet's first Lafferty site, The Lafferty Devotional Page, joins us for an interview. We also hear from two of Lafferty's former publishers, Greg Ketter of Corroboree Press and Dan Knight of United Mythologies Press. Tom Jackson gives us an interview with Lafferty himself. We have another amazing original cover by Lissanne Lake. We even have a newly uncovered photograph of Lafferty in his personal library gracing our cover, courtesy of Keith Purtell and the Oklahoma Science Fiction Writers. As with the first issue, all of this was given generously, joyfully, jubilantly in celebration of R. A. Lafferty. His writing inspires that.

And this is how it is all possible: many of us who wrote for the first Feast of Laughter wrote new pieces. Many other Lafferty fans, especially in the "East of Laughter" group on Facebook, reached out to contribute. Even more importantly, many people reached out to other fans, either to request new pieces or to ask permission to reprint a gem of Lafferty scholarship from ages past. You too can join this joyful chaos. Have you always loved Lafferty's writing and wanted a venue in which to talk about it? Do you know of some hidden gem of Lafferty commentary that needs to be brought back into the light? Have you personally known anyone who has written such gems—such as John J. Reilly, author of the great review of The Flame is Green, or the author of the review of Past Master that examines the history of the difference between Catholic and secular views of Utopia? Reach out to these writers and us at editor@feastoflaughter.org. Jump in with both feet and all ten fingers and share our enthusiasm for preserving Lafferty's place in the world of science fiction, American letters and literature in general.

> *Man, don't hang back! The crossing-over is always one of the shining things, and it never grows old. The crossing itself is worth almost everything. And then it's to arrive at the second greatest adventure of them all, and you don't even have to die to achieve it. There are one billion oysters that are yours for the opening, and every one of them is a world. Pick one!*
> R.A. Lafferty, "Company in the Wings"
> (*Heart of Stone, Dear and Other Stories*, 1983)

We plan to add a "Letters to the Editor" section in all future issues. Please contribute! Send your questions and comments to letters@feastoflaughter.org.

We may try to arrange future issues around specific themes, like Lafferty and the Mind of Man, God in SF and Literature, and Cosmogony. As with the first two issues, this will depend on the contributions we receive.

There is no specific theme for this issue, except Lafferty scholarship and appreciation. There is something in his writing that calls for scholarship and deep study. He works with ideas that force us to examine our history, our theology, our language, and our place in the universe. His stories seem to open the door into a new, bigger way of seeing the world, and he invites us in to look around. It is up to us to use our eyes, and more than just our eyes, to truly see what's inside. It's like the invitation by e e cummings:

> *listen: there's a hell*
> *of a good universe next door; let's go*

K.C. / 2015

Contents of the Table

Inventions Bright and New: Original Essays

All the People: International Fandom

Those Who Know Everything: Interviews

Oh, Whatta Ya Do When The Well Runs Dry: Reprinted Essays

You're On The Right Track, Kid: Reviews

The Emperor's Shoestrings: Works Inspired by R. A. Lafferty

Primary Education: Lafferties

Working With Ray:
My Experiences with R. A. Lafferty
By Greg Ketter

R. A. Lafferty is unquestionably one of the most unusual and recognizable voices in American fiction. He has generally been called a science fiction writer and published mostly in genre magazines and by genre publishers, but, in truth, he is nearly without category. He sometimes used the tropes and conventions of science fiction, he wrote stories with ghosts (not the type you would consider spooky as in regular supernatural fiction), he wrote fantasy but without fairies, elves or magic swords. He wrote tall tales of mighty people and mighty strange people at that.

I can't remember the first Lafferty story I read (as many others seem to be able) but when I first encountered Ray in person, I knew who he was and what types of stories he wrote. I had read many Roger Elwood and Damon Knight anthologies and it seemed that neither could possibly publish an anthology without presenting a Lafferty story.

At the 1976 World Science Fiction Convention in Kansas City, Missouri, the autograph session was held poolside of the Muehlebach Hotel. The writers all wore straw boaters to identify them as writers but, sadly, someone forgot to supply lighting. It was dark. You had to know what the person looked like you were looking for since there were no tables or name plates; authors and fans just wandered around a bit lost.

One pot-bellied old gentleman in a boater staggered through the crowd, weaving this way and that, smiling and mumbling, getting closer and closer to the edge of the pool. It seemed much of the crowd was watching to see if the old codger would indeed belly-flop into the pool in a drunken display of derring-do. I asked the nearest person who this man was and was told, "That is R. A. Lafferty." I didn't have any of his books with me for signing, but I did hurry over to him and took his arm. He looked at me with some gratitude, still smiling, and asked if I could lead him to his room. I was happy to oblige.

He shuffled along like Tim Conway in one of his old man comedy sketches and eventually we made it to the room number he had told me. At the time he was only in his 60s but he seemed much older to my own still-teenage gaze. His eyes were bloodshot and he reeked of alcohol, but that queer little lopsided smile never seemed to leave his face. I dropped him at his room with a raspy "Thank you, young man" and no other conversation. That was my introduction to a great writer who would one day become my friend.

The following spring I opened my own bookstore in St. Paul, Minnesota. I specialized in science fiction, fantasy, comics and anything else that interested me. I was barely 20 years old. The first few years were difficult: juggling college, the store, and another job to pay for the first two, and life in general. The store also moved around; I had not yet learned the adage "Location, Location, Location" and so kept trying to find the proper storefront. But because I was young and still too full of energy, two friends of mine and I decided to start a publishing company, Corroboree Press. We all agreed that R. A. Lafferty was the author we most wanted to see published.

At this time, Ray was publishing stories in many of the magazines and anthologies but little to nothing in the form of novels or collections was available. Little did we know as we started working with Ray and his agent, Virginia Kidd, that there was soon to be quite an explosion of works specifically devoted to Ray.

Corroboree published *Golden Gate and Other Stories*, which was sort of a favorites collection. Ira M. (Mitch) Thornhill, Rhip Thornhill, and I read dozens of previously published stories as well as unpublished manuscripts before choosing 16 stories, 6 which were original to the collection. We printed 1000 copies in a signed, numbered hardcover edition. We hand-tipped in four color plates and included several B&W plates by various artists. It was quite an elegant production.

While we worked on the collection, we felt a few of the stories needed some changes. I cannot recall specific story change requests but I myself felt awkward asking an established professional writer like Ray to change anything since we were so new to the game. I do remember at one point Ray telling me we could change anything we wanted. I assured him that would never happen; I couldn't imagine re-writing or changing anything myself. It was hard enough asking him to do so.

Around about the same time we published our first book, several other Lafferty books and chapbook/pamphlets appeared. First there was the original novel *Aurelia* from Donning Publishers, illustrated by underground artist Larry Todd. It was not one of Donning's better-selling titles. Shortly after, Chris Drumm started up his chapbook series with *Four Stories* and followed that with *Heart of Stone, Dear*, then *Laughing Kelly* and a number of others. Drumm produced story collections, poetry and autobiography in small booklets of very limited numbers.

Our first collection went well enough, so we decided on a second. This time a themed collection, *Through Elegant Eyes: Stories of Austro and the Men Who Know Everything*, came into being. Fifteen stories, only one of which was original to the collection, chronicled the adventures of Austro the Australopithecus Man, Barnaby Sheen, Chris Benedetti, Harry O'Donovan, and others. This collection was illustrated by comic book artist Joe Staton.

We followed this with the previously unpublished novel *Half a Sky*, the second of the "Coscuin Chronicles" series. *The Flame is Green*, first of the series, had been published by Walker in 1971; we republished it AFTER publishing the second. *Sardinian Summer* and *First and Last Island*, the rest of the series, have yet to see print. Ray gave me his original manuscripts for these two novels and told me to do with them as I pleased. Because these two books (250 signed and numbered copies, 500 trade copies) sold only moderately well, we did not immediately publish the other two in the series. Someday, perhaps.

Corroboree published two more books, Philip K. Dick's *Ubik: The Screenplay* and Kate and Richard Wilhelm's *The Hills are Dancing,* and then became moribund. Somewhere during this time I went to Tulsa to visit with Ray and spend a little time with him. It was an education, at once exciting and also frustrating. Ray was a very difficult person to talk with; at conventions he was usually drunk and mostly incoherent.

At home, where he did not drink, he was quiet and determinedly busy. When he did speak, it was still mostly unintelligible, partly from his raspy croak of a voice and partly due to his habit of muttering obscure non sequiturs. At least they were non sequiturs to me; I always had the impression that Ray lived in another reality than we mortals and his comments and jokes were brilliant bon mots that I just didn't understand. I wish I could have visited Ray's reality for a while.

After Corroboree stopped publishing and Chris Drumm slowed down, other small presses stepped up and offered more of Ray's obscure and/or unpublished works: Morrigan from the UK and United Mythologies from Canada. Broken Mirrors Press published a couple of books and Fairwood Press did one. Each brought out significant works but still in limited quantities that seemed to more than fulfill market desires.

Other than a few more convention meetings throughout the 80s, I had one more publishing contact with Ray at the 1991 World Science Fiction Convention in Chicago. I was just starting to publish under my own banner, DreamHaven Books, and had agreed to do a book edited by Stephen Jones and Neil Gaiman. It was a poetry anthology called *Now We Are Sick: An Anthology of Nasty Verse*. We had settled on doing a trade edition along with a signed limited edition of 250 copies. We would have all of the contributors sign the pages to be bound into the finished book. I decided to start the first page with Ray.

We met at the bar of the Hyatt Hotel. Ray had a significant head start in the drinking department. I sat with him, feeding him page after page as he signed; Ray would occasionally fall asleep in the middle of a signature. After a minute or three, he would jolt awake and begin signing all over again, spoiling the page he had already signed with part of his name. I had lots of extra copies of the page printed for just this reason. I was very thankful that Gene Wolfe came by to talk to Ray while he signed. He was far better able to keep Ray on track than I had been and I eventually got the number of plates I needed.

I never saw Ray after that but I would hear from him sporadically. He would send a short note or a box with some papers or manuscripts. He said he really wasn't writing anything new and his appearances in magazines and anthologies slowed quite a bit. You had to approach his agent, Virginia Kidd, if you wanted to publish anything; she and her agency were not terribly active in selling Ray's work. I don't think I heard from Ray the last five years or so of his life.

I'm very happy to see a bit of a revival of his work. Since the Locus Foundation bought the estate[1], and so many authors are championing his work (Neil Gaiman, Gene Wolfe, Michael Swanwick, Harlan Ellison) Ray's legacy is secure for a while longer. His unique voice and vision should continue to find a loyal audience who like to laugh loud and often, be amazed and amused, and appreciate a storyteller who never fails his readers.

This work is © 2015 Greg Ketter.

Greg Ketter's independent Minneapolis publisher and bookstore DreamHaven Books specializes in new and used science fiction, fantasy, horror, film and media books, comics and graphic novels at http://dreamhavenbooks.com.

---

1 This was something Neil Gaiman and I pursued shortly after Ray's death. I have to admit I didn't try very hard, since it seemed that the estate was nearly hopelessly entangled with distant relatives, but I was very happy to see Locus do the deed and attempt to bring Lafferty to the attention of a new generation.

Ray's Recycling Rewards Program:
Lafferty's Junkyard Poetic
By John Owen

But his destruction is also always in the context of carnivalized creation—whether as writer, bard, or pseudo-ursine, he dismembers so that we may all re-member.

Andrew Ferguson

When and where others won't let go and let die, Lafferty slaughters stories joyously. But the old is not abandoned; it is always the raw material of the new. A story's life, *followed importantly by its necessary death*, is the precondition for the new. Without death, there can be no new life.

In his excellent dissertation *Lafferty and His World*, Andrew Ferguson ably demonstrates Lafferty's literary habit of "carnivalized creation." Ferguson achieves this through a close reading of the short story "Snuffles" followed by an examination of *Space Chantey*'s Laestrygonian feasting and fighting. Rightly focusing on the gleeful death and destruction in these tales, Ferguson adds the necessary qualification that all of this death and destruction is *so that* new creation can be had.

Ferguson quotes Bakhtin: "Death, the dead body, blood as a seed buried in the earth, rising for another life—this is one of the oldest and most widespread themes."

There is nothing new under the sun.

Blood. Seed. Stories. All is recycled.

Truly, truly, I say to you, unless a grain of wheat falls into the earth and dies, it remains alone; but if it dies, it bears much fruit.

John 12:24

One prominent failure of the present moment is our insistence on extending copyright indefinitely. Since Mickey Mouse isn't allowed to die, we are stuck with one sad recurring mouse. What we need is this icon dead and buried so that a plague of happy mice might rise up in his tired place. We need this kind of plague!! This sort of proliferation of new stories could only be the result of a culture that is free to do what it wants with any and all of its dead stories. This is the model that Lafferty gives us. Lafferty was such a free man, the product of a free culture. Classically educated in a Catholic context, Lafferty was the product of the Western Tradition that he saw lying dead all around him. What other response than resurrection? The dead forms and characters were raised to new life, new stories.

Lafferty recycled the dead stories and dormant characters of others throughout his oeuvre. How was he able to do this? He had a deeper knowledge of the vast field of stories than our shriveled pop sensibilities allow for. The old worked very well. It had died often.

This plundering of the past is not unique to Lafferty. Many of the characters and settings that Lafferty uses have also been filtered through pop culture. Have you never seen Popeye fight Ali Baba's Forty Thieves? What about Mickey acting out Twain or Dickens? The best of these were and are new and vital. The worst examples were little more than the walking dead refusing to die. At their best, these proven stories have died and borne fruit many times over in high and low places. Lafferty, a lifelong walker, walked the length and breadth of this great field of stories many times over; in the end, he proved himself a master harvester.

This harvesting of the Western Canon is present in the short stories (and often, in the stories there is an explicit interaction with 20th century sf, the inheritor of the Classic Story). This harvesting and sowing new seed is most obviously present in his novels.

Past Master is political thriller, utopia, Renaissance farce/morality tale. *Space Chantey* is *Odyssey* and space opera. *Reefs of Earth* contains Twain-like boyish Americana, tall tale, and alien invasion. *The Devil is Dead* is sailor story, Irish bender, and Neanderthal race relations. *Sindbad* is *The Arabian Nights*, pawn shop electronics, and spy thriller. *Fourth Mansions* is secret societies, conspiracy theories, Campbellian psionics, and Saint Teresa. Those are examples from the novels I've read.

From the rest of the novels, I see a potential vision of Argonautics, Thomism, Realism, Autobiography, Historical Survey, Fairy Tale, and quite possibly an indecent amount of Swashbuckling. Heck, who am I kidding? Most of those things are already in the books previously mentioned. It's all there. The entire junkyard of civilization is Lafferty's playground.

Lafferty was running one of the largest wholesale recycling rewards programs that this world has seen so far. The man understood how to turn trash into treasure. He admitted that despite all appearances, despite the End of the World that had recently happened, a Golden Age had already begun and was continuing. This Golden Age is not in spite of all of the trash of a dead culture; it is precisely because of it. The dead stories of the past were being taken up and recycled, retold and killed and born again, faster than ever before.

> *But where had all the gold come from? And where had the charged atmospheres and the tension-balances of the arty meteorologies and lightnings come from? Oh, the gold had been transmuted from trash… From splendid trash.*
>
> *It's nostalgic trash, all the better part of it. That's one test of the quality of trash: that it be remembered with affection, and that it be remembered as better than it really was.*
>
> *It has been said that our present age will not be remembered since that would be no more than a nostalgia for a nostalgia, since ours is a backward-looking age with no quality of its own. But that isn't the case of it at all. Nostalgia is the remembering of one's depth, and the real transmuting-nostalgia is one of the most amazing of all chemical or alchemical actions. And it is in no way new, or unique to our own age.*
>
> *There must have been a lot of layers of transmuting-nostalgia in Homer: the camp-fire and palace-fire smoke of many retellings and reworkings of the material. There must have been the remembering of it as better than it was, and then the making of it better than it was. There must be a lot of layers of trans-*

> *muting-nostalgia in anything that comes through canny and*
> *clear. These layers are the living roots, and the bedamned and*
> *bedazzled arts and styles and lives and sciences will not grow out*
> *of anything else.*
>
> R. A. Lafferty, "Notes from the Golden Age" (unpublished)

Relating this back to science fiction and Ferguson's discussion of how Lafferty transforms his sf material and context, I'd like to mention Sturgeon's Law: "90% of everything is crud." Of course it is. Finally, we can think of this as a positive law. The 90% of "fecundating manure" (to steal a wonderful phrase from Lafferty's essay) is the necessary fertilizer that produces a rich harvest.

Lafferty again: "There were more than a hundred years of pulp novels and pulp magazines in a wide spectrum. Who remembers *St. Nicholas Magazine*? Who remembers *Black Mask Magazine*? Who remembers Oliver Optic? Or Oliver Onions? The transmuting nostalgia remembers them."

> *This process of dismemberment and re-creation, destroying the*
> *old to make possible the new, is central to the grotesque mode*
> *of perception, and it recurs throughout Lafferty's corpus as he*
> *continually chews together pieces to create new things. Time and*
> *again, Lafferty carnivalizes and dismembers whole subgenres of*
> *sf to provide fodder for his reconstruction of artistic and ideo-*
> *logical perceptions.*
>
> Andrew Ferguson, "Lafferty and His World"

Yes to this! And not *only* whole subgenres of sf! As I attempted to illustrate above, Lafferty "carnivalizes and dismembers" the entire Western Canon! Science Fiction is exhausted. The Modern Novel is exhausted. Yes and yes. Also, Doggerel is exhausted. The Trickster Tale is exhausted. Adventure is exhausted. It is all exhausted. But there is also nothing new under the sun. We receive the happy junkyard playground, all of this splendid trash, and we must make good of it.

But, wait. Maybe there is one astonishing *new* thing.

There is small hope in maybe one other kind of story, rarely tried but once achieved.

In his essay "The Shape of the S. F. Story," Lafferty examines Aristotle's reasonable assertion that "A whole is what has a beginning and middle and end." Lafferty writes that "The three parts, for a long while, held good for all stories except one." The essay continues with some good-natured jabs at the New Wave and concludes with reserved admiration for the classic "almost perfect" classical shape, of which there "has always been much that is strong and noble." Almost as an aside, though, before concluding, Lafferty returns to that mention of the one story that is the exception, the "one story that didn't accept the killing as the final end, that maintained (with compassionate irony) that death may only be an interlude or anticlimax; this was the story of which we were permitted to hear the part that comes after the end. But this story hasn't been of strong literary influence."

Lafferty's stories often have that strong "almost perfect" classical shape. Just as often, though, the endings don't quite seem to work. They shift and shake and somehow point beyond themselves toward further stories. These non-endings can leave a reader unsettled and maybe even disappointed at a lack of expected resolution. This is intentional. Lafferty's endings are often so "weak" because his entire work of intertextuality is precisely one valiant attempt at a literary approximation of an endless story, one that could move forward because it was dying to itself in each one of its iterations. This attempt at an endless story is most certainly grounded in that one story that is the exception. May its literary influence continue to grow. We who have been permitted to hear the part that comes *after* the end can no longer tolerate endings. They are not fitting for our story. The death or ending of any person, place, or thing united to this one exceptional story is no longer final, only an interlude or anticlimax on the way to the next greater story. Death has no sting, endings no final reality.

Or, as Lafferty put it:

Destroyed? His road is run? It's but a bend of it;
Make no mistake, this only seems
the end of it.

This work is © 2015 John Owen.

John Owen comes home each evening to the golden cliché: the u.n.d; the p.h.; and l. and u.w.; and the s.c. (seven more would have been too many). Just to live is a happy riot. He is well known in the future for having barely succeeded in establishing the Northeast Lafferty League, which has grown to cover the Northeast quadrant of this galaxy. On all of the planets, his name has become a byword for any grand success achieved based on wild enthusiasm coupled with poor planning and lack of any applicable skill set. John blogs infrequently about R. A. Lafferty: failingevenbetter.blogspot.com.

Valery's Really Eyes and the Parade of Creatures;
Or, Lafferty's Animal Fair Comes to Town;
Or, You Are a Pig Made Out of Sticks
By Daniel Otto Jack Petersen

Mostly the animals understand their roles, but man, by compar-
ison, seems troubled by a message that, it is often said, he cannot
quite remember, or has gotten wrong.
　　　　　　　　　　　Loren Eiseley, *The Unexpected Universe*

An anarchist of shaggy trees,
A great red gleam that flies,
A rearing buck, a rampant breeze,
A girl with really eyes.

　　　　　　　　　　　　　　　　　　　　Eco-Log

These epigraphs begin Lafferty's short story "Animal Fair" (1974), a
cautionary tale about the biotic community and our ways of seeing
the world. They serve well to introduce the present shaggy essay
on the same themes right across Lafferty's fiction. (I haven't the
requisite "really" or "valid" eyes myself, but I hope to show you that
Lafferty does at least.)

In my previous essay I surveyed Lafferty's habit of turning his
narrational gaze onto the environment of non-human objects in
which we are all embedded, especially as exemplified in his recurring motif of making long, erudite lists of fauna, flora, and manu-
factured objects.[1] Here I want to narrow that study into sampling
Lafferty's portrayal of animals in particular. I could almost as easily
have chosen geological formations, meteorological phenomena, flo-

---

1 See Petersen, Daniel Otto Jack, November 2014. "The Epic of Man and His
Friends; or, Slumming It With the Ontic Outcasts; or, May Our Eyes Be Big Enough
To Take In the Nine Hundred Percent Gain in Everything!" *Feast of Laughter* Issue 1
(Ktistec Press), pp. 67-100.

ra (the guy loved to make lists of types of grass!), or equipment. But Lafferty perhaps does more with animals than any other aspect of the non-human environment. The present essay can, of course, only paw and snuffle at the surface of this deep and pervasive subject in Lafferty's fiction. I can only hope it helps open up the topic to a proliferation of further investigation, by others as well as myself.

ANIMALS RAMPANT WHERE THERE ARE NO ANIMALS

Animals are so frequently and almost casually woven into Lafferty's fiction that their presence might, ironically, go slightly unnoticed at first, especially if you have mainly only read his early collections of stories. Readers may only semi-consciously notice the recurring references to animals embedded in, say, the dialogue and descriptions. In the short story "Nine Hundred Grandmothers" (1966), for instance, Manbreaker Crag puts his aggressive economic mission in terms of butchering a farm animal:

> What we go out for every time, Ceran, is to cut a big fat hog in the rump—we make no secret of that. But if the hog's tail can be shown to have a cultural twist to it, that will solve a requirement.

At another point Manbreaker goes into a rage that is described as his "dying buffalo act" where he "stomped and pawed and went off bull-bellowing." This particular story contains the actual appearance of no animals, and yet our mind's eye has been made to see quite vividly a curly-tailed pig and a charging buffalo (and later, bees, when the tiniest grandmothers are described as being comparable in size). Furthermore, these lively animal evocations help achieve in swift strokes both plot and characterization. So they are like all good animal metaphors: they simultaneously put us in mind of the animals themselves and also enliven the storytelling.

Or take "Ginny Wrapped in the Sun" (1967), where the noise the titular little girl makes coming down the mountain is described as "broken roaring, rhinoceros runting!" At the end of the story it is "Hound-dog hooting! Hissing of badgers, and the clattering giggle of geese! Shag-tooth shouting, and the roaring of baby bulls!" Animals are also evoked when the girl first visually enters the scene: "she came to them with a movement that had something of the breathless grace of a gazelle and something of the scuttering of a little wild pig." There is both poetry and a sense of the naturalist's astute observation of animal behavior in this description. And again, the animals, though not physically present in the tale, are rather rambunctiously evoked to help sketch human characteristics. This is done by other writers, of course, but perhaps rarely as frequently and vivaciously as in Lafferty.

All such "zoomorphisms"[2] are monstrous, for they are forms of transmogrification or shape-shifting. The imagery hybridizes a human with another animal, sometimes more than one kind of animal as with the girl-gazelle-pig conflation above. But more on the monstrous below. Suffice it to say here that reading Lafferty can, at the very least, make us feel like Barnaby Sheen in "Animal Fair" when he says: "I seem to see animals where there cannot be any such animals. I get the impression of a Congress of Creatures or of an Animal Fair." Even in Lafferty's stories where there are no actual animals, the animal metaphors insist on connecting us to the rest of beastkind.

Such instances of a rather deep weave of animal evocation in dialogue and description could be multiplied almost *ad infinitum* from Lafferty's short stories, as well as from many a passage in the novels (perhaps most memorably the metaphorical/metaphysical snakes and toads and badgers and falcons in his 1969 novel *Fourth Mansions*). Lafferty's readers will likely also have noticed the animals featured in many of the rather totemic *titles* of his short stories: "Land of the Great Horses," "Frog on the Mountain," "Name of the Snake," "Hog-Belly Honey," "Rainbird," "Camels and Dromedaries, Clem," "About a Secret Crocodile," "Pig in a Pokey," and so on.[3] These stories are not about actual horses or frogs or snakes or hogs or camels or crocodiles, but about people and ideas that Lafferty memorably

---

2 A zoomorphism is basically the opposite of an anthropomorphism: where the latter projects human qualities onto the non-human, the former projects animal qualities onto the human.

3 "The Transcendent Tigers" was an editor's title in place of Lafferty's own title, "Needle," as was "Among the Hairy Earthmen" in place of Lafferty's "A Pride of Lions." It's an odd and interesting side note that animals were both added and subtracted in these editorial changes.

captures by invoking the names of these animals. Nevertheless, the more you read of Lafferty, the more this richly zoomorphic conceptual field also provokes you to remember that these actual animals exist in the world. Of course, Lafferty by no means only includes animals as metaphors for human characteristics as we'll see. Before we get to that, however, let's first try to understand a little more just why in the world animals are so pervasive in his fiction at all.

FAUNA-BUILDING

Lafferty is a very complete sort of thinker, so you'd expect to find that this animal inclusiveness fits into a grander scheme, and it does, in several ways. One way to understand it is to look at the world-constructive agenda in Lafferty's fiction.

Andrew Ferguson has recently argued that Lafferty is always world-building with his stories and calling on his readers (and fellow writers) to join him in doing so.[4] Ferguson notes that, in his Guest of Honor speech ("The Day After the World Ended") for the 1979 DeepSouthCon, Lafferty claimed that the cognitive world came to an end in the 20th century and, as a result, humans were now worldview-less Flatlanders (a term for two-dimensional people in Edwin A. Abbott's 19th century romance *Flatland*). Though now cut off from the worldviews of ages past by the "amnesiac fog" of modernism, Lafferty urged that modern/postmodern people may yet build a new fully-dimensioned world from the rubble of the old, turning this post-apocalypse from "The Day After the World Ended" into the "First Day On a New Planet." But, Ferguson explains, since mimetic realism is dead in an age where there is no real world to mimic (because we have no cognitive consensus by which to view it), Lafferty urged narrative world-creation as the constructive way forward. Ferguson points out that Lafferty's speech is resonant with Paul Ricoeur's concept of a "disclosure of possible worlds" through a "third dimension of language," the poetic.

Ferguson shows that in addition to frequently performing

---

4 Ferguson, Andrew, 2014. "R. A. Lafferty's Escape from Flatland; or, How to Build a World in Three Easy Steps," *Science Fiction Studies* 41, pp. 543-561.

comic-grotesque destructions of faulty models, which made way for this world-creation[5], Lafferty also intentionally held back from properly ending many of his stories in order to build into them a radical openness to Ricoeurian possible worlds. This habit of Lafferty's invited (indeed, self-reflexively *instructed*) the reader to collaborate with the texts in order to fulfill their function. In so doing, cooperative readers may help bring about a new world and, as Ricoeur put it, new ways of *being in* the world.

I think Ferguson's insightful analysis applies quite readily to Lafferty's frequent inclusion of animals in his fiction. After all, if you are going to create and populate a new or renewed, fully-dimensioned world, then ecology in general and fauna in particular would be a crucial element of that. Thus Lafferty's fiction is calling on us to participate with him in (re)populating our (re)new(ed) world with animals (that is, a revived consciousness of, and meaningful connection to, animals). But why should we need to do so? What has our modern amnesia cut us off from in humanity's past as regards animals?

RETURNING ANIMALS TO THE CENTER WITH US

In his essay "Why Look at Animals?" (1980)[6], John Berger observes that the modern world has marginalized animals by a variety of means and with a variety of effects. The 19th century started (and the 20th century completed) a process "by which every tradition which has previously mediated between man and nature was broken," he argues. This breakage includes, of course, our connection to animals.

> *Before this rupture, animals constituted the first circle of what surrounded man. Perhaps that already suggests too great a distance. They were with man at the center of his world (Berger: 12).*

Berger acknowledges that much of this pre-modern view of

---

5 Lafferty's short story "Snuffles" (1960) is the paradigmatic example.
6 Collected in Berger, John, 2009. *Why Look at Animals?* (London: Penguin Books).

animals was due to economic and productive concerns, but denies that it can be simply reduced to such pragmatic necessities. "Animals first entered the imagination as messengers and promises," Berger avers, citing the magical, oracular, and sacrificial functions of animals in human thought and practice, in addition to their usefulness for food and work (Berger: 12).

Today, each of us birthed into a world that has long since abandoned such "ways of seeing" (to borrow the title of Berger's popular 1972 BBC TV series and book), we are uneasy about animals in a number of ways. For example, at the zoo, wanting so desperately to connect with these captive animals but feeling vaguely as if we haven't, Berger thinks that our deepest underlying and unexpressed question is: "Why are these animals less than I believed?" (Berger: 33). The answer, he maintains, is that "*you are looking at something that has been rendered absolutely marginal*; and all the concentration you can muster will never be enough to centralize it" (Berger: 34, emphasis his). Indeed, we are visiting the grave of a loved one. The animals aren't dead, but our mutual connection is. "Modern zoos are an epitaph to a relationship which was as old as man" (Berger: 30). The irony, says Berger, is that the more the real animals in their real lives receded from us, the more we started to populate our world with caged and stuffed and animated and photographed animals. "Zoos, realistic animal toys and the widespread commercial diffusion of animal imagery, all began as animals started to be withdrawn from daily life" (Berger: 35). He argues, moreover, that these trends are not "compensatory" but rather help further marginalize real animals, ratifying and reifying our disconnection to them.

In light of Berger's account, Lafferty's frequent inclusion of animals in his fiction may be seen as his world-building way of returning animals to the center of life with humans. Lafferty does this in a manner, I would maintain, that avoids the pitfalls of zoos and toys and the like, mainly by rendering neither readers nor the animals as passive. Lafferty's ubiquitous animal metaphors, for example, begin to recover the magical and oracular function of animals as *messengers* to us. Lafferty's animals reveal us to ourselves as we sacrifice their diverse bestiality on the altar of our descriptive need to understand our own characteristics. (Again we approach the monstrous here in that the Latin root *monstrum* means a portent or revelation, which connects to the oracular role these animal metaphors play.) Berger notes that this "universal use of animal-signs for charting the experience of the world" is something now almost lost to us (Berger: 17). For pre-moderns, however, it was pervasive, and in a manner resonant with Lafferty's animal metaphors. "The examples are endless. Everywhere animals offered explanations, or, more precisely, lent their name or character to a quality, which like all qualities was, in its essence, mysterious" (Berger: 18). Looking at animals and weaving what we observe of them into our descriptions of the world, we find that animals help us plumb the mysteries of existence.

The seeming paradox is that if we thus consciously *use* animals, they thereby sit at the center of the world with us, and we even begin to appreciate and understand them for their own sakes. The metaphors get us *involved with* animals (even to the point of shape-shifting and hybridity, as I mentioned above). One cannot employ a beast metaphor as an astute picture of human behavior without first gazing long and sympathetically on animal behavior in order to know and make the comparison. Lafferty's readiness to slap an apt animal metaphor on a human characteristic, or a scene, or an idea, seems to exhibit just such a habitual gaze on animals at a deep and persistent level. Nor can one appreciate the metaphor so given unless one enters into some imaginative sympathy with the animal behavior evoked, in delight or horror or wonder or tenderness and so on. We get involved, we get our hands dirty (it is no coincidence that offhanded mention of animal feces recurs frequently in Lafferty's writing). So Lafferty's fiction seeks not merely another artificial setting (zoo) or simulacral companion (toy), but a move toward genuine recovery of animals themselves and our relation to them.

MORE THAN A BIT PART FOR THE BIOTA

As a student of English Literature I have encountered almost no attention to animals in literary criticism, save in the relatively recent theoretical movement called "ecocriticism."[7] The pioneering ecocritic Lawrence Buell notes that the history of literary criticism has tended, for example, to deprecate the likes of Thomas Hardy's evocation of Egdon heath as too "place-saturated" and instead praise Henry James' Paris where there is, as one critic put it, "the barest minimum of detail and the maximum of personal reflection on these details."[8] Introspection trumps extrospection for such critics (and novelists). Lafferty, of course, sees no need for the disjunction. Indeed, as I mentioned in my previous essay, for Lafferty our inner and outer ecologies illumine one another: looking outward to the faunascape can help us better understand the beasts inside our own humanity; and tending to those inner beasts helps us better relate to the ones outside of us in the environment. (*Fourth Mansions* and *Serpent's Egg* are two of Lafferty's novels dealing overtly with these themes in blatantly ecological, and especially faunal, motifs.)

Buell perceives in such literary trends the environmentally dismissive values of many modern writers as well as their critics: "In 'good' writing, then, it would seem that the biota has only a bit part" (Buell: 85). Lafferty's writing is nothing if not good (by accepted standards of style, depth, and so on). Yet he brings the biota back to the center by a number of strategies, providing the biota with far more than a bit part in his fiction.[9]

INTIMACY WITH AN ALIEN PRESENCE—DARK ECOLOGY

This animal metaphor facet of Lafferty's prose would alone be enough to furnish material for a book-length study of animals in his fiction. But there is far more! And far stranger. To explore this takes us into the territory of an aesthetic strategy that I call the "ecomonstrous."[10]

---

7 For a brief and helpful introduction to the field, see Garrard, Gregg, 2012. *Ecocriticism* (New York: Routledge).

8 Buell, Lawrence, 1995. *The Environmental Imagination: Thoreau, Nature Writing, and the Formation of American Culture* (Cambridge: Harvard University Press), p. 85.

9 It's an interesting side question whether genre fiction such as SF and fantasy fare any better in inclusion of biota than does "literary" or "mainstream" fiction.

10 The reader not overly interested in literary theory can probably skip the next two sections and still follow the discussion when I resume talking more directly

To flesh out this aesthetic I draw on the "dark ecology" of Timothy Morton[11]. Morton criticizes "ecomimesis," a "realistic" form of ecological writing that claims to be a direct and nearly unmediated representation of the environment. This "realism" is based on "correlationism," which Morton defines as "the belief that things can only exist in relation to (human) minds or language" and that as such correlationism is "anthropocentrism in philosophical form."[12] Morton argues that ecomimesis thus fails to come to grips with the true otherness of the non-human.

Morton's dark ecology counters ecomimesis with a recognition that the "dark interiors" of non-human objects are always receding from our perception and comprehension.[13] Every object withdraws into a secret "irreducible dark side" (the seemingly infinite ways in which it has not yet been encountered or unleashed.) The more we know about a thing, the more it withdraws into what we don't yet know about it. All objects thus relate, to us and (importantly) to each other, as a "mesh" of "strange strangers."

> Strange stranger *names an uncanny, radically unpredictable quality of life-forms. Life-forms recede into strangeness the more we think about them, and whenever they encounter one another—the strangeness is irreducible. Ecological philosophy that does not attend to this strangeness is not thinking coexistence deeply enough* (Morton 2011: 165).

We can only hope to provisionally meet such strange strangers, he argues, by means of grotesquely and apocalyptically exaggerated attention to detail (*ekphrasis*) and the evocation of a sense of

---

about Lafferty's work.

11 See, for example, Morton, Timothy, 2007. *Ecology Without Nature: Rethinking Environmental Aesthetics* (Cambridge: Harvard University Press).

12 Page 164 of Morton, Timothy, 2011. "Here Comes Everything: The Promise of Object-Oriented Ontology," *Qui Parle: Critical Humanities and Social Sciences* 19, pp. 163-190.

13 Morton is here drawing on Graham Harman's "Object-Oriented Ontology," which I briefly introduced in my previous essay; see *FoL* 1. Harman in turn is drawing on (his novel interpretation of) Heidegger's analysis of "tools" or "equipment." See, for example, Harman's "Speculative Realism" (2010).

"transport" or "getting high" (*hypsos*). These "unrealistic" (or rather, "speculatively realistic") aesthetic strategies weirdly and paradoxically put us into some measure of rapport with our environment, where we can hear, as Morton puts it, what oil spills and erratic weather patterns are "saying" to us. That is, through a recovery of the strangeness of our environment, we begin to have ears to hear it and eyes to see it. Environmental writing that exhibits this speculative realism performs an "antiecomimesis," says Morton, which *amplifies* the imaginative encounter with the environment. All of which can result in "intimacy with an alien presence" (the non-human).

ENCOUNTERS OF THE ECOMONSTROUS KIND

Morton's dark ecology resonates with the work of monster theorists such as Jeffrey Jerome Cohen and Timothy Beal, according to whom the monstrous is an uncanny evocation of categorial confusion: monsters are "harbingers of category crisis" who come to us in the shape of a "freakish compilation" of incompatible parts (Cohen). The uncanny (*unheimlich* or "unhomely") is that which threaten us from within our own home or house, conceived as widely as needed, even "the world ecology as 'house'" (Beal). All of this signals alterity, the Other, that which differs from us. We fear this Monstrous Other, yet it invokes our sense of wonder as well as our sense of dread, making it impossible to be entirely xenophobic. Monstrosity enthralls as well as appalls since it may evoke both the diabolical and the sublime. Monsters thus arouse not only a sense of malevolence and threat but also of beauty and desire. The monster, therefore, threatens to bring not only destruction and transgression, but also revelation and expansion of consciousness. It is, after all, the *monstrum*, the portent or omen.[14]

---

14 This précis of monster theory is drawn mainly from Cohen, Jeffrey Jerome, 1996. "Monster Culture (Seven Theses)" in *Monster Theory: Reading Culture* ed. by Jeffrey Jerome Cohen (Minneapolis: University of Minnesota Press), pp. 3-25; and from Beal, Timothy K., 2002. *Religion and Its Monsters* (New York: Routledge). A continuing study of Lafferty's work will eventually transform even our notions of monsters and the monstrous, but for now we will draw on some of these standard explications of monstrosity. In this regard, I hope to make one more entry in this series of essays next issue, completing a small trilogy: 1) Lafferty and Objects, 2) Lafferty

Combining insights from dark ecology and monster theory, we may grope toward an emerging theory of the *ecomonstrous*: it is a way of representing the environment that eschews mimetic, correlation-ist "realism" and instead embraces the (often comic) grotesquery of "category crisis" and alterity and apocalypse in its description of the non-human. It recognizes the non-human as irreducibly *non-human* at a profound level, acknowledging that the more we know of it, the more it recedes into its dark interior, into some side of it that we have not accessed. An ecomonstrous aesthetic thereby evokes a sense of the uncanny and the alien in order to provoke fresh and freakish encounters with ecology. These ecomonstrous encounters can both terrify and tantalize readers into radical humility about their own place in the ecosystem and yet renewed curiosity about the non-human world. The ecomonstrous paradox is that its por-trayal of the environment as alien can yet achieve some level of rap-port with that same environment.

As I mentioned above, I think Lafferty already moves into the ecomonstrous with his zoomorphisms for scenes and actions and ideas. His frequently recurring animal metaphors begin to create an uncanny atmosphere in which the movements and shapes and sounds and smells and so on of a wide variety of animals are contin-ually naming and revealing human behavior at the individual and corporate level.[15] Now we will look at how Lafferty employs the eco-monstrous in other ways.

The Turtles Have a Sound Basic Philosophy

One way Lafferty goes beyond mere animal metaphor is by glancing from time to time into an imagined animal consciousness (in his characteristically "tall story" manner, of course). For it's not only humans who speak by use of animal metaphors in Lafferty's fiction. Sometimes the animals themselves speak. John Berger notes that

---

and Animals, 3) Lafferty and Monsters.

15 For an example of Lafferty's corporate (in several senses) zoomorphisms recall the phrase "the Crocodile"s Mouth" and the line "somewhere the Secret Crocodile lashed its tail in displeasure," which describe a bureaucratic enclave that shapes mass media and popular opinion in "About a Secret Crocodile" (1970).

speaking with beasts was a recurring mythical motif in pre-modern thought, when animals still co-inhabited the center with humans.

> *Such an unspeaking companionship was felt to be so equal that often one finds the conviction that it was man who lacked the capacity to speak with animals—hence the stories and legends of exceptional beings, like Orpheus, who could talk with animals in their own language* (Berger: 15).

In Lafferty's "First Day On a New Planet," the animals sometimes speak again and we can understand them—to an extent.

Take, for example, his story "The Weirdest World" (1961). The narrator is an alien blob marooned on Earth who, like Orpheus, talks to birds and snakes (e.g. "My cell mate was a surly python named Pete," the blob remarks when placed in a cage with a snake) and describes humans as "walking grubs." The blob is eventually placed in a tank with turtles, of whom he makes this observation:

> *The turtles in the tank I was put into did have a sound basic philosophy which was absent in the walking grubs. But they were slow and lacking inner fire. They would not be obnoxious company, but neither would they give me excitement and warmth.*

This little psychological sketch of the turtles surprises and enchants the reader with the sense of an inner life for animals, one that in some ways is more "sound" than our own. Coming from Lafferty, this unfavorable comparison is probably theologically driven. We are meant to feel the irony that those of the biotic community who do not share our divinely implanted "inner fire" should yet have a sounder basic philosophy than us (our unsound state being due to our primordial "Fall" in the garden of Eden, which is alluded to earlier in the story during the blob's conversation with the snake).[16]

---

16 This is an idea widely evoked in the imagery of biblical poetry and wisdom sayings where the non-human creation is often portrayed as looking to the Creator for provision as well as praising the Creator by just being themselves in their ecological cycles and seasons, whereas only humans seem to really struggle with being

But the turtles here are not featured merely to make an anthropological, or even a theological, point. We are given a sympathetically imagined glimpse of the integrity of their own inner life (their "dark interior" that withdraws from us as Morton would have it). The turtles are not "obnoxious company" even though profoundly different from us in certain ways.

In characteristic fashion, Lafferty turns up both the oddity and comedy in a subsequent scene, one that again highlights the difference between us and the turtles and yet portrays it in a way richer than we might expect, re-enlivening our engagement, piquing our curiosity:

> *I talked to the turtles while Eustace was painting my portrait on tent canvas.*
>
> *"Is the name of this world Florida?" I asked one of them. "The road signs said Florida."*
>
> *"World, world, world, water, water, water, glub, glug, glub," said one of them.*
>
> *"Yes, but is this particular world we are on named Florida?"*
>
> *"World, world, water, water, glub," said another.*
>
> *"Eustace, I can get nothing from these fellows," I called. "Is this world named Florida?"*

That alien speech (world, world, water, water, glub) has its own sort of rudimentary poetry that elicits both laughter and wonder in the reader. In this linguistically rendered glimpse we actually get a *feel* of what existence could look like from a chelonian point of view. There is a split-second of genuine "transport" (*hypsos*) here, even though (indeed, *because*) it is into a "lower" life form than our own. And just so Lafferty has drawn us into "intimacy with an alien presence" (as Morton puts it). And the alien presence with which we now feel weird rapport is not that of the extra-terrestrial of the story. No, instead we have brushed uncannily against the Alien Inside The House, the *terrestrial* aliens in our own "home ecology," the

---

grateful and trusting toward the Creator (and hence also are the unique perpetrators of ecological disrespect and damage to the creation). Cf. *Bible and Ecology* (2010) by Richard Bauckham.

strange strangers that are the turtles. These fellow-beings suddenly look deeper to us than before now that their "irreducible dark side" has been illumined in a fast-fading flash. The turtles' unique relation to water is glimpsed, for example, which humans can hardly imagine and certainly cannot share, signified by the repeated emphasis on water but also by the out-of-the-way English words "glub" and "glug" and their evocations of gurgling liquid. This is the ecomonstrous leap of imagination that shocks (and tickles) us into rapport with animals on levels that mere mimetic reportage cannot achieve. And even though we have briefly accessed their interiority, they still recede and withdraw from us into the integral uniqueness of their own being—almost as if they want us to chase their ontology, though we cannot exhaust it. (I for one have been unable to stop thinking about this imagined glimpse of turtle consciousness and my wonder spurs me to further investigation.)

Spirit of Catfish, Nymph of Sewer

It is easy to forget the weird human-animal and animal-animal "category confusion" in a story like "Boomer Flats" (1971), where catfish inhabit snakes and men are shaped like bears.[17] A waitress by the name of Crayola Catfish (note too the animals embedded in so many of Lafferty's character names) explains why the green snakes in the drinks she's serving evaporate after a time: "All the snakes are spirits of catfish just out for a little ramble." Lafferty again ups both the oddity and hilarity of this already funny and weird thought by adding:

> *"Interesting," Velikof said, and he noted in his pocket notebook that the vermis ebrius viridis is not a discrete species of worm or snake, but is rather spirit of catfish. It is out of such careful*

---

17 There are often so many elements or threads in just one short story by Lafferty (some of them very potent, if only briefly glimpsed—e.g. the Comet in "Boomer Flats") that without multiple readings, you won't readily recall them all. In this way (and others) Lafferty's fiction exhibits a monstrous quality even at the narratological level: his stories often bristle and jostle with characters and phenomena and intersecting plots the way the monstrous body is, as Cohen puts it, a "freakish compilation" of incompatible parts.

notation that science is built up.

The animal-animal "category crisis" pushes our gaze outward into the lives of animals themselves as they relate to one another and not just to us, and where the possibility of their own sort of animal spiritual life is broached.

Dr. Velikof's combining of scientific method and a spiritual realm is itself a kind of "category crisis" for many modern minds and Lafferty wryly nudges the reader into that monstrous notion. In his story "Animal Fair," another of Lafferty's characters avows that if we won't see spirits in things, then we at least should recover the veiled truth of pre-modern man's anthropomorphic projections upon nature:

> *I believe that we should see a nymph in every tree and stream once more, in every field, ah, in every factory. If only we could realize that every object contains the whole of the spirit! But, since we cannot, then why can we not see a personification of the spirit in every object? What we need is more nymphs. Even the sewers should have nymphs: then they would realize that there is no shame in being a sewer, not in being a good and transforming sewer.*

I have my doubts as to whether the ecophilosophers I'm drawing on would want to follow Lafferty into either direct or indirect spirituality. Nevertheless, I think there is an interesting and fruitful conversation to be had between these perspectives, both of which are trying to recover a truly deep and "subjective" dimension in non-human things and humanity's understanding and connection to this.

ANIMALS OF THE MIND
AND THE EMPTYING OF ANTHROPOMORPHISM

The lively, spirited animals in Lafferty's fiction can connect to popular contemporary representations of animals, but, unsurprisingly, the Laffertian Bestiary will also challenge Pop Animalia. Berger notes that though we have removed most of the actual animals from our view in modern life, the animals inside our thought-forms are harder to marginalize. "The animals of the mind cannot be so easily dispersed. Sayings, dreams, games, stories, superstitions, the language itself, recall them" (Berger: 25). Even if much of modern mainstream literature does not recall them, and even if we now use them far less to name ourselves and our world, the animals nevertheless continue to show up in these other areas of culture. In his essay "Through the Red Fire" (1980) Lafferty concurs. He cites popular SF as yet another example of the persistence of "animals of the mind":

> *The idea of a humanity both taller and deeper and more inclusive than now, of the time when animals were somehow contained in mankind, is echoed in the Tarzan stories, in the Planet-of-the-Apes pieces, in the Island-of-Doctor-Moreau pastiches.*

How do Lafferty's animals compare to the anthropomorphised animals of cartoon animation? As we'll see from examples below, many of Lafferty's animals certainly share with cartoons the trait of being anthropomorphised. But the commonality might stop there. In a passage that discusses Aristotle's ascription of certain shared emotions between animals and humans, Berger reinforces what I noted in the previous essay, that anthropomorphism is actually essential to human-animal empathy[18]:

> *Until the 19th century, however, anthropomorphism was integral to the relation between man and animal and was an expression of their proximity. Anthropomorphism was the residue of the continuous use of animal metaphor. In the last two centuries, animals have gradually disappeared. Today we live without them. And in this new solitude, anthropomorphism makes us doubly uneasy (Berger: 21).*

But why do, say, Disney's animated anthropomorphisms not make us uneasy as Berger describes?

---

18 See *FoL* 1, p. 82ff.; Bauckham, p. 53.

Men and women were formerly portrayed as beasts, says Berger, in order to highlight a central human characteristic (e.g. courage of the lion, vanity of the peacock). "The device was like putting on a mask, but its function was to unmask" (Berger 28). In the 19th century, however, epitomized in J. J. Grandville's illustrations of various animals dressed and acting like people, the animals began to serve less to unmask anything about us through our sympathetic understanding of their animality (as I argued is the case with animal metaphors above) than to simply stand in for us as caricatures that make no real comparison between ourselves and other animals. In Grandville's illustrations dogs are not canine and bears are not ursine, Berger argues, but are simply humans doing human things, though with animal faces. He then notes rather ominously: "The movement that ends with the banality of Disney began as a disturbing, prophetic dream in the work of Grandville" (Berger: 29).

Berger cites Disney and Beatrix Potter as examples of how animals are "co-opted into the family" by modern folks in a way similar to pets, but since such imaginary animals don't even need physical maintenance like pets, "they can be totally transformed into human puppets" (Berger: 25). Such anthropomorphized animals are not giving us feedback or resonance. They are mere costumes for the acting out of our mundanity. "In such works the pettiness of current social practices is *universalized* by being projected on to the animal kingdom" (Berger: 26, emphasis his). Berger cites a scene from Donald Duck as an example:

> DONALD: *Man, what a day! What a perfect day for fishing, boating, dating or picnicking—only I can't do any of these things!*
> NEPHEW: *Why not, Unca Donald? What's holding you back?*
> DONALD: *The Bread of Life, boys! As usual, I'm broke and its eons till payday.*
> NEPHEW: *You could take a walk Unca Donald—go bird-watching.*
> DONALD: *(groan!) I may have to! But first, I'll wait for the mailman. He may bring something good newswise!*

> *NEPHEW: Like a cheque from an unknown relative in Moneyville?*

There's something very depressing about this use of animals. There is no metaphor here, only mask.

Whatever the complex truth may be about current popular anthropomorphized animals, we may ask: are Lafferty's "fancy dress" talking beasts just more emptied anthropomorphisms? Not at all. In Lafferty's stories, the anthropomorphized animals are usually outsiders, not easily absorbed and assimilated and co-opted into the human contingent of the biotic community. Sometimes, for example, they communicate differently than us or have strange powers. Indeed, they do not even usually serve the purpose of illuminating human characteristics, as do Lafferty's animal metaphors. They tend to have lives very much of their own, though they exhibit "category confusion" in their sharing of certain capabilities and habits normally only found in humans (such as speech and clothing). Let's look at a few of them.

FLIP O'GRADY: THE MOST PLEASANT AND MOST RESPECTED CHIMPANZEE IN THAT PART OF TOWN

Readers who have searched out Lafferty's stories beyond the early collections will have run into some of Lafferty's most spectacular examples of talking animals. One of my personal favorites is the "hot-handed chimp," Flip O'Grady, in Lafferty's short story "Jack Bang's Eyes" (1983). Flip doesn't usually speak, but rather writes down his words on a scratch pad. Like the mundane Donald Duck, he does work a job, but it is unusual to say the least: he flips pennies for hours on end to figure out odds and probabilities, and even influences those odds in a preternatural way. Lafferty sketches a portrait of Flip's work life:

> *The flipping was dogged hard work as Flip O'Grady did it, steep psychic stuff with preternatural aspects, and he sweat a lot on the assignments. He wore a T-shirt and boxer shorts when he flipped pennies. After every flipping session he took a brisk five*

> *minute shower. Then he put on horn-pipe pants and sports jacket*
> *for a forty minute coffee-and-doughnuts break.*

And we are given also a sketched portrait of Flip's equally idiosyncratic home life:

> *Flip was a flower person and a gardener in his off hours. At*
> *home, away from his penny flipping assignments, he wore a*
> *saffron yellow robe when working with his yellow roses, a*
> *luxurious red robe when working with his red roses, and a black*
> *robe of midnight velvet when working with his moon lilies. He*
> *was the most pleasant and most respected chimpanzee in that*
> *part of town. He was also a statistical prediction apparatus that*
> *contained an uncertainty factor.*

And these are just meandering asides from the main narrative, which is really about human characters. (The story is, however, about the possibility of humans making an evolutionary jump into a heightened awareness of everything, including the non-human, so the sidelight on Flip is relevant.)

Also, compare the weary dialogue between Donald and his nephew above to the following lively exchange between Flip and another character (in which we also see a humorous instance of Lafferty's attention to zoological accuracy):

> *"I've heard that he uses a monkey flipping pennies as a basis*
> *for his statistical analysis," a lady said. "You know him, young*
> *fellow—" (This to Flip O'Grady)— "Is that the truth of it?"*
> *"I get so damned tired of explaining the difference between a*
> *monkey and an ape!" Flip wrote wearily in his notebook. "Other*
> *than that, it's true."*

So what *is* Flip O'Grady in this story? He's an actual chimpanzee, whatever else he is. He's not even much of an anthropomorphism really. He's more like an exception to the rule of apedom. He serves neither to unmask us, as in the older tradition, nor as a modern empty puppet. He is like us in his showering after sweaty work and coffee breaks and a quiet gardening home life. Yet he's simply his own person with his wonderfully offbeat wardrobe habits and the poetry of his green thumb pastimes. There is alterity and intimacy both in this gently ecomonstrous portrait. We may not so much glimpse Flip's "dark interior" as we did with the turtles, but it is implied. Who but a sensitive soul could have such habits? I suspect his portrait partly expresses a human longing to treat animals with the respect we would give a kindly, if irascible, eccentric: curiosity, tolerance, even collaboration and partnership.

TALKING-ANIMAL JOKES—TRUE EXACTLY AS TOLD

Lafferty's short story "And Name My Name" (1974) reverses the roles of who is in the sidelight. It is a tale where such talking animals take center stage and we humans are the ones who play the bit parts. The story begins with a traveling band of seven apes from different regions of the world. The apes are robed and shod, though slightly uncomfortably we are told, as if they are not used to it (for they are not: it is only for a special occasion). They are discussing the paradigm-shifting event they are journeying toward, reminiscing on various ages of the world where various species of animals had their Day (Day of the Elephants, Day of the Whales, Day of the Dolphins, Day of the Apes, Day of the Hyenas, and so on). Each animal in its Day named the other fauna of the world, just as humanity later did. For instance, "the Day of the Whales was a big one," or so the apes have heard through animal rumor:

> For showiness it topped even our own takeover. The account of it is carved in rocks in whale talk, in rocks that are over a mile deep under a distant ocean; it is an account that no more than seven whales can still read. But there are several giant squids who can read it also, and squids are notoriously loose-mouthed. Things like that are told around.

Just what is this we are granted a glimpse of? It's a funny scenario. And weird. It's as if we are inducted for a moment into a world that has little or nothing to do with us, where the biosphere talks amongst itself and we humans are deaf to it. The fauna inscribe and read annals of which we remain wholly ignorant. Lafferty has created (in this story and elsewhere) a richly ecocentric myth that at once acknowledges humanity's current uniqueness in some respects (this is our "Day"), yet relativizes that special status of humanity by enfolding it into a similar kind of special status possessed by each species of animal.

The story later provides a humorous vignette of an encounter between humans and this temporary phenomenon of beasts dressing and talking:

> *There were of course the Bears that walked and talked like men and were reported as coming out of the Russias. One of these bears, so the joke went, entered a barroom in Istanbul. The bear was nattily dressed, smoked a cigar, laid a hundred lira note on the bar and ordered a rum and cola.*
>
> *The bar-man didn't know what to do so he went back to the office and asked the boss.*
>
> *"Serve the bear," the boss said, "only don't give him his ninety lira change. Give him ten lira only. We will make prodigies pay for being prodigies."*
>
> *The bar-man went and did this, and the bear drank his drink in silence.*
>
> *"We don't get many bears in here," the barman finally said when the silence had gotten on his nerves.*
>
> *"At ninety lira a throw I can understand why you don't," the bear said.*

It's funny again, but the joke is on us. The vignette reveals our discomfort with animals really returning to the center of life with us. We sense little or no interiority to the bear as we did implicitly with Flip O'Grady. The bear's integrity of independent being can only be glimpsed by his silence, his reticence to commune with the humans who refuse to commune with him. The surface details of the bear's debonair dress sense (conveyed by a solitary adverb where

Flip's varied dress habits were given in some detail) and his dry re-mark on the bar's inhospitable behavior toward him serve only to bar us from access to his ursine essence.[19] We are not even given the bear's name (as we are with the seven apes earlier—Mary Rain-wood, Joe Sunrise, Linger Quick-One and so on). Prodigies must pay for being prodigies, say the humans, the same stingy ontology we saw in my previous essay with Quine's philosophy.

This talking bear scene could have been an instance of merely a sort of "eco-comic" approach. But Lafferty never leaves things at the merely humorous. He pushes further, into ecomonstrous "cate-gory crisis," here again at the narratological level in addition to the "freakish compilation" of beasts having the power of speech. In this story, "jokes" like the one about the bear won't stay in their prop-er category: "There were hundreds of these talking-animal jokes in those days. But they had a quality different from most jokes: they were all true exactly as told." As ever, world-building Lafferty is opening up Ricoeurian possibility ("disclosure of possible worlds"), making flatlanders squirm—here in regard to our loss of connec-tion to animals and its possible recovery in a way more genuine than mere cartoonish puppetry. But this story takes these possibilities to an even more disturbing level.

The World is a TV Set and We Have Become the Animals' Cartoons

Berger notes that animals are "transformed into spectacle" by photo books and the like (Berger: 26). (This is all the more so in contem-porary TV shows that feature cinematic documentary footage of animals.) "In the accompanying ideology, animals are always the observed. The fact that they can observe us has lost all significan-ce"(Berger: 27). In "And Name My Name," however, we glimpse not only the animals' view of the world, but also of *us* and our present "reign." And it is not favorable. The apes, for example, consider the

---

19 I wish there was space to go into a full survey of the *Ursus Laffertius*—for, among his many ursine portrayals, Lafferty even sketches how an anthropomorphized bear might uniquely wink (*Serpent's Egg*) or speak (*Annals of Klepsis*) in non-human ways, oddly mixing bits of realism into the flights of fancy—but that will have to await its own separate essay.

human age to be "a step backwards or at least sideways." Humans are "interlopers" who can be replaced.

There is a scene in the story that has an odd and uncanny resonance with Berger's argument mentioned above, that we have ironically lost true kinship to animals in our proliferation of animated cartoons featuring them (such as Disney produces[20].) In "And Name My Name" the situation is the obverse: *humans* are becoming the cartoons as they fade to the periphery of life. A group of seven humans is assembled and summoned to the paradigm-shifting event just as with the apes and other species. These seven persons represent the very best that humanity has to offer in intelligence and depth. They try to assume they are the apex of the animal kingdom and secure in this position. Yet they are uneasy as they discuss the situation with one another:

> *"But I am very edgy about all this, and I believe that we are really coming to the edge. There is something wrong with the setting and the set."*
>
> *"What do you say, Helen?" Jorge asked. "What is wrong with the set?"*
>
> *"The set is off; it is gone wrong. Both the picture and the sound seem doubled, Jorge."*
>
> *"Cannot it be fixed? But what am I talking about? I do feel for a moment that we are no more than animated cartoons on a screen. But this isn't a TV set; it is something larger."*
>
> *"This set is the whole-world set, Jorge," Helen Rubric muttered. "And it has gone too far wrong to be fixed by ourselves. It may be fixed by this New Fixer who comes. But I feel that we ourselves are diminished and demoted, that we are put into a shadowy box now and confined to a narrow corner."*

Our TV set mentality is projected to a worldwide scope and we are now the ones pushed to the margins. We are the animated cartoons now, not the animals. This aspect of the story, though one

---

20 *Regular Show* and *BoJack Horseman* are recent examples of anthropomorphic animal cartoons that are arguably more sophisticated, yet still seem totally surface-oriented in their evocation of animals.

of its most comic in imagery, is yet the most nightmarish in notion. By the end of the tale, the humans are indeed demoted (to "secondary ape") and commanded to fade off the scene/screen. It's a grim ending. But it's only one possible future in Lafferty's way of seeing things, as we'll see. It is a warning, not yet a condemnation.

RE-JOINING THE AEVITERNAL PARADE: LAFFERTY'S THEOLOGICAL ECOLOGY

This all comes out of, as we would guess with Lafferty, a rather ornate theology[21], which he once outlined in an interview.[22] One of the pillar-like phrases Lafferty used to describe his theological worldview was the "Distinction and Adornment of the World" (which he tells us is a scholastic phrase). The Distinction indicates our unique world "apart from the billions of other worlds, all special, but not all special to us." It indicates simply "the scale and site we are on." The Adornment then, says Lafferty, is the "process and movement and composition, and finally the Flora and Fauna (including ourselves)" of this world. There is thus, undergirding Lafferty's ecological gaze, a majestically metaphysical order that bestows both significance and humility on humanity (and on all the other animals). Cosmically and ontologically, humans come rather late in the game in this schema and we are embedded in the rest of the ecology, not above or over it. Yet we are meant to be here. I think Lafferty's theological ecology here can accommodate Timothy Morton's view that "*human* being is just one way of being in a mesh of strange strangeness—uncanny, open-ended, vast: existence is (ecological) coexistence" (Morton 2011: 165-66, emphasis his)[23].

Lafferty then further elaborates that Roman Catholicism also teaches about an existential "procession," first in terms of Trinitarian monotheism: the Son proceeds eternally from the Father, and the

---

21 I began to look at Lafferty's theological ecology in the previous essay, drawing on G. K. Chesterton's popular account of the theology of Thomas Aquinas.

22 Walker, Paul, 1978. *Speaking of Science Fiction: The Paul Walker Interviews* (Oradell: Luna Publications), pp. 21-23.

23 It's worth noting that Morton is a Buddhist and thus he and Lafferty no doubt differ theologically. Yet it seems to me that, in their respective "weird universes," they have some provisional common ground on which a discussion may take place.

Holy Spirit proceeds eternally from both the Father and the Son. In turn, he says, "every creature proceeds aeviternally (having beginning but not end) from the Holy Trinity."[24] This, Lafferty tells us, is the "Procession of Creatures," which he also calls the "Parade of Creatures."

This Procession of Creatures, I would suggest, even underwrites the "open-ended" receding into strangeness that Morton claims for all objects, a kind of aeviternity in the depth as well as the continuation of each being. Lafferty's theology thus posits two ends to the "mesh" of existence, processional as well as recessional, the Great Dance (to borrow C. S. Lewis' phrase at the end of his 1943 novel *Perelandra*).

In the shambles and shards of the modern/postmodern world, I suppose Lafferty would say the Parade is proceeding more like a drugged, half-hearted Riot/Orgy with the rest of the fauna on the margins and ourselves alone at the center, lost and listless, unable to effectively name either the animals or ourselves. That is why he does what he does in his fiction and urges us to participate, to parade again ontologically rampant, animals and humans and all else.

The Parade in Lafferty's evocation across his fiction is by no means solemn or dull. It is a festive (and even monstrous) revel to be sure, but a "structured" one (to borrow a key term from his 1973 short story "And Walk Now Gently Through the Fire"). The Parade of Creatures may not always be orderly, but it is *ordered* (in the high metaphysical sense outlined above). It is for Lafferty as it was for Chesterton when the latter said: "And the more I considered Christianity, the more I found that while it had established a rule and order, the chief aim of that order was to give room for good things to run wild."[25]

Of course, our being out of step with the Parade of Creatures is, for Lafferty, theological also, as one of his characters remarks in his short story "Animal Fair" (1974). We have already seen a passage

---

24 See Gregorio Montejo's excellent essay in the previous issue for an explication of aeviternity: "Aeviternity: R.A. Lafferty's Thomistic Philosophy of Time in the Argo Cycle," *FoL* 1, pp. 102-114.

25 Chesterton, G. K., 1908. *Orthodoxy* (many editions), chapter 6 "The Paradoxes of Christianity."

from that story calling for at least a return to seeing nymphs in every object if we can't see the spirit. This passage explains why:

> *"One of the things that has gone wrong is that you no longer recognize the spirit in things," the seed-man said. "The spirit of the Shaper, of course, is in everything, whether living or unliving, in every person, animal, plant, tree, pond, rock, house, factory. But your minds are not able to comprehend this. Once you saw a nymph in everything, every tree, every stream, every stone. At another time you saw an angel in each thing. Now you the lords do not see the spirit in anything at all. You are not holy enough to see the Shaper, not holy enough to see the angel, not even holy enough to see the nymph. Ah, most of you are not holy enough to see the stone."*

The Spirit of the Creator ("the Shaper") is in all things since all things proceed from the Creator. But this goes undiscerned by us and thus we are disconnected and alone at the center of our world when we are meant to be part of a procession there.

"Animal Fair" goes on to suggest rectifying this problem by a sort of spiritual recycling[26], using spiritual "good and transformative sewers" to reverse the spiritual pollution inside us that leads to our disrespect and disconnection to our outer environment. As always with Lafferty, restoration of inner ecology leads to restoration of outer ecology (and it was the pollution of the inner that led to the pollution of the outer). I think it's an assessment that to some degree comports with Berger's.

WARNING: YOU CAN BE REPLACED, YOU KNOW

One must remember that time works in a "multiplex" way (as "And Name My Name" puts it) in Lafferty's fiction and the futures we are shown are only possible futures, thus warnings or encouragements.[27] Whereas in "And Name My Name" we get a glimpse of genuine

---

26 Cf. John Owen's essay in this issue.

27 See both Ferguson's and Montejo's respective articles for sophisticated elucidations of Lafferty's highly complex philosophy of time.

judgement and our subsequent demotion to secondary ape and of the reins being handed over to other "lords," in "Animal Fair"[28] we are only "put on notice" by the rest of the animal kingdom:

> *The Animal Fairs here and all over the world have put you on very short-term notice. Your unwritten contract will not even be on a yearly basis now. It will be on a weekly, even a daily basis. The creatures have been doing all the work, they say: they have furnished the forming eyes, and you the deforming. You must see with more valid eyes, with more interlocking eyes. You can be replaced, you know.*

We must see the world better. We must again see animals, for example, as more than empty anthropomorphisms that entertain us with our own image in costume. We must recover both their alterity and their centrality. The stakes are high. We are currently weighed in the scales and, though not just yet "found wanting," Austro writes in glowing red words: "Sure is going to be close."[29]

So. It's time for new eyes.

CONCLUSION: THROUGH VALERY MOK'S EYES— HOW CAN ONE NOT LOVE ANYTHING?

Like Barnaby in "Animal Fair" seeing through Chiara's and Austro's "really eyes"[30] ("valid" or "interlocking" vs. "incomplete" eyes as the story also puts it), Lafferty's readers are given the opportunity to see the world through his eyes... *and there is so much more to see,*

---

28 It is interesting to note that these two stories with alternate endings for humanity were both published in the same year.

29 Reminds one of the "Repent!" messages etched redly into exhumed stained glass in the ending of "In Deepest Glass"; see my previous essay for a brief discussion of that story and Craig May's essay in this issue for a thorough and enlightening treatment.

30 Austro is accused of being an anarchist by a neighbour in the story because his richer "really eyes" view is so rampant compared to modern reductionisms. But he is actually an archist as the story argues in one of Lafferty's interesting expositional digressions, which connects informatively to Lafferty's Procession of Creatures theology.

including animals and our deep relation to them.

This is a central theme of his early and celebrated short story "Through Other Eyes" (1960). By means of a "Cerebral Scanner," characters in the story are able to view the world through each other's powerfully subjective points of view. When Charles Cogsworth sees the world through Valery Mok's eyes he is shocked at her deeply sensual view of things and calls her a pig to another character, Gregory Smirnov. Gregory remarks to Charles: "I doubt if you understand pigs any better than you understand women." Gregory then informs Charles that by use of the Scanner he had recently experienced "a pig's-eye view of the world":

> It is a dreamy world of all-encompassing placidity, almost entirely divorced from passion. It's a gray shadowy world with very little of the unpleasant. I had never before known how wonderful is the feel of simple sunlight and of cool earth. Yet we would soon be bored with it; but the pig is not bored.

Like the turtles in "The Weirdest World," the pig is imagined as having a unique relation to other non-human things in the world (sunlight, earth) that humans cannot have.

But Valery herself is more alive to these animal's-eye views of the world and they have become part of her own. Her view is thoroughly ecomonstrous, in her case sensuous to a degree that shocked Charles. Indeed, the whole planet is a monstrous "harbinger of category crisis" for Valery. Flora and fauna and land and body and myth and monster and machine all writhe together in empathic hybridity in her vision of the world:

> And to her the grass itself is like clumps of snakes, and the world itself is flesh. Every bush is to her a leering satyr, and she cannot help but brush into them. The rocks are spidery monsters and she loves them.
>
> [...]
>
> She worships every engine as a fire monster, and she hears sounds that I thought nobody could ever hear. Do you know what

worms sound like inside the earth? They're devilish, and she would writhe and eat dirt with them.

Charles, like the bartender in "And Name My Name," does not welcome such proximity to prodigy. He does not feel friendly toward monsters as Valery does. He does not relish the "intimacy with an alien presence" that she so obviously does.

The more open-minded Gregory again interprets Valery's vision to Charles:

> *And yet, Charles, she is but a slightly more than average attractive girl, given to musing, and with a love of the world and a closeness to it that most of us have lost. She has a keen awareness of reality and of the grotesqueness that is its main mark. You yourself do not have this deeply; and when you encounter it in its full strength, it shocks you [...] But to move into a pristine universe is more of a difference than you were prepared for.*

Valery loves the world and does not fear its grotesquery. And note that her ecomonstrous vision of the universe is called "pristine." If we could see clearly, it is implied, this would be the way the world really looks in its "natural state"—not a reductionist vista of magnetic fields and superstrings or the like; nor a tidy pastoral collection of safely separated surfaces; but a roiling blend and dance of interweaving and happy monstrosities harbouring ontic depths and heights. The Parade of Creatures is definitely a wild affair.

After his initial shock, Charles pursues the matter again. Provoked by Valery's view to keep looking through other eyes he "nibbled at the edges of mystery with his fantastic device," trying a variety of viewpoints, even those of the non-human he initially so loathed:

> *He saw with the eyes of other men. And of animals: the soft pleasure of the fox devouring a ground squirrel, the bloody anger of a lamb furious after milk, the crude arrogance of the horse, the intelligent tolerance of the mule, the voraciousness of the cow,*

the miserliness of the squirrel, the sullen passion of the catfish.
Nothing was quite as might have been expected.

Nothing was quite as might have been expected. Lafferty has a very poetic touch in these observations of wildlife, mixing the passions and actions differently than we would normally combine them, ecomonstrous in freshly unexpected ways.

This further research prepares Charles for Valery's rebuke when she says to him: "You are a stick with no blood in it. You are a pig made out of sticks." While he had conducted his research, Valery had used the Scanner to see Charles' point of view in turn: "I saw the world the way you see it. I saw it with a dead man's eyes. You don't even know that the grass is alive. You think it's only grass." Charles' responses are rather bemused as Valery continues:

> "I don't think you have any eyes. You can look at a hill and your heart doesn't even skip a beat. You don't even tingle when you walk over a field."
> "You see grass like clumps of snakes."
> "That's better than not even seeing it alive."
> "You see rocks like big spiders."
> "That's better than just seeing them like rocks. I love snakes and spiders. You can watch a bird fly by and not even hear the stuff gurgling in its stomach. How can you be so dead? And I always liked you so much. But I didn't know you were dead like that."
> "How can one love snakes and spiders?"
> "How can one not love anything? It's even hard not to love you, even if you don't have any blood in you."

The two of them are husband and wife by the time we reach Lafferty's novel *Arrive at Easterwine* (1971), featuring again the members of the Institute for Impure Science. We too may eventually fall in love with Lafferty's love of the world and become married to it. As the narrator goes on, focalising in on Charles' view of this strange Valery:

And after all, how can one not love anything? Especially when it becomes beautiful when angry, and when it is so much alive that it tends to shock by its intense awareness those who are partly dead.

This is what Lafferty's "ecomonstrous" writing does: it shocks we who are partly dead into being more alive by its intense level of awareness: of the animal world, the non-human world in general, and many other things.[31]

This work is © 2015 Daniel Otto Jack Petersen.

Daniel Otto Jack Petersen is married to fine art and fashion photographer Flannery O'Kafka. They have five children, the youngest in her first year in school and the oldest in her second year at art college. Daniel has accepted an offer from the University of Glasgow to begin doctoral research this October on the theme of the "ecomonstrous" in the works of R. A. Lafferty and Cormac McCarthy. He blogs about Lafferty at antsofgodarequeerfish.blogspot.co.uk. He also blogs about a few other things at a few other places and is known to occasionally record strange noises with his mouth, sometimes even for public consumption: e.g. laminarexcursion.bandcamp. com/album/lem-volume-20-october-2010.

---

31 You'll no doubt have thought of other short stories and passages in the novels that bear directly on this topic and will have wondered how I could leave them out. Please write to *FoL* at editor@feastoflaughter.org and have your contribution added to *FoL* 3 in the new "Letters to the Editor" section that will begin to be featured in that issue.

"This Was More Than a Spectacle, More Than an Illusion, It Was a Communicating Instrument":

R. A. Lafferty and Hans Urs von Balthasar
on the Relational Form of Being

By Gregorio Montejo

Anyone with even a nodding acquaintance with the work of Raphael Aloysius Lafferty can attest that the author was captivated with the fecund multiplicity of the universe, often taking verbal delight in describing, arranging, and recording the sheer bewildering variety of objects that comprise the universe. As Daniel Otto Jack Petersen has eloquently shown, no entity was too apparently small or mundane to be lovingly delineated in his prose, no phenomenon too exotic or grand to find a humble home in one of Lafferty's eccentric taxonomies.[1] Implicitly, everything in the world could plausibly find a home in one of these poetic agglomerations, many of them inventories as homely as a laundry list, and yet on closer inspection often as epic in their implicit meanings as the Homeric catalogue of ships in the *Iliad*.[2] For example, in one of Lafferty's narratives, an encounter with a spring is the commencement of a passionate, even

---

1 See Daniel Otto Jack Petersen, "The Epic of Man and His Friends; or, Slumming It With the Ontic Outcasts; or, May Our Eyes Be Big Enough To Take In the Nine Hundred Percent Gain in Everything!," *Feast of Laughter* 1 (Ktistec Press, 2014), pp. 67-100.

2 Cf. John Crossett, "The Art of Homer's Catalogue of Ships," *The Classical Journal* 64:6 (March, 1969), pp. 241-245; Tilman Krischer, *Formale Konventionen der homerischen Epik. Zetemata* 56 (Munich: Beck, 1971); Jan Felix Gaertner, "The Homeric Catalogues and Their Function in Epic Narrative," Hermes 129:3 (2001), pp. 298-305; Benjamin Sammons, *The Art and Rhetoric of the Homeric Catalogue* (Oxford and New York: Oxford University Press, 2010). Recent scholarship convincingly demonstrate that this technique of poetic cataloguing has its roots in the ancient pre-literate tradition from which the Homeric poems emerged, which bears features of both a mnemonic and a rhetorical character, and an acknowledgment that these catalogic structures also serve a significant compositional purpose for the author, who employs this recurring "classifying principle" as a fundamental method of organizing information in narrative form. Lafferty similarly employs older oral and folk idioms and methods—including a reliance on catalogic structuring—in his fiction.

dangerous enchantment with the natural order, one that evokes a rapturous response from the protagonist, who evinces his ardor by enumerating various corresponding springs in loving detail:

> *Ranwick enjoyed the gushy small spring which was really quite loud at this short range, and he tried to place the spring with her kindred. All the springs share a sort of cousinship, but there are degrees of kindred. She was a bit like Iron Mountain Spring which would always remain as a type. There was the sexiness of the iron-water sparkling in the daylight, and there was flint-stone derision and mockery in the crooked grin of the spring. Ranwick could feel the mist-water on his face and hands. He could smell the brittle and blue skin of the snake-doctor dragon flies as they hovered over this new-hatched pool. He could empathize with the shock of this born-blind water breaking out of its underground darkness to its first dazzling daylight, and he could hear interior rocks being rattled by the resonance of the tumbling water.[3]*

In his essay exploring Lafferty's use of elaborate enumerations, Petersen rightly calls our attention to the deeper philosophical implications of these catalogic structures, especially with certain affinities between Lafferty's elaborate cataloguing of things in the world and the contemporary philosophical movement known as Object-Oriented Ontology (OOO).[4] Petersen is particularly adept at finding deep resonances between Lafferty's depictions of inanimate objects that are capable of communicating their being to other

---

3 R. A. Lafferty, "Love Affair With Ten Thousand Springs," *Odyssey* 1:2 (Summer, 1976), p. 34.

4 Petersen, "The Epic of Man and His Friends": "It is fascinating to note that Lafferty's wide-angle and deeply layered view of physical existence bears some similarity to the vision advocated by a recent philosophical movement known as "object-oriented ontology" (OOO). Graham Harman's writings on OOO, for example, are often replete with rhapsodic lists of non-human objects, which serve as vivid reminders of the physical surfaces and entities that surround, uphold, and impinge on every one of us during every single second of every single day—and also of more remote entities that yet share this universe with us. Lafferty's writing has a habit of frequently and lavishly enumerating such lists as well," p. 70.

objects, and which are in turn open to receiving such communications from other entities, and Object-Oriented Ontology's emphasis on the encounters between non-human objects predicated on the inexhaustible ontic depths of all beings. The onus of this comparison is that both Lafferty and OOO share a common vision of the repleteness of existence and the rich abounding mystery of being which resides at the heart of every entity. In part, this essay attempts to show that despite several intriguing areas of confluence, any Object-Oriented Ontology has inherent conceptual drawbacks which limit its usefulness in analyzing Lafferty's thought-world. Petersen himself tacitly admits that OOO has to be at the very least supplemented by looking at other philosophical traditions, most importantly the Thomism that infused much of Catholic intellectual and imaginative life during Lafferty's formative years. Indeed, Petersen begins to lay the groundwork for just such a creative retrieval of Lafferty's Thomistic roots at the conclusion of his piece.[5] The bulk of this essay, then, will be devoted to exploring how contemporary strands of Thomism, particularly those inspired by the work of the Swiss theologian Hans Urs von Balthasar, may be useful in further elaborating the ontological context of R. A. Lafferty's fiction.

The (Relative) Metaphysical Paucity of Things in an Object-Oriented Ontology

The origins of Object-Oriented Ontology can be traced back to its foundational text, Graham Harman's *Tool-Being: Heidegger and the Metaphysics of Objects*. As the titles indicates, Harman begins to delineate a new ontology—a new conceptualization of being—by examining a specific aspect of Martin Heidegger's metaphysics, viz. tool-analysis, and applying it to all entities in general. According to Heidegger, a tool (*das Zeug*), or a piece of equipment, or any object whatsoever—in its broadest sense—is any object in the world with which we have meaningful dealings. Objects are the way that the world we find ourselves in presents itself to us. However, out of all the countless objects that we may encounter, not all will contribute

---

5 Cf. Ibid, pp. 92-95; 98-99.

to our own authentic being-in-the-world, but only those objects that Heidegger identifies as having a readiness-to-hand (*Zuhandenheit*) for us. In order to understand this distinction between objects, perhaps it is best to illustrate how a rock is encountered by persons in general, in contrast to how that very same object will present itself to a stone-mason. The mason's relationship to that object is one of readiness-to-hand, a relation in which the stone reveals its inner being, its pure ontic *thereness* to the mason in a manner that is intrinsic to the way the mason, as another being-in-the-world, as *Da-sein*, is called upon to utilize the things of this world in its own act of existence.[6]

Harman reverses and universalizes this Heideggerian notion by transforming readiness-to-hand into presence-at-hand, a phenomenon not restricted to the intentionality of *Da-sein* towards objects as ontologically constitutive *pragmata*, but applicable to any relation among any objects in the world. For Harman, the central fact about existence is the undeniable existence of discernable things, and the way in which such "concrete entities tear away from the shapeless totality" of *das Zeug*, and the "stance in which specific beings take up a relation to their own being."[7] This irreducible facticity of things means that, as Harman goes on to explain, a tree, a star, a boulder need not be experienced by an intentional consciousness in order to function in the world as an integral, distinct object, a star or a stone or a tree manifesting specific powers and qualities as something integrally its own in relation to other boulders, stars, trees or anything else in the world. Indeed, it is through these sorts of encounters that objects are torn out of the undifferentiated mass of stuff and constituted as individual entities. What precludes our ability to perceive the true reality of things as they are is that we are prejudiced by our notion that objects reveal their true existence only in their readiness-to-hand for us, in other words, by their tool-being. But this intentional relation of *Da-sein* to objects as tools is only one particular manifestation of rationality in general. As Harman

6 See, for example, Martin Heidegger, *Being and Time*. Trans. J. Stambaugh (Albany: State University of New York Press, 1996), pp. 67-71.

7 Graham Harman, *Tool-Being: Heidegger and the Metaphysics of Objects* (Chicago: Open Court, 2002), p. 44.

concludes, we are no more or less perspectival than such inanimate things as trees, stones, or stars:

> *Ontologically speaking, there is no difference between the activity of a trained human eye and the crash of two colliding boulders. In other words, conscious awareness can no longer serve as one of the basic orienting poles of reality. Explicit awareness is not a special negating instrument, not one that perceives where less fortunate beings only interact in their blind physical way. The idea that perception or freedom work by negating is a myth: we never manage to free ourselves from the plenum of tool-being, not even partially.*[8]

Harman's wish to protect the integral distinctiveness and full reality of objects apart from any existential utility they may hold for human beings is admirable. However, as the book approaches its climax, Harman's argument takes a disturbing path, proposing that this ontic distinctiveness is ultimately grounded in an abandonment of all relationality. As Harman phrases it, "far beneath any prehension" *of* the object or *by* the object, the inscrutable object itself lays hidden, "silently resting in its vacuum-sealed actuality (a.k.a. 'vacuous actuality)."[9] This is the case since no particular relation or matrix of relations could plausibly exhaust the complete reality of an object, nor any perception comprehend the actuality of a thing in its entirety. As a consequence, the being of an "object is the reality of that object quite apart from any of its specific causal relations, and unexchangeable for any grand total of such relations, so that if we were to catalog exhaustively the exact status of every object in the cosmos vis-à-vis this" object in the world, nevertheless "it would still be possible to conceive of other entities that might occupy a different stance or relation to it"—in the final analysis, Harman's Object-Oriented Ontology "withdraws not just behind any perception, but behind any form of causal activity as well."[10]

---

8 Ibid, p. 225.
9 Ibid, p. 283.
10 Ibid, p. 225.

ONTOLOGICAL PLENITUDE:
TO BE IS TO BE SUBSTANCE-IN-RELATION

In sharp contrast, Thomist-based ontologies acknowledge the in-exhaustible and integral depth of things in themselves, but refuse to abrogate notions of authentic relationality and causal efficacy. The key to understanding this two-fold affirmation is to be found in Aquinas' understanding of being as intrinsically—that is, essen-tially—dynamic. For Thomas, things which possess being are not 'just there' (*Da-sein*) as in Heidegger, they are not "lumps of static essence, inert, immovable, unprogressive and unchanging."[11] The act of existence (*esse*) should not be seen as state, it is an act, the act of all acts, and, therefore, must be understood as act and not as any static and definable object of conception. *Esse* is dynamic impulse, energy, act—the "first, the most persistent and enduring of all dynamism, all energies, all acts. In all things on earth the act of being (*esse*) is the consubstantial urge of nature, a restless, striving force, carrying each being (*ens*) onward, from within the depths of its own reality to its full self-achievement."[12] Any analysis of Thomas' metaphysic has to take in account his adage *agere sequiter esse* ("action follows being" or better yet "activity flows directly from a thing's act of ex-istence").[13] For Aquinas, the first actuality (or first act) is existence of a real being, whereas the second actuality (or second act) is the actions (the actualization of the potencies) which flow from the first act. So, as the noted Thomist scholar Norris Clarke points out, "to be" and "to be active" are inseparable: "A non-acting, non-com-municating being is for all practical purposes equivalent to no being at all. To be real is to make a difference."[14]

As many of Aquinas' own texts demonstrate, "it is the nature of every actuality to communicate itself insofar as it is possible."[15] In fact, "communication follows upon the very meaning of actu-

---

11 Gerald Phelan, "The Existentialism of St Thomas," in *Selected Papers*, ed. A.G. Kirn (Toronto: Pontifical Institute of Mediaeval Studies, 1967), p. 77.

12 Ibid.

13 Aquinas, *Summa Contra Gentiles*, III, 69, 20: Agere sequitur ad esse in actu.

14 W. Norris Clarke, S.J., *The One and the Many: A Contemporary Thomistic Meta-physics* (Notre Dame, IN: University of Notre Dame Press, 2001), p. 32.

15 Thomas Aquinas, *De Potentia*, q.2, a.1.

ality,"[16] for "each and every thing shows forth that it exists for the sake of its operation; indeed, operation is the ultimate perfection of each thing."[17] Clarke points out that for Thomas, "to be" and "to be active" are inseparable; that is, being is revealed in and through action. Moreover, this dynamic understanding of being makes communication and community intelligible: "since every action on others produces cause-effect relations all around it, it follows that every real being is somehow related to others [...] Hence *to be real is to be related*."[18] Therefore, relationality itself is a primordial dimension of every substance; that is, of every extant thing considered in its integral and unfathomable individuality.

> *Relationality and substantiality go together as two distinct but inseparable modes of reality. Substance is the primary mode, in that all else, including relations, depend on it as their ground. But since "every substance exists for the sake of its operation," as St. Thomas has just told us, being as substance, as existing in itself, naturally flows over into being as relational, as turned towards others by its self-communicating action. To be fully is to be substance-in relation.*[19]

Revealing the Form

On this Thomistic account, reality is comprised of a plenitude of things, each of which actively presents itself to other real beings through its own *esse*, with its characteristic self-manifesting and self-communicating activities, and in return each one receives the actions of other entities upon itself, thus becoming a member of that vast interconnected community of real existents that is the universe. It is a view of existence which is echoed throughout Laf-

---

16 Thomas Aquinas, *In I Sent.*, d.4, q.4, a.4.

17 Thomas Aquinas, *Summa Contra Gentiles*, III, 113.

18 W. Norris Clarke, S.J., "The Integration of Personalism and Thomistic Metaphysics in Twenty-First-Century Thomism," in *The Creative Retrieval of St. Thomas Aquinas: Essays in Thomistic Philosophy, New and Old* (New York: Fordham University Press, 2009), p. 228. Italics in the original.

19 W. Norris Clarke S.J., *Person and Being. The Aquinas Lecture*, 1993 (Milwaukee: Marquette University Press, 1998), p. 14. Italics in the original.

ferty's fiction, where all manner of beings, from stones, to dolphins, to stars not only display their unique ontic features, but are equally receptive to the existential qualities communicated by other objects which are ordinarily seen as uncommunicative, inert, and unreceptive. Yet the humblest, most mundane of natural objects, even the stones of the fields themselves, can be the most receptive recorders of the intra-cosmic dialogue, that interplay of natural phenomena communicating and receiving the multitudinous qualia of the countless acts of existence which bind reality together:

> "I have heard it said by an erudite man that it would be wonderful to have located recording microphones at various spots in the time and place of history. Oh, but it has been done. We use such microphones all the time! I have never found a dingle or dale on this earth in which there were not many such microphones. Stones are the most common recorders. Everywhere, to a person with informed eyes and ears, these stones shine and shout their presence. It is in their thin (but not so thin as a non-historian might imagine) patinas that we may read complete histories.
>
> "We commonly lift or peel off transparencies at six-second intervals. Each such transparency will give a detailed and accurate analysis of the air for its period, temperature, direction of wind, light intensity (whether in shade or sunlight or dark night or bright night, even, from the angle of the shine, the hour of the day, and the day of the year), sulphur content of the air, significant pollen, aroma, and quality generally. Do you realize that it would take fewer than three hundred billion such six-second intervals, fewer than three hundred billion such transparencies to carry us back through the last fifty thousand years of history, the period in which we are interested, the period since our own first appearance? We can go deeper, of course, but frankly we have not the technique to go more than ten times deeper, or to about half a million years. Beyond that, we lose accuracy. But why should we go deeper than our own period? In those murky depths, we find only animals and uncouth creatures and peoples who are not ourselves.

"But we can slice the transparencies much thinner than six seconds. We can slice them down to a hundredth of a second for any period we wish to focus on. The six-second interval is merely cruising speed or hunting speed. The patinas deposited on good rock surfaces can be lifted down to the thickness of a single molecule.

"Complete visual pictures, from any aspect or direction, can be reconstructed of anything whose light or shadow fell even indirectly on one of our stones. We can get detailed pictures of animals, of plants, of people as they lived and moved thousands of years ago. We can reconstruct color pictures of the clouds moving overhead, and we can read the spectra of those clouds. We can reconstruct anything that was ever visible, that was ever to be discerned by any of the senses that was ever subject to any sort of analysis. Give us a dozen tuned stones (they resonate to each other, and those of the same locale will always know each other) and we can reconstruct a complete countryside for any period we wish. Nor would upheavals which seem to scramble the record make as much difference as you might suppose.

"We can trap sounds and play them back with perfect fidelity. We can play the song of the ancestral cicada that had two more chromosomes than have its descendants. The old cicada (it is only coincidence) has two more notes to its song. We can say what the two disappeared chromosomes were. We can even, by very advanced technique, duplicate those chromosomes.

"And smells! Of course they are even more simple than sounds to lift in the transparencies. We can go back and pick up nearly every scene complete for the last fifty thousand years. We can do it at ten times that depth, if there were anything interesting happening there. And patinas and deposits on stones are only one of the dozens of tools that we have for such historical reconstruction."[20]

In these passages we have the basis for an aesthetics grounded

---

20 R. A. Lafferty, "From The Thunder Colt's Mouth" in *In the Wake of Man: A Science Fiction Triad*, ed. R. Elwood (Indianapolis and New York: The Bobbs-Merrill Company, 1975), pp. 24-25. Cf. Petersen, "The Epic of Man and His Friends," pp. 75-78.

in an ontology of self-communicative being. Not just a notion of beauty, but an account of seeing (*aesthesis*) as the apprehension of the hidden depths of *esse* in all objects, a modality of vision holding the promise of increased powers of discernment to anyone with suitably "informed eyes," organs empowered by an expanded awareness, and attuned to the way that even stones "shine" forth their glorious existence, and "shout their presence" for those with ears to hear. It is the bold claim that perceptual Form, when it is experienced in all its profoundly rich and expressive clarity, lays open that object to us, not just in regard to its outward appearance but to its inner nature, and beyond that to a disclosure of the hidden depths of the very world in which that object and its observer are situated. It is the very claim of the theologian Hans Urs von Balthasar, who traces his own aesthetic to the transcendental metaphysics of Aquinas.

For von Balthasar, following in Thomas' footsteps, "truth is as evident as existence and essence, as unity, goodness, and beauty."[21] Hence, Balthasar identifies truth not merely as a mode of epistemic justification but as one of the transcendental aspects of being. In metaphysical studies, a transcendental is one of the basic properties of anything that exist, thus leaping over or transcending all particular existential categories, such as quantity, place, and time. Every list of such trans-categorial properties would include the *one*, or unity, that property of integrity or inner coherence that makes a being to be undivided in itself and divided from everything else; the *true*, or the intrinsic intelligibility of all being; and the *good*, or being considered as capable of fulfilling a desire, or under the aspect of perfection. Any transcendental property is a positive attribute that can be predicated of every real being, so that it is convertible with being itself. Balthasar, in accordance with the thought of Thomas Aquinas, adds *beauty* to the list of transcendentals.[22] In beings, then,

---

21 Hans Urs von Balthasar, *Theo-Logic: Theological Logical Theory I: Truth of the World*, trans. A.J. Walker (San Francisco: Ignatius Press, 2000), 35. All further citations to this volume will be given parenthetically in the body of the essay. This book was originally published as Wahrheit der Welt in 1947, and then subsequently reprinted as the first volume of Balthasar's three-volume *Theo-Logic* (Theologik: Erster Band: Wahrheit der Welt (Einsiedeln: Johannes Verlag, 1985).

22 See Jorge J.E. Gracia, "The Transcendentals in the Middle Ages: An Introduction." *Topoi* 11 (1992), pp. 113- 120; and Jan A. Aertsen, *Medieval Philosophy and the*

there is only a conceptual differentiation between beauty, goodness, unity, and truth; they are all convertible aspects of existence, considered under distinct epistemological modalities. As we shall seem in some more detail below, Aquinas distinguishes the modes of beauty and goodness by indicating that the beautiful simply adds to good a reference to the cognitive faculty. We may further elaborate that precisely because a beautiful object is rationally intelligible, it can also be identified with the property of truth. In addition, because that beauty emanates from an integrally unified subject, it is recognized in the manner of the transcendent one. Hence, the beautiful must be included among those universal properties that transcend all particular categories of being.

To the extent that they suffuse all aspects of existence, the transcendentals give a unique access to being as being. This is especially the case when we examine the relation of truth to being. According to Balthasar, even a thoroughly methodical skeptic, in the manner of Descartes, who doubts the veracity of his own thoughts, is sure that he doubts and "in being certain of his doubt, he is implicitly certain that he is thinking, and in being certain that he is thinking, he is certain that he exists." (36) This primordial truth of existence disclosed in every being's thinking act, even in a thinker that radically doubts the truth of his own thought, already discloses the essence of truth. For in the act of thinking, a consciousness is unveiled in two distinct ways, not only of being *conscious*, but also of *being* conscious. Hence, the existential ground of being is unveiled in thinking and it indicates that being, precisely as being, can be both disclosed and understood. Therefore, for Balthasar, adopting an observation by Martin Heidegger, the initial description of what is true, of the being of truth, is *aletheia* or unveiledness. This "unveiledness is [...] an absolute property of being," and the fact that "being is unveiled entails analytically it is also unveiled to someone who recognizes it in its unveiling." (37-38) That "someone" is the thinking subject who apprehends the truth of being precisely in its existential unveiling. A second fundamental aspect of truth is its quality of *emeth*, that is,

---

Transcendentals: The Case of Thomas Aquinas, Studien und Texte zur Geistesgeschichte des Mittelalters 52 (Leiden, New York, Köln: E.J. Brill, 1996).

of fidelity or reliability. Truth is reliable because once something has been understood and judged to be true it concludes that particular act of unveiling. Nevertheless, the apprehension of one particular truth gives rise to further questions, for once a truth has become evident "a thousand consequences, a thousand insights" spring up (39). This is because "truth is always an opening, not just to itself and in itself, but to further truth" (ibid). No one truth comprehends all of truthfulness, for the true remains transcendent, hence, "it awakens in the knower a yearning for *more*"(40).

According to Balthasar, this yearning for transcendence reveals the duality of truth. That is, "insofar as the disclosure of being is a property objectively inherent in being itself, the knowing subject is obliged to conform itself to this disclosedness" (41). Thus, knowing the truth of a thing occurs when knowledge allows itself to be determined or measured by the thing itself. Nevertheless, as Balthasar points out, the objects of being exists for the sake of thinking subjects:

> *They are offered as possible objects of knowledge so that they can be actually known; they are relative to subjects. It is the subjects that not only possess knowledge and bring it to its conclusion but that also pass judgment on truth as such. Truth in the full sense is actualized only in the act judging the truth—as the manifestness of being now possessed as such in a consciousness. The emphasis in truth thus shifts. Although the object remains the measure by which truth is measured, the agent of the measuring is now the subject . . . . But we can go even further. The disclosure of being is meaningful only if it is directed to the knowing subject. We must therefore say that the object's meaning is first fulfilled in the subject, which therefore contains the measure of the object. (ibid)*

Thus, for Balthasar, the knowing subject not only comprehends the truth, but also brings it into being. Coming to know the truth of things always consists of this twofold process: "knowledge always both gives and receives the measure," so truth is constituted by the "duality of measuring and being measured" (42). The true resides in the dynamic center of these two movements.

Truth, then, is the measure of being. This measure is inherent to being because outside of being there is nothing. Being then contains its own measure, and this measure is nothing other than being unveiling itself. In Balthasar's terminology, a "being that can measure itself because it is unveiled to itself is called a 'subject'" (43). This unveiling of self to a subject is consciousness, the knowing self to which all being unveils itself. "The coincidence of the two disclosures—that of the self and that of the world—guarantees the true objectivity both of the knowledge of the self and of the knowledge of the world" (44). In order for a subject to come to know being it has to be receptive to existence. Not a passive receptivity but rather an active potency, a ready willingness to encounter being as it discloses itself. This fundamental disposition towards truth grows increasingly active the more it comes to know being, so that each act of cognition gives the subject greater impetus to encounter existential truth. The encounter reveals a double limitation to the knowing subject. First, any object, any being, is a limited instantiation that stands out against an unlimited ground of existence that is greater than itself. Secondly, when being is revealed to a subject it realizes that its knowledge cannot be restricted to its own circumscribed subjective consciousness. The knowing subject comes to understand

> *that in applying its own measure to the knowledge of the object, it is not using a subjective measure but is privileged to participate in an objective, ultimately infinite and absolute measure. And so the subject realizes that in the act of measuring it is being measured by the encompassing truth of being . . . which comprehends the subject itself [...] [The subject's] thinking is embedded in an infinite thinking of being and so can serve as a measuring stick only because it itself is measured by an unmeasured, yet all-measuring, infinite measure [...] This infinite, unmeasurable measure is the identity of thinking and being in God. All finite subjectivity and cognition necessarily presupposes the presence of this identity. The finite subject, of course, can never wield this full measure itself, because the plenitude of being does not appear, or even come close to appearing, either in itself or in some appearing object. Nevertheless, the subject can measure*

only in the light of the measure by which it is itself measured. It therefore knows God implicitly in every act of consciousness and in every object. (51-52)[23]

The subject's apprehension of its own existential contingency and cognitive finiteness gives it an awareness that there must be a self-subsistent being-thinking-itself that grounds the very being of truth. The truth proper to finite being is not the possession of absolute truth but rather in its openness to the disclosure of the truth of being in all of its finite instantiations, an openness that is an obediential potency of the creature to the realm of the transcendent. This absolute distinction between the finite truth of the subject and the absolute truth that encompasses it "ultimately grounds the very objectifiability of objects, hence, the intentionality of knowledge." (54) Without this primary distance, the objects of cognition could be mistaken for objects residing solely in the subject's consciousness, a kind of idealism that would undermine the objective truth of being. By contrast, judgments of true objectivity affirm the "intentionality of intellectual cognition, whose primary direction is out of the subject," and they do so because, "in the primordial act in which they lay hold of themselves as subjects, they know that another, holding them in his grasp, places them in existence, over against, and at a distance from, himself." (ibid) This distinction also allows room for intersubjectivity, that is, the existence of many centers of conscious knowing, each open to the disclosure of truth in objects, and in communication with other subjects regarding the being of truth.

Knowledge is thus intentionally directed towards objects that are inherently measurable and intrinsically knowable, but for an object to be knowable it must not only be measurable only in principle but also measured in fact. The object does not measure itself and the subject only knows an object to the extent that is in fact already measured. This paradox leads Balthasar to explain that the conditions for knowability are established by the fact that they are already perfectly known by being itself. However, God, the creator

---

23 In this last sentence Balthasar quotes Thomas Aquinas, *De Veritate*, q.22, a, 2, ad 1: Omnia cognoscentia cognoscunt implicite Deum in quolibet cognito.

of Forms "does not take the measure from an already existing object; rather, the object gets its measure from the idea God has of it. Insofar as the object accords with this idea, it participates in truth." (57) In other words, the idea or Form of the object is already immanent in the object itself. This Form is not to be reduced to an object's outer shape, since Form is an entity's inner principle of being. In living entities, the Form animates the object so that it will actualize its potential for being, and it facilitates the disclosure of that potentiality because being is inherently dynamic. So, the knowing subject does not come to know a static conception of existence through the Form, but rather the moving, ever-shifting entelechy (*entelecheia*) that drives being toward its transcendent fulfillment. The subject, in apprehending being and judging its truth through Form participates analogically in God's creative knowledge of being. The term *entelecheia* denotes the fact that every Form has an inner nature or principle of operation which makes it to be precisely what it is and nothing else, along with a concomitant characteristic set of potentialities, which informs not only all of its present actions, but which impels it to fulfill its ultimate *telos* or goal. Perhaps the best way to understand entelechy is to think of it as an immanent dynamic purpose that is encoded into our very essence. This inner dynamism is evident in any complex organized state, in any Form, that persists against all internal and external events that would divert it from its ultimate natural fulfillment. Narrative as Lafferty practices it— Drama, to use Balthasar's favored phrase—at its most general can perhaps then be seen as the story of a universe of objects with their respective entelechies as they unfold over time, a universe which in and of itself, as a totality, has in turn its own teleological Form, its own destiny to fulfill.

As both subjects and objects, Forms can be considered apart from each other, yet in reality there is a cognitional reciprocity between both poles of knowing. Objects find their essential completion, as objects of knowledge, only outside themselves, that is, only within the interior world of a knowing subject. This subjective interiority is the space that objects need in order to come fully and truly into being. A tree, for example, needs to be experienced by a subject in all its leafy objectivity so that it can fruitfully achieve its arboreal essence. A tree that is not experienced has not fully actualized its tree-Form. "It needs the sensorium as a space in which to unfurl itself. It unveils its color within an eye that sees color; it whispers in an ear that hears sound; it presents its unique flavor only in the mouth of another capable of tasting." (63) Moreover, a tree that is not known by a subject remains a mere material substrate.

> *The concept that expresses the full essence of the tree needs something more than that substrate; it needs someone to conceive it, someone whose heterogeneous, though analogous, space holds ready the complementary factors required alongside its already existing vital principle for the full, organic, unitary concept of the plant's essence [...] This concept alone utters what the tree truly is, in other words, the truth of the tree. This truth is the unveiledness of its being, but the unveiling in which the truth is constituted calls for the joint operation of subject and object. It is not a property inhering in the object alone that merely needs to be discovered; rather, this discovery, which is something that the subject does, is an essential component of the unveiling of the object. The latter's objective truth lies partly in itself and partly in the space of the subject whose activity helps it become what it is meant to be. (64)*

According to Balthasar, in a "naively realistic world view, which unreflectively regards sensory qualities as inherent in the object even apart from the space opened by the sensorium, the object has no need to unfold in a subjective space;" in other words, the object is epistemologically self-sufficient and "at most emits images of itself to enrich subjects with a view of its essence," but these "images are mere duplicates of the objects, not the deployment of their essence" (65). In such a world, Balthasar contends, the subject comes to know only reflections of being, not being in its undisclosed truthfulness. Conversely, in the idealist critical philosophy associated with Immanuel Kant, knowledge resides almost exclusively in a knowing subject that never comes into full contact with things-in-themselves, so that "in the end the truth of things is reduced to a few abstract, nonsensory . . . concepts" (66). However, in an account of knowledge that appreciates the constitutive role of both subject and object in the epistemic—and perhaps even more importantly—the aesthetic or creative process, the object only comes fully into being when it is cognized in the apprehension of a knower, and a knower only becomes truly conscious as a subject by recognizing itself in the work of coming to know being. Rather than needing to free itself from the prison-house of solipsistic subjectivism, for Balthasar, the knowing subject is "always already plunged into the richest fullness of 'truth in itself,'" and so, it need only actualize its receptive potentiality in "order to transform truth into 'truth for itself'" (69). The self and the world constitute each other correlatively. None of this is to say that the knowing subject exhausts the meaning of that which is known, for the true measure of being only resides in the transcendent Knower wherein being is measured. The process of unveiling is never concluded in this world, and even the lowliest object processes a boundless ontic richness. As Aquinas himself wrote, "Our manner of knowing is so weak that no philosopher could perfectly investigate the nature of even one little fly. We even read that a certain philosopher spent thirty years in solitude in order to know the nature of the bee."[24]

"This Was More Than a Spectacle, More Than an Illusion, It Was a Communicating Instrument"

These extensive epistemological ruminations are ultimately at the service of a fully worked-out aesthetics, a conception of beauty and creation that Balthasar traces back to Aquinas, and which has significant areas of convergence with Lafferty's own poetic practice and notions regarding the communicative relationality of the world. Very much in the manner of his epistemology, Balthasar's aesthetic focuses on the knowable, perceptual aspects of Form, particularly when such perceptive experience, effectuated by an expressive-

---

24 Thomas Aquinas, *Expositio in Symbolum Apostolorum, Prooemium*: Sed cognitio nostra est adeo debilis quod nullus philosophus potuit unquam perfecte investigare naturam unius muscae: unde legitur, quod unus philosophus fuit triginta annis in solitudine, ut cognosceret naturam apis.

ly vivid clarity, lays open the object to us, not just in regard to its outward appearance but to its inner nature (its entelechy), and beyond that to a disclosure of the interconnected world of beings in which it subsists. This kind of clarity, one that begins to reveal ever more profound levels of being within Forms, is referred to by Aquinas as "radiance" or "splendor"—it is a kind of "brightness" that evinces itself in the very *esse*, the self-communicating act-of-being of Forms. This splendor contains infinite depths, for it reveals itself as both an unlimited capacity within objects or Forms for ontic self-disclosure, but also a correlatively isomorphic capacity in us as fellow entities to grasp these formal acts of self-disclosure as an endless expanse of radiant intelligibility.[25]

On Thomas' account, beautiful things possess three qualities: *integritas*, *consonantia*, and *claritas*. *Integritas* has some affiliation with the English integrity; but for Aquinas, it primarily signifies wholeness and perfection, the idea that nothing essential is absent, nor anything superfluous present in a thing. Likewise, consonantia has parallels with the English term consonance, particularly in relation to its musical roots: that is, the combination of notes that are in harmony with each other due to the relationship between their frequencies. However, this harmonious interconnection of elements does not just refer to a relation of functional parts to one another, but even more so the quality of proportionality towards the object's teleological fulfillment. The third element, *claritas*, (precisely the el-

25 The secondary literature on Thomas' aesthetics is vast. Only a few works can be indicated: Maurice De Wulf, "Les théories esthétiques propres à Saint Thomas," *Revue néoscholastique* 1—2 (1894—1895), pp. 188—205, 341—357, 117—142; Jacques Maritain: *Art and Scholasticism*, trans. J. W. Evans (New York: Charles Scribner's Sons, 1962), originally published in 1921; Francis J. Kovach: *Die Aesthetik des Thomas von Aquin* (Berlin: De Gruyter, 1961); Cyril Barrett, "The Aesthetics of St Thomas Re-Examined," *Philosophical Studies* 12 (1963), pp. 107—124; Armand Maurer: *About Beauty* (Houston: Center for Thomistic Studies, 1983); Umberto Eco, *The Aesthetics of Thomas Aquinas*, trans. H. Bredin (Cambridge: Harvard University Press, 1988); Jan A. Aertsen, "Beauty in the Middle Ages: A Forgotten Transcendental?," *Medieval Philosophy and Theology* 1 (1991), pp. 68—97; Pascal Dasseleer, "Esthétique 'thomiste' ou esthétique 'thomasienne,'" *Revue Philosophique de Louvain* 97:2 (1999), pp. 312—335; Brendan Thomas Sammon, *The God Who Is Beauty: Beauty as a Divine Name in Thomas Aquinas and Dionysius the Areopagite*, Princeton Theological Monograph Series 206 (Eugene, OR: Pickwick Publications, 2013).

ement of Aquinas' idea of beauty that Balthasar focuses on most in his aesthetics), is the ability of an object, as Form, to communicate or reveal some aspects of its ontological reality in relation to the perceptive gaze or attentive ear of an observer or listener, who not only sees the outward appearance of an object, or perceives the surface structure of a musical composition, but delves beneath outward appearance to reach the essential features of the aesthetic object. At its most essential, *claritas* is *"the fundamental communicability of form, which is made actual in relation to someone's looking at or seeing of the object.* The rationality that belongs to every form is the 'light' which manifests itself to aesthetic seeing."[26] To summarize: Thomas posits that something is beautiful if it possesses all of its constituent elements (*integritas*), is proportional within itself and in relation to its ultimate purpose (*consonantia*), and makes manifest its hidden or essential reality to the perceptive viewer/hearer (*claritas*).

Moreover, Thomas posits that there is a proportion between the knower and that which is known, a true epistemic isomorphism, wherein forms come to be in the mind according to the mode of the knower, so that truth can thereby be understood as an adequation, received first through the senses, and culminating in a judgment, between the reality of the object known and the consciousness of the knowing subject. In addition, the beautiful, that which manifests some essential truth through *integritas, consonantia,* and *claritas,* is—as we have already seen Balthasar will later argue—the same as the good, for beauty, goodness, and truth differ in aspect only. Since, as Aquinas, following Aristotle, argues that the eudaimonistic good is what all men seek, then the acquisition of this good will be that which completes the universal impetus towards fulfillment; while the notion of the beautiful embraces that aspect of the good which satisfies the appetitive power of the senses when perceived. Hence, Thomas will famously write,

> *The beautiful is the same as the good, and they differ in aspect only. For since good is what all seek, the notion of good is that which calms the desire; while the notion of the beautiful is that*

---

26 Eco, *Aesthetics of Thomas Aquinas,* p. 119. Italics in the original.

which calms the desire, by being seen or known. Consequently those senses chiefly regard the beautiful, which are the most cognitive, viz. sight and hearing... Thus it is evident that beauty adds to goodness a relation to the cognitive faculty: so that 'good' means that which simply pleases the appetite; while the 'beautiful' is something pleasant to apprehend.[27]

The integrity, harmony, and splendor of beauty evinces itself in the very *esse* or act of being of things, revealing itself at once as both an unlimited capacity for an object's self-communication, and a corresponding receptivity in us to grasp that act of self-communication as an endless expanse of radiant intelligibility. The beautiful, precisely as *claritas*, is the meeting place of Form with transcendent light. Paradoxically, the inexhaustible ontic depth and self-transcendence of things, manifesting themselves as splendor, can also be perceived by us as a dazzling darkness, a radiance that blinds precisely because of its super-abundant transcendent clarity. If beauty is the realm of formal clarity, then the apophatic blindness of transcendent light can perhaps best be situated in the dark intervals between immanent and transcendent being wherein Forms are generated.[28]

A truly aesthetic encounter reveals, therefore, not only the beauty and goodness of things, but discloses their essential truth, the depths of their being, as well. A Lafferterian aesthetic, if indeed it followed the spirit of Balthasar's Thomism, would perforce embrace a similar account of our encounter with the beautiful. It would

---

27 Thomas Aquinas, *Summa Theologiciae*, I-II, q.27, a.1, ad.3: Quod pulchrum est idem bono, sola ratione differens. Cum enim bonum sit quod omnia appetunt, de ratione boni est quod in eo quietetur appetitus, sed ad rationem pulchri pertinet quod in eius aspectu seu cognitione quietetur appetitus. Unde et illi sensus praecipue respiciunt pulchrum, qui maxime cognoscitivi sunt, scilicet visus et auditus rationi deservientes, dicimus enim pulchra visibilia et pulchros sonos . . . Et sic patet quod pulchrum addit supra bonum, quendam ordinem ad vim cognoscitivam, ita quod bonum dicatur id quod simpliciter complacet appetitui; pulchrum autem dicatur id cuius ipsa apprehensio placet.

28 See Gregory P. Rocca, O.P., *Speaking the Incomprehensible God: Thomas Aquinas on the Interplay of Positive and Negative Theology* (Washington, D.C.: The Catholic University of America Press, 2004); Steffen Lösel, "Love Divine, All Loves Excelling: Balthasar's Negative Theology of Revelation," *The Journal of Religion* 82: 4 (2002), pp. 586-616.

honor the mysterious ontic profundity ensconced at the heart of every entity in the world, regardless of its relative size or importance, much like OOO does, but unlike that metaphysic, it would at the same time highlight each substance's innate ability to communicate its own unique act of existence, from within the relational complex that is reality, by means of its *integritas, consonantia,* and *claritas* to anyone with the vision to perceive it. Finally, the creative process itself would partake of the plenitude of being, as it generates a multitude of Forms that will manifest the good, and thus give pleasure when seen, even when that vision may finally bedazzle us with its transcendent beauty. And indeed, we have something quite akin to this in a scene from Lafferty's novel *Arrive at Easterwine,* when Diogenes Pontifex, at the behest of Valery Mok, a member of the Institute of Impure Science, conjures a new game of "Conceptualism in Contemporary Snow Design" out of the thin, cold winter air, pregnant with the possibility of new Forms:

> *Now they gazed in admiration at the results of their own meddling, and a thousand or so other people had also gathered to gaze.*
>
> *"We'll have to top them out soon, Valery," Diogenes said. "We use every trick of structure and weightlessness, but we will have to top them out soon."*
>
> *There are not words enough to say, there are not minds enough to comprehend the sublimity of the airy snow towers that were being raised. It had come on dusk now, almost dark, but the snow steeples and spires and towers glowed interiorly with blue and gold light. Genuine obelisk crystals will always glow with these colors in the dark. That the snow obeliskite did so also, shows that the glow is a property of the structure and not of the quartz.*
>
> *"Buttresses, flying buttresses, rib-vaults, arcading, triforiums, archivolts, engaged columns, ridge ribs, lantern domes, buttress arches, piers, build them in," Valery was ordering the construction to assemble itself.*
>
> *"We are using all of them, Valery, and more intricate counterparts of them," Diogenes said, "but we will still have to top it all out."*

There are not eyes enough to see the wonder that was rising. It was Cielito, the City of the Sky; it was Wolkenzwingburg, the Sky-Fastness. There were Castles and Minsters and Pleasure Palaces up there, but more open, more dimensioned, more populated than any previously conceived. Every person of the earth city was out gaping at the rising sky-towers. There was tracery up there, lacelike bridges thrown across from spire to spire, intricacy impossible, night colors incredible. Spirakite will glow red and purple in the dark; sicalite will glow yellow and orange; agukite will glow green and flame-olive: that the snow ghosts of these crystals also glowed shows that the glow-lights are properties of the structures and not of the rock-crystals.

This was more than a spectacle, more than an illusion, it was a communicating instrument.

"We will still have to top it out, Valery," Diogenes whispered, and now all the Institute people were with them. The snow-structure was the nexus of a web and it was radiating and speaking from its center.[29]

This work is © 2015 Gregorio Montejo.

Gregorio Montejo is a professor of Historical Theology at Boston College. His research interests include Thomas Aquinas, Medieval Theology, Christology, Trinitarian Theology, and Pneumatology. Gregorio is a member of the Catholic Theological Society of America, the Society of Biblical Literature, the North American Patristics Society, etc.

http://www.bc.edu/schools/cas/theology/faculty/gmontejo.html

---

29 R. A. Lafferty, *Arrive at Easterwine: The Autobiography of a Ktistec Machine* (New York: Ballantine Books, 1971), pp. 157-158.

Through a Glass Darkly: an Analysis of the Parabolic Significance and Christian Context of R. A. Lafferty's "In Deepest Glass"

By Craig May

> *"The Stained Glass Art, seemingly the most sessile of arts, was flowing powerfully. It wasn't interpreting; it was unfolding. It was pouring out the traveled and lived epic which is itself plot and narration, the Epic of Man and his Friends, of that brave company that has both angels and apes on its fringes."*
>
> R. A. Lafferty, "In Deepest Glass"

> *"The language of art is a 'parabolic' language, with a special openness to the universal: the 'Way of Beauty' is a path capable of leading the mind and heart to the Lord, to elevate them to the heights of God."*
>
> Pope Benedict XVI, from a speech delivered in Oct., 2012

"In Deepest Glass: an Informal History of Stained Glass Windows" by R. A. Lafferty has been published only once: in the *Berkley Showcase: New Writings in Science Fiction and Fantasy Vol. 4*, published in July, 1981. The story is an atypical one—not that any story by Lafferty can ever really be considered typical—in that it does not have any characters or even a standard narrative, but rather the story is presented in the format of a short history, essentially an encyclopedia article, written in the 22nd century on the history of stained glass windows. "In Deepest Glass," however, is more than a science fiction story in the guise of an historical essay; it is in fact a modern parable: a parable reflecting Lafferty's understanding of the entire history and meaning of the world. In this parable Lafferty uses images (stained glass windows) to depict the nature of the world and the significance of Man's place in it; and, since Lafferty himself has a religious worldview, it follows that the parable of "In Deepest Glass" is informed by and consistent with Lafferty's Catholicism; and, beyond that, even the very use of stained glass as a symbol within this parable is inspired by Lafferty's Catholic experience and philosophy.

I

The history presented in the story consists of descriptions of five periods of time where stained glass windows have been important in human history: the first was during the time of the Neanderthals, the second during the Medieval period, the third was during the Zurichthal Ice Age of the 22nd century, the fourth was during a three year period shortly after the Zurichthal Ice Age, and the final time mentioned in the history began ten years later. It is during this time that the history of stained glass is written.

This history of stained glass explains the differences in these periods of stained glass artistry: the first time that stained glass appears on Earth was during the time of the Neanderthals. The Neanderthals used stained glass although they did not make it, rather it was "something that happened to them as an intuitive people." Lafferty explains that the Neanderthals made the glass, itself, but that it was "wind-borne" elements of the air (arising from increased volcanic activity) that enlivened the glass with the stained glass appearance and artistry. Despite the fact that this is the first appearance of stained glass on Earth (and that it is Neanderthals using it and not modern humans), the "whole history of Man and His Friends was contained in the deep glass pictures." The Neanderthal glass is "the pristine stuff from the beginning." The Neanderthal period (the "First Age of Magic") is distinguished from the Cro-Magnon period that followed where humans lived and created art in caves. The history points out that despite the fact that the Neanderthals lived during an age of Magic—something went "wrong near the very *beginning* of the Neanderthal Era."

The second period of stained glass discussed in this future history was during the Medieval time period. This creation of stained glass here is described as different than during the earlier period. In the Medieval period, humans made the glass intentionally through ingenuity and handicraft. In the Medieval period glass pieces were put together to form larger pictures: "The result was mostly a glass mosaic. [...] it was imitative work. But it had an element that the mosaics lacked: light shining through everything, sunlight, sunlight, sunlight, that totality of color suffusing the fractured colors." Although the history notes that "If something had clearly gone wrong with the world at the very beginning of the Neanderthal Era, something had clearly gone right with the world near the beginning of the Medieval period."

The description of the third period of stained glass activity takes up the majority of this informal history of stained glass. It takes place during in the 22nd century when an ice age has occurred along with an increase in volcanic activity. The result is that colored images appear on much of the world's glass. It is recognized as being the result of the climate, but we are told it is also the result of the Spirits of the Air. Most people disliked the images that appeared on the glass for cutting down on their view or for recording their dreams of the night before. People tried to eliminate the images from the glass, but were unable to. Some of the very best images that appeared however are recognized as Masterworks of Art and are highly regarded by a few. Eventually computers secretly worked to sequence the Masterwork images into a pattern, and they began a travel agency that allowed people to go on a Grand Tour (described as a pilgrimage) to see all the Masterworks in order: to view all of the stained glass Masterworks would take eleven years. The computers realized that if the Masterworks are viewed in the correct sequence, then a story is told and revealed by the images in the glass: and the story is nothing less than the Epic Story of Mankind from beginning to end. Some people went on pilgrimage to view all or some of the masterworks, and they were ennobled by their partaking of it; but, the majority of people reject, misinterpret, or ignore the Epic; some we are told disapprove of the images because if the Great Epic told in the glass had a design (which the computers insisted it did), then the universe itself must have a design and that is unacceptable. In addition to suggesting design, the Epic revealed Man's past: the First Age of Magic where Man had transcendent powers before "the fall." After his fall, Man's mental and moral world shrank so that Man essentially lived on a narrow isthmus or island. The Epic pointed to a way to return to a Second Age of Magic ("Wake up all the world and tell the good news"), but "The Establishment had buried all its treasure on that desert island, and it could not go away and leave it." So a revolt among the anti-establishment occurs (although Lafferty wryly notes that "Both the Establishment and the Anti-Establishment...[have been]...identical for two hundred and fifty years"). So the climate is artificially warmed by humans and the volcanic activity stopped, and the window smashers destroyed most of the stained glass on Earth, after all: "What could be more popular than smashing glass! What could be more popular than smashing people! A great toll was taken on both."

The fourth appearance of stained glass windows occurs shortly after the iconoclasm which brought an end to the third appearance. This time the stained glass returned during a three year period of cold weather, and the new images appeared on every piece of glass or crystal on the planet On many of the pictures that appeared, in red ("popularly named Armageddon Red"), the words "Repent, Repent" appeared as if made by lightning.

The final occurrence of stained glass began ten years after the fourth ended, and it is similar to the second (Medieval) creation of stained glass in that it is an imitative endeavor that originates with human craftsmen. These craftsmen are "impassioned amateurs" (remember that the root of the word amateur is one who does something for love). These human imitations are created in "tenuous rapport to the Armageddon Glass of the three year period." The writer of the history wonders at the end of the story if there will be a "retrospect to our now" that can appreciate the efforts of the human craftsmen.

Can one claim that "In Deepest Glass" is an allegory? Perhaps. But it might be more accurate to view the story as a parable: a parable about the necessity of both repentance and art. "In Deepest Glass" certainly has parabolic elements to it. I think the key to understanding the story's symbolism is in the description of the fourth occurrence of stained glass: the three year period marked by the appearance (in Armageddon Red) of the command to "Repent." If one views the story as possessing Christian elements, which on the surface words and phrases like "the Fall," "repent," "Medieval," "pilgrimage," "stained glass," "Good News," and so on would suggest, then I think one can view the fourth appearance of Stained Glass within the story as suggesting or representing the three-year ministry of Christ, whose constant admonition to humanity was to repent ("to turn around" or "to return home"). If that is possible, then the fifth age of images would correspond, in reality, to our time: the time after Christ has ascended when some work as amateurs (out of love) to imitate the Masterwork. St. Paul himself frequently reminded his hearers and readers that we live in the last days; or, as the story puts it, a time when there will not be "a retrospect to our now."

If that is a possible reading, then the third age could be an age of Prophecy (Old Testament?) since this age does reveal the entire Epic, which includes events of the future—including the three year period of Armageddon Red lettering. This could suggest that the second age of stained glass (one of the two uninspired times) could suggest pagan art. The first age of stained glass, in this reading, could represent Man in his paradisal state: an Age of Magic and Wonder.

In any case, it is clear that Lafferty also intends to have the images that appear in the stained glass windows throughout the story represent art in general: both pictorial art and written art. To enter into a second Age of Magic, one must do so through Repentance, but one must also do so, incarnationally, by means of experiencing and perceiving Man's Story through the medium of images and tales.

II

Aside from the fact that the symbolism of "In Deepest Glass" (i.e., references to a Fall, Good News, repentance, Medieval stained glass, pilgrimages, etc.,) seems to be informed by Lafferty's Catholic theology, I believe the very importance of images in the story was suggested to Lafferty by his Catholic faith as well. In the Epistle to the Hebrews, St. Paul (or whoever the actual author of this inspired epistle was) says that Christ "is the brightness of God's glory, and the express image [Greek: icon] of his [the Father's] person" (Heb. 1:3). Traditional forms of Christianity (the Catholic, Orthodox, and

Oriental Orthodox churches) have always viewed the fact of the Incarnation of Christ as a mandate for the use of images in a religious context: God Himself, after all, became an image for mankind to see and worship at the Incarnation. In fact the Fathers of the Second Council of Nicaea (A.D. 787) wrote that "The Tradition of making images...existed even at the time of the preaching of Christianity by the Apostles...Iconography is by no means an invention of painters but is, on the contrary, an established law and tradition of the Catholic Church." As Lafferty would have been aware, members of the Catholic Church have, since the beginning, venerated images as a part of religious worship and used religious imagery and symbolism to communicate truth in stories. In the first millennium of the Christian era two dimensional art such as paintings (usually referred to as icons), mosaics, tapestries, and stained glass windows predominated, but in the second millennium of the Church (esp. since the European Renaissance of the 14th century) three dimensional statues have become the most popular form of pictorial art.

Lafferty, who began his own history *The Fall of Rome* with a description of an ancient Roman mosaic of Christ, would no doubt be aware of the importance and use of images to Christians throughout time. In his essay on the use of images in the early Church, Leonid Ouspensky points out that "beginning in the 1st and 2nd centuries...besides allegorical and symbolic representations, such as anchor, fish, lamb and so forth, a whole series of pictures drawn from the Old and New Testaments" would serve as the themes for the "catacomb paintings." Ouspensky continues that "From the very first centuries, Christian art was deeply symbolical and this symbolism was...essentially inseparable from Church art, because the spiritual reality it represents cannot be transmitted otherwise than through symbols." As far as pagan symbols being used in Christian artwork, Ouspensky explains that symbols "from pagan mythology, as for instance, Cupid and Psyche, Orpheus, etc." were also used in Christian artwork and "in using these myths, Christianity re-establishes their true and profound meaning, filling them with new content. This adoption by Christianity of elements of pagan art is not limited to the first period of its existence. Later, too, it takes from the world around it all that may serve it as a means and form of expression [... although ...] what the Church accepts from the world is determined not by the needs of the Church but by those of the world." The Church then, from its beginning, has used pictorial art—both of Christian and worldly origins—to reveal and unravel spiritual Truths. This is true in the early Church and continued even until modern times. If one sees pictures of or visits the Christ the King parish in Tulsa where Lafferty was a longtime parishioner, one will notice the immense stained glass windows of saints behind the altar and in other locations around the Church. Lafferty's Christ the King parish was part of a long line of Churches where images told stories that conveyed Truth. And just as Christian iconography has over its history, Lafferty uses symbols in his stories and novels from many diverse sources (pagan mythology, Jungian psychology, secular history, etc...) to create a complex tapestry which reveals a larger truth in a beautiful way.

Through "In Deepest Glass," Lafferty, a devout Catholic, utilizes the constant understanding shown in Christian art across the centuries of the truth-revealing power of images. In the story, visual icons (stained glass), which are driven by "wind borne" elements and the "Spirits of the World" appear in the glass of the world: they depict the whole epic scope, both spatially and chronologically, of a designed creation, and they remind men of Man's central role in this story: the central message in the story as well as of the story is for people to "repent" so they can experience a "Second Age of Magic" where we realize our true nature and our true home. Lafferty ends "In Deepest Glass" with the observation that the history of stained glass depicted in the story does not use "any element of the grotesque." It is an unusual sentence to end with, but I think Lafferty is drawing on the original meaning of the word grotesque which was "grotto or cave-like," which can refer either to caves or to art drawn on cave walls. But icons (esp. stained glass windows which are so full of light) are called by the Catholic Church "windows to heaven." And Lafferty, indeed, has the stained glass in his story be a window which provides not only a view of heaven, but a passage there as well: a transcendent passage out of the cave and away from the grotesque.

WORKS CITED:

Lafferty, R. A. "In Deepest Glass: an Informal History of Stained Glass Windows." *Berkley Showcase: New Writings in Science Fiction and Fantasy Vol. 4*, 1981. Eds. Victoria Schoschet and Melissa A. Singer. New York: Berkley Pub Group. Print.

Ouspensky, Leonid. "The Meaning of Icons." New York: St. Vladimir's Seminary Press, 2002. Print.

Paul, "Epistle to the Hebrews."

Craig May is a husband and father of nine, who, in his spare time, teaches language arts to 7th and 8th grade students, and reads and studies the works of R. A. Lafferty, Gene Wolfe, George MacDonald, and Sir Arthur Conan Doyle.

Exploring Themes From Catholic Theology in Two Short Stories by R. A. Lafferty

By John Ellison

"Will there be a mass this morning, Mike?" Melchisedech asked.
"There won't be any this morning," the statue said sadly...
R. A. Lafferty, "Great Day in the Morning"

The pursuit of shapes and elusive patterns in the works of R. A. Lafferty is one obvious technique for putting together any kind of textual analysis of his writings. I had been going over notes I had been making for an essay that looked at the Catholic mass as a sort of central super-narrative and how this was an influence on Lafferty's work. I seemed to have the necessary content but was struggling to get the right tone and overarching structure that would bring it to completion. Then I came across a newspaper interview with Bob Dylan in which he is talking about formative moments in the evolution of his musical style:

> *I remember listening to the Staple Singers "Uncloudy Day". And it was the most mysterious thing I'd ever heard. It was like the fog rolling in. I heard it again [...] and its mystery had deepened. What was that? How do you make that? It just went through me like my body was invisible [...] I listened to the Staple Singers a lot. Certainly more than any other gospel group. I like spiritual songs. They struck me as truthful and serious. They brought me down to earth and they lifted me up all in the same moment [...] And even at that age I felt that life itself was a mystery.*
> The Independent, 3 February 2015

This was a kind of epiphany for me. What seemed most obviously coincidental was that I had been looking at themes in two particular stories, "Great Day in the Morning" and "Incased in Ancient Rind" that were directly echoed at a number of levels in this quote from Dylan. Importantly, too, I now felt that many of the barriers had vanished in relation to this essay. I had fussed too long trying to find a smooth-surfaced discourse. If it was a bit fragmentary and rough-edged, so too, I realized, were those very moments of epiphany I was glancing at in various parts of the discourse of the essay.

Returning to the quote at the start of this essay, the conversation between Melchisedech Duffy and the statue of St Michael, it is worth noting how "science-fictional" aspects of the catholic mass may seem to a non-believer. For a regular participant in the catholic mass, like R. A. Lafferty, it really was a context where unlikely channels of communication and transformation could take place. Because the key principles of the Real Presence and Eucharist are never really softened by the qualifying descriptions of symbol and metaphor the substance of the catholic liturgy does happily conflict with the accepted laws of science.

The liturgical experience is a coming together of the eternal and the temporal in everyday life. In fact, despite all its recurring structures and familiarized forms of communication, it is a kind of constant refutation of the way "everyday life" and "the ordinary" are understood within the contemporary secular consensus. Although it is indeed the same thing over and over again, the mass always contains that transfiguring aspect of the eternal. Every regular attendee can eventually see the complex mix of experience and sensation as tinged with the colors of the transcendent. The mass, therefore, is that foundational narrative to which the faithful return to gain sustenance for every aspect of their lives. Again, the term "feeding" on the Eucharistic gifts of bread and wine means so much more than a merely symbolic act of memorial.

The sense of repose and comfort that secular critics presume is offered in communal celebrations of religion contrasts with the real sense of drama and enactment woven into the liturgy. The Catholic theologian Romano Guardini expresses this point in the following terms:

> *Christ's promise teaches us to re-evaluate the present, the better to persevere in it.*

> *How well we understand the mood that must have prevailed in the early Christian congregations. Those people knew: everything around us is uncertain, alien, edged with danger. No one knows what tomorrow will bring. Now, however, we are here, celebrating the memorial of our Lord. He knows about us, and we know about him.*
>
> Romano Guardini, *Meditations before Mass*

There has developed in Catholic thought a kind of "theological aesthetics" of the Eucharist often expressed in terms of a person's appetite and vigor in relation to the fullness of being. Lafferty's recurrence to themes of the morning and new adventures may be seen as directly connected to this:

> *To me, most of the great moments of SF are planet-falls: unshipping and setting foot on new worlds. And yet the experience of planet-fall is a daily thing, one that never grows stale...We live in a tolerably new world, and there is always the feeling of having just arrived on it.*
>
> R. A. Lafferty, "The Case of the Moth-Eaten Magician"

In "Great Day in the Morning" we are confronted with radical breaks in the continuity and flow of the normal world. Rather than an adventure this soon turns out to be a descent into an enclave from which the Eucharistic elements of communication and encounter have been excised. The mass is not taking place that morning; the motion of the sun across the sky is halted; sign systems such as newspapers and traffic lights have taken on new and opaque modes of communicating; and, finally, bodies themselves are portrayed as in various processes of transformation and disintegration.

I have tried to suggest so far that the liturgical outlook can look back in memorial and forward in anticipatory hope. This stretching and interweaving of consciousness also creates a sense of a solid present that is not just being constantly dissolved into nothingness. The assent to and reassurance in the here-and-now offers a kind of "ground of being" on which cultures and personal lives can be built. The action of this particular story shows us how the traditional cultural forms which have sustained the concrete sense of the present are now presumed to be obsolete.

> *Papers and magazines were useful only for the transition period. Now that the Great Day is here we should be doing Great Day stuff instead. [...] Be free, be unenclosed, be emancipated, be unstructured,' they all insisted to him.*
>
> R. A. Lafferty, "Great Day in the Morning"

In interpreting the significance of this general unstructuring of being it may be appropriate to turn to additional Catholic thinkers and their reflections on the body. This from Karl Adam speaking about the historical Church:

> *In acute and prolonged conflicts with Gnostics, Manicheans, Albigenses, Bogomili, and other sects, she has guarded the rights and dignity of the human body [...] She does not regard the body as a "garment of shame", but as a holy and precious creation of God [...] This reverence for the body leads the Church further to a careful consideration of man's sensible needs. Since we are not pure spirits, but spirits enmeshed in body, we grasp spiritual things by means of things visible and sensible. Hence the whole sacramental system of Christianity and the Church.*
>
> Karl Adam, The Spirit of Catholicism

It is important to reflect how this validation of bodies also offers an implied guarantee for the containing categories of time and space. This next quote is from the medieval mystic and visionary, Julian of Norwich:

> *For just as the body is clothed in its garments, and the flesh in its skin, and the bones in their flesh, and the heart in its body, so too are we, soul and body, clothed from head to foot in the goodness of God.*
>
> Julian of Norwich, Revelations of Divine Love

Reflecting on the insights of the above quote, the attacks on Melchisedech as an "old wine-skin" and the attempts to rip away his clothing clearly discloses a theological level to the story: Lafferty is trying to portray the destruction of the manifold layers of spiritual and physical reality.

While Duffy refuses any assent to these new patterns of being this is not the case for the rest of the characters in the story:

> *[...] the people were all interiorizing themselves. Some skinless, some part so, they looked blank, blank in every part of them. And they were merging. They were coming together witlessly, blankly, spherically. Dozens of them had now formed into great balls all together. These rolled, and they merged with other great balls of people substance. Soon all the people in the whole city would be coalesced into one big fleshy sphere, communicating and interiorizing like anything.*
>
> *Then all the peoples of the world would somehow roll together and become one thing, although the mechanics of this latter development were far from clear.*
>
> R. A. Lafferty, "Great Day In The Morning"

Lafferty uses the sphere here as a kind of emblem of inhuman forms of self-enclosure. Similarly, the canopy in "Incased in Ancient Rind" is shown as another form of enclosing sphere:

> *"Why should anyone want to go above the canopy?" Harry Baldachin asked crossly. "Or rather, why should anyone want to claim to do it, since it is now assumed that the canopy is endless and no one could go above it?"*
>
> R. A. Lafferty, "Incased in Ancient Rind"

The canopy in this story has closed the earth off from color and any perception of the blue sky. Corresponding with this is a shift towards ponderous and deliberate motion as bodies have become thickened and slow-moving. Over the course of the story we are shown the wearing away of the memory of the old world. In the first of the regular hundred-yearly meetings all the characters still remember and talk about the old elemental world of frost, snow, rain and thunder. By the second meeting there is a polarization of memory and opinion:

> *Charles Broadman answered, "[...] Then came the clear instant, which has been called glaciation, flood or catastrophe, when it was shattered completely and the blue sky was seen supreme. It was quite a short instant, some say it was not more than ten thousand years, some say it was double that. It happened and now it is gone. But are we expected to forget that bright instant?"*
> *"The law expects you to forget that instant, Broadman, since it never happened, and it is forbidden to say that it happened," Baldachin stated stubbornly.*
> R. A. Lafferty, "Incased in Ancient Rind"

In each of the stories there are moves towards enclosure at various thematic levels. The slogans and instructions that Duffy receives from the characters in "Great Day in the Morning" set out the new edited—down version of reality which he should conform to. In "Incased in Ancient Rind" we see the shifted relationships of time and bodies in a number of telling passages:

> *Many human minds would still have been able to master the mathematics of stellar movements and positions, if ease and the disappearance of the stellar content had not robbed them of the inclination and opportunity for such things. [...]*
> *"How could anything happen in a hundred years?" Harry Baldachin asked.*
> R. A. Lafferty, "Incased in Ancient Rind"

The stasis which weighs down on most of the characters under the canopy is a kind of living death. By contrast, Sally Strumpet and her husband are shown as still connected to the "blue sky" sources of fertility and creativity. Sally's actions of having sons and daughters and quoting from old poetry are seen, though, as a kind of riddle by the others. They can no longer comprehend what these actions are supposed to mean. When Sally's husband announces that "you destroy yourselves under the canopy," the reference point of this and other rainbow allusions are to the Old Testament account of the covenant made by God after the flood:

> *When I gather the clouds over the earth and the bow appears in the clouds, I will recall the Covenant between myself and you and every living creature of every kind. And so the waters shall never become a flood to destroy all things of the flesh.*
>
> Genesis 9:12-16

In the Catholic mass as the liturgy ascends to the high-point of Eucharistic offering there is the phrase, "This is the cup of my blood, the blood of the new and everlasting Covenant."

I want to propose here a kind of grappling in Lafferty's stories with the mystery of God's intervention into the world. In the Old Testament the rainbow's formation at the intersection of the elements of light, water and air is a guarantee that God will continue to sustain the world. The celebration of the Eucharistic rites associated with the New Covenant is also a kind of recurring configuration within history which is noted, and participated in, by God.

All of the preceding may make some sense of the way that we can say that Lafferty is not at all a world-denying writer. In fact, as many critics have noted, his texts overflow with people, food, words and happenings. At the same time we can also argue that he is a deeply spiritual writer speaking from the living tradition of Catholicism.

Can we start to see these emerging patterns as having relevance for ongoing interpretations of Lafferty and do they speak to our present cultural situation? At one level it is tempting to see our own lives resembling the sharp, fast-moving world described in "Slow Tuesday Night." But with billions rendered immobile by staring into the screens which relay the electronic narratives of the world; bodies grown pale and obese by withdrawal from the natural and social environment; consciousness desensitized by the layers of chat and imagery imposed by a digitized media "noosphere"... Are we not, perhaps, nearer the contexts of the two stories I have examined?

It may be worth exploring at this point the often strident culture-wars discourse that is played out in Lafferty stories of a certain period of the late 1960s and early 1970s. He clearly felt that—inspired by gurus such as Julian Huxley and Teilhard de Chardin—Western civilization was generally veering into lifestyles rooted in destruction and the deadening of the senses. Lafferty argues that far from being forces for liberation, these transgressive cultures were in fact agents of nihilism wanting to uproot tradition.

A comparison of another independent thinker's perception of liberalism may be helpful here. This is from a collection of essays on the thought of Lewis Mumford.

> *Pragmatic liberalism, he asserted, was "vastly preoccupied with the machinery of life" and "the only type of human character it could understand was the utilitarian one," believing that "the emotional and spiritual life of man needs no other foundation than the rational, utilitarian activities associated with the getting of a living" (CL, 569). The pragmatic liberal was color-blind to moral values and had taken "values, feelings, emotions, wishes, purposes, for granted. He assumed either that this world did not exist or that it was relatively unimportant; at all events, if it did exist, it could be safely left to itself without cultivation…"*
> Robert Westbrook,
> "Lewis Mumford, John Dewey, and the 'Pragmatic Acquiescence'"

Lafferty would presumably endorse much of this position. There is also the sense from his stories that he did see, as well, a kind of qualitative change in the emergence of particular youth cults. Far beyond the flower-carrying pacifism of the hippies there were many movements which would openly advocate violence. Taking Mao as their lead rather than Marx, and de Sade rather than Freud, this reflected a shift from secular liberalism to full-blown anarchism. To Lafferty this was all of a piece with the prioritizing of sensation through mind-expanding drugs. The fundamental categories of being such as time, space and personality were, for a time, subject to ferocious assault and often in the name of a self-regarding politics of hedonism.

This initial turning away from the will-towards-the-good does have a characteristic frisson of self-assertion and excitement. This is well illustrated in Augustine's long debate in the Confessions over his youthful episode of pear-stealing; he reflects on the motivation of his youthful self in that he did not steal the pears in order to eat them but to "taste" the reflective pleasure he felt in committing an act of rebellion. Once, though, the deformation of the will is commenced upon actions soon merge into the deadlier stage of moral inertia. This is when people feel they no longer have to make any active choice between good and evil. Lafferty certainly seemed to believe that these issues were at the centre of some kind of cosmic struggle being played out on a grand scale.

The physical representation of this is shown by the immobility of the characters in "Incased in Ancient Rind" and the insubstantial forms of the bodies in "Great Day in the Morning." We may even glance here at the similar kinds of literary techniques used by Dante. Much of his work is full of representations who are no longer recognizable as human persons and whose distorted use of the will keeps them enclosed in new and disfigured forms.

In starting to draw these reflections to a close I want to quote from a passage describing a visit of the American historian-philosopher, Henry Adams, to Europe:

> [...] he toured Normandy and the neighboring regions: Amiens, Bayeux, Coutances, Mont-Saint-Michel, Vitre, Le Mans, Chartres. He had, of course, known of the things he saw; but now, suddenly, he grasped them. Or rather these incredible churches of the twelfth and thirteenth centuries seized him and shook him until his intellectual teeth rattled. What force had impelled men to infuse stone with such striving and restlessness and to fling it high into the heaven? Why had they filled acres of windows with throbbing colors such as a Yankee had never dreamed of? Why had they enriched every portal and pinnacle with figures from earth, hell and paradise?
>
> Lynn White, Jr., Dynamo and Virgin Reconsidered

The general renewal of life and culture in the High Middle Ages was linked to a spiritual refocusing on the Trinity and Incarnation as well as the traditional model of Eucharistic theology. Cistercian spirituality flourished in this period and the particular innovations and good practices of their monastic lifestyle that over-spilled into the wider cultural life of Europe has been noted by various historians. It is a paradox, then, that the seeming "dying to the self" could lead to a revival of society at every level. The following passage is from a Cistercian writing in the 20th century:

> For in some mysterious way we died to ourselves with Christ on the cross. And to achieve the fullness of that death and the consequent resurrection to a newness of life, all that is needed is the continual action of our own will by which, renouncing our own life of self-love, we endorse the dedication of ourselves to God, and accept the subsequent life of grace in which we live for God and not for ourselves.
>
> M. Eugene Boylan, The Mystical Body

The heavenly blue sky in "Incased in Ancient Rind" and the "living water" which has gone out of things in "Great Day in the Morning" are traditional Christian symbols of grace. The above passage is significant in that it brings to the fore the Eucharistic pattern of life, death and resurrection which the Christian believer seeks to imitate in their own life. A writer like Lafferty usually witnesses to this in the way narrative becomes adventure-shaped and the exuberance of characters almost bursts out of the containing frame of the text. I have argued that the negativity and life-denying elements in the stories we have examined are still meant to signal and point us back to the main pathways which may have been temporarily obscured.

There are, of course, many passages in Lafferty which may seem either hopelessly opaque to interpretation or actually prophetic of our own times. In favor of the latter view I suggest sampling some of the content on websites dealing with the fashionable philosophy of Transhumanism and then imagine that it is Lafferty speaking to us today through the words of Melchisidech Duffy:

"It's amazing the way you predicted it all," she said, "how we would become uncontained...how we would merge with each other, how all walls and clothes and skins would be dismantled..."

She handed him The Bark *opened at the article, "Great Day in the Morning" by Melchisedech Duffy. And Duffy's hands shook as he held it.*

"But Mary Virginia," he said, "this was a comic article, a bitterly comic article."

R. A. Lafferty, "Great Day in the Morning"

John Ellison lives in England. At an early age, he selected Lafferty as a favorite author after discovering his short stories in SF magazines and anthologies in the late 1960s. John writes that at this time, Catholicism informs most of his choices in life—indeed he has shifted between the quite different milieu of Damon Runyon (he used to be a manager of betting shops) and Dorothy Day (he now works in the charity and voluntary sector). John is a frequent commenter on Andrew Ferguson's Tumblr, "Continued on Next Rock." He has had one other essay on Lafferty published in Dan Knight's fanzine, Boomer Flats Gazette.

Late Light

BY RICH PERSAUD

"On my tenth birthday my father gave me the Grolier History of the World, all eighteen, huge, double-columned volumes of it. I went through every word of it in a year, and I still remember most of it. I haven't a photographic memory now, but I very nearly had when I was ten."
R. A. Lafferty, *Speaking of Science Fiction,* Paul Walker, 1978

"Honesty. That's the thing in the theater today. Honesty... and just as soon as I can learn to fake that, I'll have it made."
Unnamed theater actor, quoted by Celeste Holm in
Morning Advocate, "The Lyons Den," Leonard Lyons,
6 April 1962

The term "conspiracy" has been successfully stripped of all meaning by various pots and kettles scratching each other's black. Yet, the chameleonesque human capacity for falsehood is neutralized by our age, race and creed-neutral capacity for subconscious distillation of sincerity.

From the epistemological roots of Moses ("these 15—*crash*—10 commandments"[1]) to the populist confidence of long division, elders have held social restraint as counterweight to unfettered button pushing by liberated fingers, as new straps of literacy are booted once again.

Still, each generation must address the transclusion of means and ends by the partially literate ("I smile therefore I am"). Thousands of years of agenda joyriding have yet to derail the expansion of literacy or the truth-colocation capacity of semantics.

Economics bequeathed special powers of modulation to the semantic device we have amicably named "price." In the absence of this most populist of social restraints, what have we reaped from our

---

1 *History of the World, Part 1,* Mel Brooks, 1981 Film

voluminously open cyberlands?

Truth? It rides near, not on, semantics.

Wisdom? Does a menu of 100 diversions eclipse a menu with 2 solutions?

Light. Courtesy of distant stars, publishing only their past. It is fitting that cyberlands arrive at our brainsteps after traversing optical fiber at light speed. The tense of cyberlands is a past of select publishers, but past photons are more numerous than their selection in our cyberlands.

With late light[2,3] from the pasts do the futures distill our presents.

This work © 2003, 2015 Rich Persaud.

Rich Persaud created www.ralafferty.org to introduce new readers to Lafferty's works. He is slowly catching up on histories and other omissions from his Math & Science education, with the help of R. A. Lafferty's fiction and free historical books from www.archive.org. He writes at www.symspaces.com.

2 "Gravitational Lensing to Observe Ancient Earth," Peter Reinhardt, www.rein.pk, March 2013

3 "Cosmic Lens Reveals 4 Views of Same Star Explosion," Charles Q. Choi, www.space.com, 5 March 2015

Lafferty's Monkey

By Clinton Reid Claussen

He's singing dust bowl ballads, and every ballad is convoluted with
clarity, holy and profane. Lafferty's monkey is climbing up in the
spires of old churches and leaping effortlessly through blown out
windows and rusted scaffolds of abandoned buildings. He's spitting
on the heads of passersby and laughing hysterically, but don't let his
laughter fool you. He's deathly serious.

Lafferty's monkey is calling out the secrets of the universe, and
we're struggling desperately to hear them over the whistling of the
Oklahoma wind through whiskey bottles. We kick our soles at those
empty whiskey bottles, but all we can find is sobriety. We call out to
him, asking him to repeat himself, but he just mumbles *You're on the
right track, kid* from the top of a space station, and then he's gone
again, leaving townships and universes crumbling in his wake.

Even from faraway planets, we still hear him mumbling words
between feigned and unfeigned bouts of unconsciousness, words
that the greats struggle to hear and the ungreats don't bother to pay
attention to. We beg him to elaborate, we need more clarification.
But Lafferty's monkey leaves us laughing gravely, with those same
empty bottles, that same sobriety, and he says *Misunderstandings can
be agreeable. But there is something shattering about sudden perfect understanding.* Then he's nodding off again, smiling smugly to himself
with a frivolity, a humming, drumming excess of perfect, greater
understanding, and the howling of that Oklahoma wind is louder
than ever.

Lafferty's monkey pulls us into the dingiest bookstores searching red-handed and feverish for words. And when we finally find
them, these high, glorious words, these glowering, towering for-
tresses of words, Lafferty's monkey pulls us back out again. He drags
us along with these high words through the gutter with a swing
of his spindly arm, but on the upswing he scrapes them, dripping

folksy, sewered and sea-chantyed, across the cosmos. During that swing, through the grime and across the buildings into the heavenly, we saw hints of those great truths that Lafferty's monkey mumbled, but not from slapping against the cosmos, that great glowing celestial inconsequential, but from sliding through the gutter. And we find that those high words we so crave, so great, so high that they are, contain nothing compared to the low words, and we leave the cosmos behind, traipsing through the muck for treatise, tearing apart tumbleweeds and pulling up the sodden earth, for maybe after all the truth is to be found in the rust and the dust, in those low and lovely words.

Beware, however, of the winding of that otherworldly warmness, that seductive sentence that simultaneously waxes and wanes, giving you the high and the low until they are indistinguishably one bewildering body of words that works at every angle of your brain until it deteriorates into a higher plane, and you finally realize that the harrowing importance lies in the lyrical, the lunatic, the cartoonish and buffoonish. *Great mother of ulcers!* Beware. This is right where he wants you. This is when Lafferty's monkey moves in for the kill.

Then Lafferty's monkey swings away again, leaving behind deadly comical treatise and absurdly accurate and authentic Apocrypha crumbling in codices hideously rare or unavailable altogether that we so pitifully, desperately need. These immortal epigraphs come clamoring down canyons in the harmonious hostility of an avalanche, flattening us in the form of enchantments, aphorisms, and epigrams, entrancing epigrams, ravishing in their repulsion. We arise sick and pallid for prose. Lafferty's monkey has infected us with the fervor, the delirium to dig up words, and we have no other choice. We need to find them all. He has given us no recourse. We realize, frustrated, manic, that we could be worse off. We feel the necessity to uncover everything, read every word, knowing fully well it could be impossible, but most people will be doomed to never read the greatest (or possibly any of his) works. *I look for a happier doom.*

Lafferty's monkey takes you on to strange tangents through

back-woods that go on indefinitely, then down main roads, roads you swore led somewhere of vast importance, that end abruptly. Though they are deliberate, these back paths seem so swerving, wild and winding. As though sensing your incertitude, he calls out to you quietly. *Not a drop in two days now, though your world always seemed a little bleak without it,* but behind his words you hear that lonely whiskey wind again.

You go again down those narrow back-roads, those weaving corkscrews in and out of time, to the end of avenues that bend through sea-side shacks overflowing with salty air and saltier chanteys. He'll take you on silly, shaggy planets with sillier, shaggier deities that infiltrate your brain, adorable and abhorrent. You'll go through time, space, places of horrible solitude and more horrible overpopulation, and even through other minds, minds more sensuous than you can possibly imagine. You'll wonder how you could ever *watch a bird fly by and not even hear the stuff gurgling in its stomach.* If you follow Lafferty's monkey down the very roads he chooses, he'll take you even further in, and some of those places can't even be explained, but let him lead you when he chooses to, and try to keep up with him when he leaves you behind. As you go, stumbling and bumbling along, you may find some wonderful weatherbeaten signposts along the way. This is where you'll find the beauty, the bounty, for along the way, you'll encounter divisions, diversions, but never delusions. *And perils pinnacled and parts impossible. And every word of it the sworn-on gosipel.* Behind these gnarled sign-posts hover apparitions of surety, phantasms of actuality and optical assurances parading as illusions. In these phantasies, in these tall tales, lie the trickery, for behind them are astounding visions of reality.

Keep at it, Lafferty's monkey will tell you. When the silliness is grave and serious, and when the seriousness is absurd, despicable and roll on the floor, rip out your guts and sputter on yourself laughing hysterically, don't be too surprised. For that too is where the truth lies. At these moments you'll often find familiar places and people that Lafferty's monkey will take you past again and again. It'll seem as though the paths are wrapping you in a circle, but that's just when you've gone in too far. These glimpses, these moments are when *you're on the right track, kid.* At these places, at these times, you witness *time heaped up, bulging out in casing and accumulation, and not in line sequence.* Before this point, there may have been a fork in the road that you could have taken, a fork that would have led you who knows where, but it doesn't matter anymore. You didn't take it. You followed Lafferty's monkey this far and now it's far too late. You think at this point you can follow this far and not keep going? You think you can turn back now? You could have taken that fork that was maybe back there in the road, but you didn't, so the best you can do is keep trying to keep up. But don't worry too much. *There are worse places to live than in tall stories.*

Lafferty's monkey will take you to the most insane and painfully sanest of places, but be aware that his retracts and protracts always divulge into brass tacks. Tearing you through the furthest reaches of outer space and the vastest, overextended expansions of time, he'll snap you back like a rubber band pulled to the very stretches of its extremities, closer to the present and the befuddling research of the Institute for Impure Science. With a bewildering wink from Valery Mok, you'll be snapped away again to odder plains, to the metaphysical, the mortifying and mystifying histories and mysterious mythos, before being snapped away yet again. Lafferty's monkey, swinging from vines and trees, weaves you in and out of his foci, but in the defining moments, you're shot with his dead-eye, blown full of tall tales with his dusty, distinct folk eye.

Remember though, that what matters most here are the words, as you crawl with Lafferty's monkey over mountainous mounds of manuscripts, displacements of esoteric words to make way for accessibility unachieved. Follow him reluctantly through fugue states clouded into gaseous spirits and clammy, clamoring typewriters in the pursuit, the cruel chase and attainment of import, trifling with deliriously laborious, saberous words. Lafferty's monkey swung us, kicking and screaming, into the absurdity of the twenty-first century, made even more absurd by our yellowed, dog-eared sacred works molding into obscurity. He takes us on the outskirts of knowledge, treatise, mythos and tall tales, but lets the cipher allude but so few, leaving us turning out our pockets and ordering, flipping, scouring, leafing, overturning, climbing, pulling and pushing aside dusty volumes in dustier bookstores and ordering dusty boxes from dustier websites in desperation, exasperation, to piece together, to finally solve an as yet unsolvable, unfinished puzzle. We look for that nexus tying all the glorious absurdity together. Though we may not find it, he implores us to *put the nightmare together,* assuring us, *if you do not wake up screaming, you have not put it together well.* Lafferty's monkey knows we'll continue, for we're all desperate for that long, winding, irretrievable "ghost story" that will finally, ecstatically, euphorically unravel our universe.

Clinton Reid Claussen was born in Atlantic, Iowa. His pursuit of great literature was initiated by the writing and philosophy of his grandfather, Reid Wilson. Clinton's dreams of seeking out fantastic places, his Midwestern sensibilities, and an absurdist slant have been forces which are continuously channeled through his writing as well as his life. Fate has led him to New York, where he currently resides in Brooklyn, with his wife, Yvette and their hoard of books.

Lafferty: An Appreciation
BY PATRICK MAY

R. A. Lafferty wrote parodies of things I never knew existed. Long relegated to what Kurt Vonnegut once called the "ghetto" of science fiction, in his prime Lafferty produced works that blended strange humor with lyrical wordplay. His meandering novels are plotless drinks some of us dare dip into, and the more foolhardy of us drown in.

It is impossible to talk about Lafferty's appeal without talking about his biography. Catholic and ornery in the vein of Flannery O'Connor, he was a mail-order certified electrical engineer who only turned to writing in his 40's, he says, to fill in the time freed by cutting back on drinking. An eternal bachelor, he lived his entire life in Tulsa, Oklahoma, which to my New England ears strikes me as an exotically dull-sounding place.

Most of his literary output was corralled to the markets of paperbacks, the back aisles of drugstores and hobby shops. I imagine it was in these deceptively generic environs an unsuspecting young person might have purchased one of Lafferty's tomes, expecting to read a Jocks in Space yarn of the Buck Rogers variety, only to instead be confronted by, say, Thomas More falling in love with a future society that takes his parody of Utopia seriously (the "plot" of *Past Master*), or a supercomputer tasked with finding the true shape of the universe (as in *Arrive at Easterwine*).

It feels strange to recite these plots, as if the recitation of the facts of these novels moves anywhere towards explaining them. Kingsley Amis once wrote that science fiction stories won't come of age until the synopsis of their plots is not interchangeable with the experience of reading them, and it is true most science fiction stories are more concerned with expressing neat ideas than the style in which those ideas are unloaded. To which I would argue, there are books too filled with purple prose of majesty, clever tricks employed by pretentious hacks who flourish their nothing insights in the shadows of typography. Lafferty is of neither world, he is his own world.)

I used the word "confronted" above because Lafferty's novels are indeed confrontational (his short stories are another matter entirely, but I prefer the wild jungles of his novels to those manicured parks). To enjoy Lafferty, you must suspend your dependency on rational chronology, and allow normal novel conventions (i.e., character motivation) to remain unexplained, or if ever explained, only in the most frustrating of ways. You must be able to enjoy subtle (and not so subtle) word games and etymology, and understand everyone is a double of someone else. Characters are operatic drunks; esoteric trivia (some real, some invented) is expounded, vast conspiracies unearthed, and an alienating and unfathomable cosmology charts the fate of man. On the sentence level, Lafferty turns clichés on their heads on their heads on their heads on their heads.

Lafferty is the proprietor of a world of lies. His stories are categorized as science fiction because that club of outcasts is the only one which would have him; but even so, he is a fringe member. He writes in the tradition of the trickster, the yarn-spinner, the folklorist who speaks of myth and dream while riding the back of a shaggy dog. His novels are long digressions, and seem to culminate as one endless tale of which we have only the most tantalizing of pieces.

Even his history books are lies! I have looked up weird facts found in *The Fall of Rome*, ostensibly his history of the end of that empire. The facts are not true, yet they are presented so eloquently and authoritatively one still believes after finding them out to be lies they are true, or at least should be. Lafferty seems to want us to challenge truth, to research his tales, to lead us down blind alleys. Like most people, I don't like feeling like an idiot, and I usually don't like books that make me feel like an idiot. Yet Lafferty often leaves me feeling like an idiot, a happy fool who thought he understood the world when like some denizen of Plato's cave I really only understood a very small slice of a shadow of it. And, just when I believe I am starting to understand, that shadow moves and I am once more grasping for it, searching for another angle.

The bulk of Lafferty's output still remains obscure and out of print, though I feel now he is on the verge of being rediscovered. There is a Facebook group devoted to him 130 members strong (most of them eternal bachelors), and there are fanzines sprouting up in Japan, and both pirated and unpirated new editions of his stories. I wonder sometimes if he will live up to the scrutiny that comes with being rediscovered by the secular, if part of the enjoyment one gets from him derives from the fact he is so obscure, a fountain of the arcane. But I for one can never imagine a criticism of him; it would be like criticizing the God of the Bible for being too opaque. An imperfect Lafferty story is still a thousand times more interesting than anything else.

I have so far abstained from offering any examples of his prose. Here then, finally, are two examples. The first is the previously-mentioned supercomputer from *Arrive at Easterwine's* response to a rejection slip he received from a literary magazine that refused to publish his story (and something I wish I could write to any who refuse to publish mine):

> *Not quite what you had in mind? Who asked you? It is what I had in mind or I wouldn't have written it. Misses the mark? Move the mark then. Where this hits is where the mark should be. Listen, you, I have your person-precis before me. I see that you have talent only and no genius at all. Whose fault is it that you are overstocked? Am I responsible for your inventory control? I do not ask you to publish these things. I tell you to. These are parts of the High Journal itself.*

This here next is the opening passage to *The Fall of Rome*, and I include it because I believe it shows Lafferty's love of etymology:

> *The sub-title of this study 'The Day the World Ended' is not meant to be extravagant. It was not the orbis terrarum, the globe, that ended; but the mundus, the ordered world. Mundus, as an adjective, means clean, neat, or elegant. As a noun it may mean the ornamentation, the vesture; but it also means the world. It*

is like the Greek cosmos which not only means the world and the universe, but likewise means the order, the arrangement, the beauty: for cosmetic, the beautifier, and cosmos, the beauty, are of the same root.

Both before and after the mundus, the ordered world, there is chaos. But in its bounds it was one thing. It is redundant to speak of the Roman world; the mundus was the Roman world, and there was no other. It was one of the great things that have happened but once. It has been a living person, and now there were but the sundered limbs.

Patrick May is an MFA student in creative writing at the University of Florida, but his heart belongs to Rhode Island, his homeworld. He randomly picked up a copy of Not to Mention Camels in a public library ten years ago and has been spreading the Gospel of Lafferty ever since.

Question: Why?
Excuse: Because Monsters
By Rich Persaud

Can you see a narrative projected by glimmers of times and stories elsewhen, spilling color onto trusses silently shiny, as they move to predict your choice of perceived paths?

Each glimmer from a nearby black rectangle expects your questions and perusals of rectangular answers. At the terminus of each glimmer lies experience encoded, paths prioritized and geometry unnamed.

Lafferty causes more—many—nows, thens and if-thens.

As you navigate nows and nexuses, do not run from monsters, but from the excuse "Because Monsters."

Nada: "Put on the glasses."
Frank: "I told you. I didn't want to be involved."
Nada: "Take a look. Put them on."
Frank: "No!"

They Live (fight scene), John Carpenter, 1988 Film

Lafferty: "There is a secret society of only four persons that manufactures all the jokes of the world. One of these persons is unfunny and he is responsible for all the unfunny jokes."

"About A Secret Crocodile," R. A. Lafferty, 1970 Story

Wesley: "And you say this demon wanted cash? That's very unusual."
Giles: "Demons after money. Whatever happened to the still-beating heart of a virgin? No one has any standards anymore."

Buffy the Vampire Slayer, Joss Whedon, "Enemies," 1999 TV series

Michael Corleone: "Discontent for money is just a trick of the rich to keep the poor without it."

The Godfather II, Francis Ford Coppola, 1974 Film

Gaiman: "If you are protected from dark things then you have no understanding of dark things when they show up."

Toon Books interview of Neil Gaiman, Oct 2014 Video

Lafferty: "It is only very good people who have no fear at all of the unknown."

"The Six Fingers of Time," R. A. Lafferty, 1960 Story

Col. Jessup: "You want answers?!"
Lt. Kaffee: "I want the truth!"
Col. Jessup: "You can't *handle* the truth!

A Few Good Men, Rob Reiner, 1992 Film

Nikita: "Sometimes the devil is the only one open for business."

La Femme Nikita, Joel Surnow, "New Regime," 1998 TV series

Hauser: "I am something you will never be. I'm pure. I believe in evil. You and your friends, you're conflicted. You're confused. We're not."

Angel, Joss Whedon and David Greenwalt,
"Conviction," 2003 TV series

Sitterson: "They have to make the choice of their own free will. Otherwise, [the] system doesn't work."

The Cabin in the Woods,
Drew Goddard and Joss Whedon, 2012 Film

Leroy: "I knew the White Swan wouldn't be a problem. The real work will be your metamorphosis into her evil twin."

Black Swan, Darren Aronofsky, 2010 Film

Dawn: "This is blood, isn't it? It can't be me. I'm not a key. I'm not a thing."

Buffy the Vampire Slayer, "Blood Ties," 2001 TV series

Milton: "I'm a fan of man! I'm a humanist. Maybe the last humanist. Who, in their right mind, Kevin, could possibly deny the 20th century was entirely mine? All of it, Kevin! All of it! Mine!"

The Devil's Advocate, Taylor Hackford, 1997 Film

Lewis: "There are two equal and opposite errors into which our race can fall about the devils. One is to disbelieve in their existence. The other is to believe, and to feel an excessive and unhealthy interest in them. They themselves are equally pleased by both errors, and hail a materialist or magician with the same delight."

The Screwtape Letters, C.S. Lewis, 1941 Novel

Lafferty: "Learn the true topography; the monstrous and wonderful archetypes are not inside you, not inside your consciousness; you are inside them, trapped and howling to get out."

The Devil is Dead, R. A. Lafferty, 1971 Novel

Number 6: "I am not a number. I am a person."

> *The Prisoner* (UK series), Patrick McGoohan, 1968 TV series

Veil: "No matter how much you take away, everyone has something that belongs to them, to them and nobody else."

> *Nowhere Man* (US series tribute to The Prisoner),
> Lawrence Hertzog, 1996 TV series

The Economist: "Evolution has equipped [the Ood[1]] with two brains—one in their heads, the other carried around in their hand… the smartphone is changing the way people relate to each other and the world around them… the world's smallest slot machines."

> *The Economist*, "The Truly Personal Computer," Feb 2015 Article

Anna: "I need the number of a suicide hotline."
Smartphone AI: "National Suicide Prevention Line: Call 1-800-273-8255."
Zimmerman: "I need the number of a suicide hotline."
Smartphone AI: "5 Painless Ways to End One's Life."

> *Person of Interest*, Jonathan Nolan, "Q&A," 2015 TV series

Ivanovas: "'How long is the coast of the British island?' It is a typical undecidable question. The answer is: It depends on the ruler. The finer the measuring ruler the longer is the coast, finally becoming infinite. It is a metaphysical act to decide on a ruler."

> "From Autism to Humanism," Georg Ivanovas, 2010 Ph.D. Thesis

Lucy: "One plus one has never equaled two. There are, in fact, no numbers and no letters. We've codified our existence to bring it down to human size to make it comprehensible. We've created a scale so that we can forget its unfathomable scale."

> *Lucy*, Luc Besson, 2014 Film

---

1   The Ood are a fictional alien species from the TV series *Dr. Who*.

Lafferty: "The mind has its erosions and weatherings going on along with its deposits and accumulations. It also has its upthrusts and its stresses. It floats on a similar magma. In extreme cases it has its volcanic eruptions and its mountain building."

"Continued on Next Rock," R. A. Lafferty, 1964 Story

Thamus: "If men learn this, it will implant forgetfulness in their souls; they will cease to exercise memory because they rely on that which is written, calling things to remembrance no longer from within themselves, but by means of external marks. What you have discovered is a recipe not for memory, but for reminder."

Phaedrus, Plato, BC 360 Dialogue

Mace: "Memories are meant to fade. They're designed that way for a reason."

Strange Days, Kathryn Bigelow, 1995 Film

Lafferty: "The human memory of the thing was blocked by induced world amnesia. This was done hypnotically over the broadcast waves, and over more subtle waves. Few escaped it. The deaf moron mentioned in one of my items was one of those few."

"What's The Name Of That Town," R. A. Lafferty, 1964 Story

Hawksquill: "Practitioners of the old art discovered some odd things about their memory houses the longer they lived in them... the symbolic figures with vivid expressions, once installed in their proper places, are subject to subtle change as they stand waiting to be called forth [...] also, as the memory house grows, it makes conjunctions and vistas that its builder can't conceive of beforehand."

Little, Big, John Crowley, 1981 Novel

Amanda: "We can't know where we're going until we know from where we came... Our memories can be unreliable narrators. You may think you know with absolute certainty what's in your past. And then you find out you don't know the past at all."

Nikita, Craig Silverstein, "Guardians," 2011 TV series

Sheppard: "Memory is crucial for a strong sense of self. We are mythical beings. We only know ourselves by memories of what we've done and what has happened to us. Those memories have formed through a sense of story. In an absolute sense, identity is the story of our lives."

Story Alchemy, David Sheppard, 2014 Book

Ressler: "Rowan passed the lie-detector test."
Keen: "That's because Rowan's unaware of Nora and Nora's unaware of Rowan. That's how dissociative identity disorder works."

The Blacklist, John Bokencamp, "Lord Baltimore," 2014 TV series

IASB: "Material Omissions or misstatements of items are material if they could, individually or collectively, influence the economic decisions that users make on the basis of the financial statements."

International Accounting Standard 8, IFRS, IASB, 2009 Guide

Lafferty: "The Camiroi child will have failed in business once, at age ten, and have learned patience and perfection of objective by his failure. He will have acquired the techniques of falsification and conmanship. Thereafter he will not be easily deceived by any of the citizens of any of the worlds."

"The Primary Education of the Camiroi,"
R. A. Lafferty, 1966 Story

Nikita: "What's Amanda trying to do with this lie about the secret account?"
Michael: "Establish a context. Create a narrative for Spencer's assassination."

Nikita, "Dead or Alive," 2013 TV series

Abbott: "Narrative is the principal way in which our species organizes its understanding of time [...] our narrative perception stands ready to be activated in order to give us a frame or context for even the most static and uneventful scenes."

The Cambridge Introduction to Narrative, H. Porter Abbot, 2008 Book

Zak: "My lab was the first to discover that the neurochemical oxytocin is synthesized in the human brain when one is trusted and that the molecule motivates reciprocation... By measuring how your peripheral nervous system responds to a story, we can almost perfectly predict what you'll do before you do it... The U.S. Department of Defense's funding of the emerging science of narrative jump-started the field."

> "Why Inspiring Stories Make Us React: The Neuroscience of Narrative," *Cerebrum*, Paul Zak, Feb 2015 Paper

Lafferty: "There is no particular virtue in using a word to mean its opposite, though the trick has had tremendous success in some fields of opinion forming."

> *Speaking of Science Fiction*, Paul Walker, 1978 Interview

Dr Rutledge: "Source Code is not time travel. Rather, Source Code is time re-assignment. It gives us access to a parallel reality."

> *Source Code*, Duncan Jones, 2011 Film

Peter: "We think of time as linear, right? Life is a journey. You're born, and then you die. And to get from one end to the other, there's only one way through. Unless you look at it like this and then you can see at any point. It's all happening at once... It's more like they're observing time. I think these guys show up at important moments—historical, technological, scientific."

> *Fringe*, J.J. Abrams, "August," 2009 TV series

Lafferty: "Genesis, and all of the Old and New Testament, are full of things that haven't happened yet, and God used scribes who were open to the past, and to all the presents, and to all the futures."

> Letter to *The Wanderer*, U of Tulsa Ms 12:9, R.A. Lafferty, 1987

Knight: "The Argonaut's main strategy against evil is to slip into the probable future and effect changes there so that when the World arrives the obstacles will have already been dealt with."

> "A Richness of Endings," Dan Knight, 1993 Essay

September: "If we can send the boy into the future to that moment… they will realize all that he is: Living proof that they don't have to sacrifice emotion for intelligence, and they will never go down that path."

Fringe, "The Boy Must Live," 2013 TV series

Lafferty: "A person old enough to have learned the lore and techniques of time travel must hurdle at least thirty years of closed-off time before he begins his exploration… reincarnation… are memories of early time travel with the young traveler identifying himself with someone he observed on that travel."

"Bank and Shoal of Time," R. A. Lafferty, 1987 Story

Nicole: "You know how everyone's always saying seize the moment? I don't know, I'm kind of thinking it's the other way around, you know, like the moment seizes us."

—*Boyhood*, Richard Linklater, 2014 Film

Borges: "Any life, no matter how long or complex it may be, is made up essentially of a single moment in which a man finds out, once and for all, who he is."

"The Life of Tadeo Isidoro Cruz," Jorge Luis Borges,
tr. Norman Thomas di Giovanni, 1968 Story

Somni-451: "To be is to be perceived. And so to know thyself is only possible through the eyes of the other. The nature of our immortal lives is in the consequences of our words and deeds that go on apportioning themselves throughout all time."

Cloud Atlas, Andy and Lana Wachowski, 2012 Film

Atlas: "If I put you out of my mind for a moment, then you are not. By my attention I hold it all in being. Nothing exists unless it is perceived. If perception fails for a moment, then that thing fails forever."

Space Chantey, R. A. Lafferty, 1976 Novel

Rabelais: "Time, which gnaws and diminisheth all things else, augments and increaseth benefits; because a noble action of liberality, done to a man of reason, doth grow continually by his generous thinking of it and remembering it."

Gargantua, Rabelais, 1534 Novel

Marquez: "Life is not what one lived, but what one remembers and how one remembers it in order to recount it."

Living to Tell the Tale, Gabriel Garcia
Marquez, 2002 Autobiography

Belloc: "The moment a man talks to his fellows he begins to lie."

The Silence of the Sea, Hilaire Belloc, 1941 Collection

Calvin: "History is the fiction we invent to persuade ourselves that events are knowable and that life has order and direction. That's why events are always reinterpreted when values change. We need new versions of history to allow for our current prejudices."

Calvin & Hobbes, Bill Watterson, 1994 Comic

Mencken: "Explanations exist; they have existed for all time; there is always a well-known solution to every human problem—neat, plausible, and wrong."

Prejudices: Second Series, H.L. Mencken, 1920 Collection

Denker: "My favorite proverb of all is the one that says for every proverb, there is an equal and opposite proverb... Sometimes the best way to get your eggs from point A to point B is to put them all in a basket and take really good care of that basket."

"Security Recommendations for Any Device that Depends on
Randomly-Generated Numbers," John Denker, 2013 Essay

Guenon: "The truth is that there is really no 'profane realm' that could in any way be opposed to a 'sacred realm'; there is only a 'profane point of view', which is really none other than the point of view of ignorance."

"Initiation and Spiritual Realization,"
Rene Guenon, 1952 Essay

Sir Thomas More: "The maxim is 'Qui tacet consentit': the maxim of the law is 'Silence gives consent'. If therefore you wish to construe what my silence betokened, you must construe that I consented."

A Man For All Seasons, Fred Zinnemann, 1966 Film

Thomas Jefferson: "Just a moment, Mr. Thomson. I do not consent. The king is a tyrant whether we say so or not. We might as well say so."

1776, Peter H. Hunt, 1972 Film

Lafferty: "Rise again and fight some more, dead people!"

Galaxy: Thirty Years of Innovative Science Fiction,
R. A. Lafferty, 1980 Collection

The Beast: "In the world of kung fu, speed determines the winner."

Kung Fu Hustle, Stephen Chow, 2004 Film

Eve: "Come on! Isn't anybody excited? This is a crazy time of fun. The most powerful evil around has given a pivotal position over to its sworn enemies. You're not scared, are you?" *(Angel stares at Eve and bites into the apple.)*

Angel, Joss Whedon, "Conviction," 2003 TV series

Marquez: "Our greatest good fortune was that even in the most extreme difficulties we might lose our patience but never our sense of humor."

Living to Tell the Tale, Gabriel Garcia
Marquez, 2002 Autobiography

Calvin: "[I pray for] the strength to change what I can, the inability to accept what I can't, and the incapacity to tell the difference."

Calvin & Hobbes, Bill Watterson, 1988 Comic

Miéville: "He walked with equipoise, possibly in either city. Schrödinger's pedestrian."

The City & The City, China Miéville, 2009 Novel

Du Chaillu: "The great gift given to every creature is knowledge of how to protect itself from its enemies, and how to approach its prey."

The world of the great forest : how animals, birds, reptiles, insects talk, think, work, and live, Paul Du Chaillu, 1900 Book

Harry: "Most people live life on the path we set out for them. Too afraid to explore any other. But once in a while, people like you come along who knock down all the obstacles we put in your way. People who realize free will is a gift you'll never know how to use until you fight for it."

The Adjustment Bureau, George Nolfi, 2011 Film

Lafferty: "There are no really new things or new situations. There are only things growing out right, or things growing out deformed or shriveled. There is nothing new about railways or foundries or lathes or steel furnaces. They also are green-growing things. There is nothing new about organizations of men or of money. All these growing things are good, if they grow towards the final answers that were given in the beginning."

The Flame is Green, R. A. Lafferty, 1971 Novel

Illustration by Joseph M. Gleeson, page 78, The world of the great forest: how animals, birds, reptiles, insects talk, think, work, and live, *1900, courtesy of Internet Archive Book Images collection on Flickr, www.flickr.com/photos/internetarchivebookimages/14564367749*

Rich Persaud created www.ralafferty.org to introduce new readers to Lafferty's works. He apologizes to the indomitable Mrs. Blake of Queens College, Guyana, for leaving behind English in favor of Math & Science. He is attempting to revisit that if-then, a few decades later, writing at www.symspaces. com. He thanks Gregorio Montejo for introducing him to the catena form of commentary.

Seven-Story Dream on Terschelling
BY PETER SIJBENGA

The Youth Theater School Friesland was about to spend the weekend doing workshops on Terschelling.

Terschelling has gained a reputation because of Oerol, an annual Theater Festival; this mainly tourist island then transforms into a ship of fools. Experimental shows, open-minded audience. In Friesland the saying goes that "as soon as you leave Harlingen harbor by ferry and head for Oerol you leave behind more than the shore." You immediately travel into a different dimension. When you disembark two hours later in West-Terschelling you're willing to open up to anything you would have frowned upon two hours before.

There are disadvantages. Many times I attended a show during Oerol which totally enthralled me as if I had experienced a speech by Professor Aloys Foucault-Oeg. Once I got back to Harlingen there was not much left; a lick of body-paint, a flickering reminder of fire-eating and jabbertalk and the general feeling of "What was it all about then?"

Because of this sensation I once suggested fellow Oerol-travelers to create a T-shirt reading "I did not understand anything..." at the front and "but far out, man!" at the back. I guess Burning Man in the United States has a comparable effect on people.

Wait, I am a bit too negative. Not only are there many artists doing wonderful performances on Oerol (surviving the return to Harlingen masterfully), I want to emphasize the importance of... let us call them havens. Physical havens, havens of the mind. There are not that many left. And we need them to wrestle with the Gods.

So that's why the Youth Theatre School Friesland decided to do the workshops on Terschelling. Goal: to disconnect from the regular lessons, mix up the classes, and work towards short presentations. The theme for the weekend: "Who dunnit?"

So that's why I chose the murder of Minnie Jo Merry.

A group of students was assigned to me (age 12 to 17), a location was chosen (an old farmers' shed) and over the weekend, we sung, danced and developed short acts.

In the first act we witness (the audience is inside the shed) Minnie Jo, standing outside by the small window. She is smiling. Then she carefully covers the window in tomato ketchup. She is now pressing her face against the window. Slowly she is slipping down. Soon she disappears from view.

Luckily she'll be reappearing from time to time to provide us with clues on how she was murdered. "Maybe I was shot, or strangled, or stabbed to death."

One suspect, Captain Izzard, has to do a rather long monologue. The young actor is not yet ready for that and his fellow actors support him, having established some kind of human bow of a ship while continuously chanting "Izzard! Izzard!" and moving from left to right on the waves... In the end Izzard nails his monologue.

Then we go all musical 40s (including choreography), a chorus line singing "Minnie Jo Merry, she was a pretty girl, just like you and me! Who me? Yes you!"

When pitiful neighbor Lamprey states she "has killed nobody, she's all the time afraid to be killed," it goes all silent. The actors succeed in prolonging this silence for over an uneasy minute. In a shed. On Terschelling.

I have no recollection whether we succeeded to solve the Merry murder case in our presentation or not. (Those who know their Lafferty know that Gilford Gadberry was the culprit. He 's a painter and unable to bear imperfection. Since Minnie is so tantalizingly close to perfection she has to die.) Should we not have managed to find the murderer that beautiful weekend, I dare to say, in the spirit of Lafferty, that solving a murder case is not of pressing importance.

What I know: we were outside of time that weekend. We had six fingers on each hand. We were in an old shed on Terschelling and only Lafferty could have described what was all piled up in there. If you'd have perceived the shed from the outside (even when you'd carefully covered the windows in tomato ketchup) you would not have believed it all fit in.

It was a great shed. Terschelling was great and totally Oerol that weekend. We had Lafferty to dress ourselves in. A haven within a haven inside a haven. Maybe when I am in a more reflective and analytic mood, I will properly explain why Lafferty makes for such great workshop material. Why junior actors can sing, dance and act Lafferty. In the meantime I just assume Lafferty kicks open the door to one's fantasy so rigorously that resistance is futile. Before you realize it you taste freedom. And it may taste a bit spicy, like blood or even better.

Peter Sijbenga (Leeuwarden/The Netherlands, 1964) is a musician, composer, copywriter and translator. He sings and plays bass in It Dockumer Lokaeltsje. *He first read Lafferty in Dutch translation, since his dad held the short story collection* Negenhonderd grootmoeders *on the bookshelf. He considers his work to be an escape route through life. Nobody has caught him yet, he thinks. His projects include www.sexettek.com, www.kohlemainen.com and www.rosesandrecords.com.*

The Lafferty Centennial In Japan

By Kenji Matsuzaki

2014 was Ray's centennial year, and we Japanese Laffertians celebrated his 100th anniversary. Just before the birthday, Hayakawa's SF Magazine: The Lafferty Centennial memorial issue was out on October 25th. A celebration event "One at a Time" was held in Tokyo on November 7th, his birthday; the Lafferty fanzine "The Next Rock Continuum" was out on November 24. In the list that follows, a * symbol signifies that I have translated the names of the articles from the original Japanese.

Hayakawa's SF Magazine:
The Lafferty Centennial memorial issue
"Happy 100th Birthday, R. A. Lafferty!"

Vol. 55, No. 705, 2014 December
Guest editor: Shinji Maki
Cover illustration: Fumihiko Shiozawa

["Introduction"] pp. 25-28, Shinji Maki

SHORT STORIES:
["St. Poleander's Eve," R. A. Lafferty] pp. 9-24, Trs. Kiichiro Yanashita, Ill. Toshiko Tsuchihashi

["The Only Tune That He Could Play," R. A. Lafferty] pp. 29-41, Trs. Hiroo Yamagata, Ill. Ryoichi Iso

["Cabrito," R. A. Lafferty] pp. 42-46, Trs. Kenji Matsuzaki, Ill. Yukiko Arai

ESSAYS:
["Shape of the S. F. Story," R. A. Lafferty] pp. 47-51, Trs. Nozomi Ohmori

["Lafferty Love," Hisashi Asakura] pp. 52, Trs. Yoshimichi Furusawa

["Despair and the Duck Lady," Michael Swanwick] pp. 62-65, Trs. Shinji Maki

INTERVIEW:
["An Interview with R. A. Lafferty" by Darrell Schweitzer (From *Cranky Old Man from Tulsa*, 1990)] pp. 53-61, Trs. Teruyuki Hashimoto

CORRESPONDENCE:
[Correspondence with Lafferty 1979-1993, Hiroshi Inoue] pp. 66-69 (Hiroshi Inoue has translated: *The Devil Is Dead*, Sanrio, 1986; *Past Master*, Seishinsha, 1993; *Serpent's Egg*, Seishinsha, 2013; *Among The Hairy Earthmen* (Japan original collection, ed. Hiroshi Inoue), Seishinsha, 1982; *The Last Astronomer and Other Stories* (Bequest of Wings) (Japan original collection, ed. Hiroshi Inoue), Seishinsha, 2011.)

REVIEWS:
["Translated Novels in Japan"] Maki Oono, Toshiya Okamoto, Ryuichiro Nakafuji, Tetsuya Hayashi pp. 70-73

Past Master (T.H.), *The Reefs of Earth* (T.O.), *Space Chantey* (M.O.), *Fourth Mansions* (M.O.), *The Devil is Dead* (T.H.), *Arrive at Easterwine* (R.N.), *Serpent's Egg* (T.O.)

["Untranslated Novels in Japan"] Hiroshi Inoue pp. 74-79

Archipelago, Dotty, Okla Hannali, The Fall of Rome, The Flame Is Green, Half a Sky, Not to Mention Camels, Apocalypses ("Where Have You Been, Sandaliotis?" / "The Three Armageddons of Enniscorthy Sweeney"), *Aurelia, The Elliptical Grave, More than Melchisedech, Annals of Klepsis, Sindbad: The Thirteenth Voyage, East of Laughter, My Heart Leaps Up*

["All 106 Translated Short Stories in Japan: And Reading the Flesh Between the Lines"] Yuichi Sakanaga pp. 80-89

["Recommendations: Untranslated 20 Short Stories in Japan"] Kenji Matsuzaki pp. 90-91 ("Bubbles When They Burst," "All Hollow Though You Be," "Great Tom Fool," "Flaming Ducks and Giant Bread," "Quiz Ship Loose," "In Outraged Stone," "Smoe and the Implicit Clay," "Tongues of the Matagorda," "Royal Licorice," "Magazine Section," "The Skinny People of Leptophlebo Street," "Oh, Those Trepidatious Eyes!," "Endangered Species," "This Boding Itch," "Gray Ghost: A Reminiscence," "Assault on Fat Mountain," "Marsilia V," "Lord Torpedo, Lord Gyroscope," "And Walk Now Gently Through the Fire...," "Thou Whited Wall")

"Has Anybody Seen Junie Moon?" (Gene Wolfe's Lafferty Story)

COLUMNS:
*["About the Neon Genesis Secret Crocodiles: Laffertian News from Overseas"] Kenji Matsuzaki pp. 92-93

*["The Astigmatic Reader's Thousand and One Novels: Continued on Next Issue"] Tadashi Wakashima pp. 94-95, Ill. Ryoichi Iso

*["Hard Facts of Lafferty Stories"] Kiichiro Yanashita pp. 96-97

*["The Voyages of *Archipelago*"] Hiroo Yamagata pp. 98-99

*["Lafferty's Eschatology"] Shinji Maki pp. 100-101
*["Lafferty's 'Tale'"] Masahiro Yamamoto pp. 102-104

THE NEXT ROCK CONTINUUM: AN R. A. LAFFERTY TRIBUTE ANTHOLOGY (EDITED BY THE HARVESTERS)

R. A. ラファティ生誕百周年記念
トリビュート小説集

つぎの岩
[The Next Rock Continuum]

編：六人の愉快な収穫者の会

STORIES:
*["The Next Rock"] by Yuichi Sakanaga
*["Next Century Modern"] by Kazuhito Funato
*["Nine Hundred Trillion Granddaughters"] by Yusuke Kurei
*["Garatea Looked Back"] by Kaeru Shunmin
*["Tinyhands Always Together"] by Ren Hanna

ILLUSTRATIONS:
Yuichi Sakanaga (Cover), Kaeru Shunmin (1st. edition), Itachi Shirakata (1st. edition), Takashi Kurata (2nd. edition)

The Next Rock Continuum anthology contains 5 Lafferty tribute short stories with essays projected by Yuichi Sakanaga and was out on November 24. The contributors are members and ex-members of KUSFA (Kyoto University SF and Fantasy Association).

ONE AT A TIME

"One at a Time" was Lafferty's 100th year birthday celebration event, held at "Café Live Wire" in Tokyo on November 7. Shinji Maki and Hiroshi Inoue had a talk show. Kiichiro Yanashita also joined to the discussion. In Japan, many Lafferty's works had been published in fanzines. At the event, a lot of fanzines were shown to the participants.

Thanks to Dr. Funkenstein for his blog article about the event: http://funkenstein.hatenablog.com/entry/2014/11/24/005919

This work is © 2015 松崎健司 (Kenji Matsuzaki)

Kenji Matsuzaki (in the apparent world) is a radiologist at a University hospital and, in the real world, is a wild Japanese Laffertian.

Continued on Next Book:
100 Books to Read After Lafferty
By 7 Japanese Laffertians: Kenji Matsuzaki, Tetsuya Hayashi Shinji Maki, Kiichiro Yanashita, Hayato Kato, Teruyuki Hashimoto, and Yuichi Sakanaga

This booklist was created by 7 Japanese Laffertians for a panel at "Kyoto SF festival 2010," a Japanese SF convention, and translated by Kenji Matsuzaki.

"KISOU" is a Japanese word which is often used in referring Lafferty's works. "KI" means Odd, Strange, Off-beat, Cranky, Bizarre, Surreal, Eccentric, Queer, Ridiculous, Weird, Twisted, Eerie, Unbelievable, Crazy, Rummy... and possibly Lafferty. "SOU" means imagination. So, the recommenders may use [KISOU] when they feel some Lafferty-tastes in the books.

Sorry! Some books (marked with a * symbol) are in Japanese only.

Recommendations by Kenji Matsuzaki:
The American Imagination at Work, Ben C. Clough [American tall tales]

Shinka Shita Saru Tachi, Shinichi Hoshi [American cartoons]

Dreams That Burn in the Night, Craig Strete [SF with Native American view]

Change the Sky and Other Stories, Margaret St. Clair [Strangeness and humor]

Bumberboom (Japan original collection), Avram Davidson [KISOU]

Space-time for Springers (Japan original collection), Fritz Leiber [KISOU]

Over Flat Mountain (Japan original collection), Terry Bisson [KISOU]

The Third Policeman, Flann O'Brien [KISOU and Satire]

Teskeré, Lucio Ceva [KISOU and Satire]
Self-Reference ENGINE, Toh EnJoe [KISOU]
The Thackery T. Lambshead Pocket Guide to Eccentric & Discredited Diseases, Mark Roberts & Jeff VanderMeer [KISOU]
*Tottemo Shonen Tanken-Tai, Hiroshi Aro [KISOU, comic]
*Scrap Gakuen, Hideo Azuma [KISOU, comic]
*Kininaru Bubun, Sachiko Kishimoto [KISOU]
*Dainana Joshi-kai Houkou, Tsubana [KISOU, comic]
*Margaret to Goshujin no Soko-nuke Chin-douchu, Yasuko Sakata [KISOU, strange travel, comic]
Monday Begins on Saturday, Arkady and Boris Strugatsky [Strange institute, KISOU and Satire]
*Ichigo Jikken-shitsu, Sawako Yamana [Strange institute, KISOU]
Adventures in Unhistory, Avram Davidson [Pedantry and KISOU]
*Kai-tai shin-sho, Karasawa Shoukai [Pedantry and KISOU, comic]

RECOMMENDATIONS BY TETSUYA HAYASHI:
The Illuminatus! Trilogy, Robert Anton Wilson & Robert Shea [Occultism and Myth]
*America Hora-banashi, Kazuo Inoue [American Tall Tales, Folklore]
Anansi Boys, Neil Gaiman [Occultism, Myth and Folklore]
Bumberboom (Japan original collection), Avram Davidson [KISOU and Folklore]
The Steam-Driven Boy (Japan original collection), John Sladek [KISOU]
Anywhere But Here, Tori Miki [KISOU, comic]
*Shiori to Shimiko to Yoru no Sakana, Daijiro Morohoshi [KISOU, comic]
*AMACHA ZURUCHA, Hone Fukabori [KISOU]
*Doronkorondo, Yusaku Kitano [KISOU]
*Mushi Zukushi, Minoru Betsuyaku [KISOU]
*Saru, Daisuke Igarashi [KISOU and Folklore, comic]

The End of Mr. Y, Scarlett Thomas [KISOU]
El Grimorio, Enrique Anderson Imbert [KISOU]
The Paradise Motel, Eric McCormack [KISOU]
Il Babbo Di Kafka E Altri Racconti, Tommaso Landolfi [KISOU]
The Helmet of Horror, Victor Pelevin [KISOU]
Captain Jack Zodiac, Michael Kandel [Slapstick]
Slow Birds (Japan original collection), Ian Watson [Slapstick]
**Uchusen "Viekuri"-Gou no Bouken,* Shinji Kajio [Slapstick]
The Brightonomicon, Robert Rankin [Slapstick]

RECOMMENDATIONS BY SHINJI MAKI:

Mimsy Were the Borogoves (Japan original collection), Henry Kuttner [KISOU SF]

A Pale of Air, Fritz Leiber [KISOU SF]

Over Flat Mountain (Japan original collection), Terry Bisson [KISOU SF]

Time Out, David Ely [Extraordinary unique]

Cosmicomics, Italo Calvino [Extraordinary unique]

NASTYbook, Barry Yourgrau [Extraordinary unique]

The Life of Gargantua and of Pantagruel, François Rabelais [Destructive humor]

The Cyberiad, Stanisław Lem [Destructive humor]

Exercises in Style, Raymond Queneau [Destructive humor]

Catch-22, Joseph Heller [Humor and Satire]

The Third Policeman, Flann O'Brien [Humor and Satire]

The Palm-wine Drinkard, Amos Tutuola [Primordial tale]

Industrias y andanzas de Alfanhuí, Rafael Sánchez Ferlosio [Primordial tale]

Ведьма, N. A. Teffi [Folklore and Imagination]

Quiroga collection (Japan original collection), Horacio Quiroga [Folklore and Imagination]

The Man Who Was Thursday, G. K. Chesterton [Secret society]

The Crying of Lot 49, Thomas Pynchon [Secret society]

Life Among the Savages, Shirley Jackson [Enfant terrible]

La Decouverte australe, Restif de La Bretonne [Finding utopia]

Le Mont Analogue, René Daumal [Travel to unknown worlds]

RECOMMENDATIONS BY KIICHIRO YANASHITA:
The Napoleon of Notting Hill, G. K. Chesterton
The Dalkey Archive, Flann O'Brien
The Loved One, Evelyn Waugh
A Good Man Is Hard To Find, Flannery O'Connor
The Very Horrific Life of Great Gargantua, Father of Pantagruel,
François Rabelais
Legenda aurea, Jacobus de Voragine

RECOMMENDATIONS BY HAYATO KATO:
Arrival, Shaun Tan [Strange places]
HAV, Jan Morris [Strange places]
Sinai Tapestry, Edward Whittemore [Strange places]
Phosphor in Dreamland, Rikki Ducornet [Strange places]
Ghostwritten, David Mitchell [Strange places]
The People of Paper, Salvador Plascenci [Strange people]
As She Climbed Across the Table, Jonathan Lethem [Strange people]
Someone Comes to Town, Someone Leaves Town, Cory Doctorow
[Strange people]
Pfitz, Andrew Crumey [Strange people]
Blackwater Days, Terry Dowling [Strange people]
The Exploits of Engelbrecht, Maurice Richardson [Strange people]

RECOMMENDATIONS BY TERUYUKI HASHIMOTO:
Psychological Methods To Sell Should Be Destroyed, Robert Freeman Wexler
Scorch Atlas, Blake Butler
Instruction Manual for Swallowing, Adam Marek
Other City, Michal Ajvaz
La Compagnia dei Celestini, Stefano Benni
Shamrock Tea, Ciaran Carson
Through the Arc of the Rain Forest, Karen Tei Yamashita
Un Lun Dun, China Miéville

RECOMMENDATIONS BY YUICHI SAKANAGA:

The Unreasoning Mask, Philip José Farmer [KISOU SF]

Desolation Road, Ian McDonald [KISOU SF]

El Mundo Alucinante, Reinaldo Arenas [Strange travel]

L'interprete, Diego Marani [Strange travel]

Les Flamboyants, Patrick Grainville [Strange travel]

Dr. Adder, K. W. Jeter [Strange travel]

Lullaby, Chuck Palahniuk [Strange travel]

The Hearing Trumpet, Leonora Carrington [Roaring Apocalypse]

Saint-Glinglin, Raymond Queneau [Odd celebration]

Bats out of Hell, Barry Hannah [KISOU in Southern America]

A Dozen Tough Jobs, Howard Waldrop [KISOU in Southern America]

Nights at the Circus, Angela Carter [Tales]

The Paradise Motel, Eric McCormack [Grotesque, Tales]

The Book of Wonder / Tales of Wonder, Lord Dunsany [Traveler's tales]

The Master and Margarita, Mikhail Bulgakov [Humor and Irony]

*Baseball Book, Kyoichi Imura [Tropical strangeness]

*Nettai, Tetsuya Sato [Tropical strangeness]

*Sakana zukushi, Minoru Betsuyaku [Jokes w/ KISOU]

Without Feathers, Woody Allen [Jokes w/ KISOU]

Le petit savant illustre, Pierre Thuillier [Occultism and Science]

Kenji Matsuzaki is the webmaster of "Toriaezu Lafferty (Japanese Laffertian Page)," which is a Lafferty fan site (in Japanese and English) to be found at http://hc2.seikyou. ne.jp/home/DrBr/index.html. His translation work includes "Cabrito" on Hayakawa's SF Magazine #705, 2014

Tetsuya Hayashi is a SF reviewer and the webmaster of "Himitsu no Lafferty ni tsuite" ("About a secret Lafferty"), which is a Lafferty fan site in Japanese: http://www2s. biglobe.ne.jp/~ttsyhysh/lafferty.html

Shinji Maki is a SF critic and the guest editor of Hayakawa's SF Magazine #705, the Lafferty Centennial memorial issue. Translation works: "The Wagons" in Hayakawa's SF Magazine #556, 2002, and "Despair and the Duck Lady" by Michael Swanwick in Hayakawa's SF Magazine #705, 2014.

Kiichiro Yanashita is a translator. Translation works: "Fourth Mansions," Kokusho Kankou Kai, 2013; "The Reefs of Earth," Kawade Shobo Shinsha, 2002; "Space Chantey," Kokusho Kankou Kai, 2005; "Brain Fever Season" on Hayakawa's SF Magazine #556, 2002; "St. Poleander's Eve" on Hayakawa's SF Magazine #705, 2014.

Hayato Kato is a SF reviewer.

Teruyuki Hashimoto is a SF reviewer. Translation works: "An interview with R. A. Lafferty by Darrell Schweitzer" on Hayakawa's SF Magazine #705, 2014

Yuichi Sakanaga is a SF writer.

Russia discovers R. A. Lafferty —
to be continued on the next rock?
By Sergei Sobolev and Yakov Varganov

In 1965 an unusual short story appeared in August's issue of *Yuniy Technik* ("Young Mechanic"), a popular magazine for young readers. The humorous tale entitled "Sem Strashnih Dney" ("Seven Days of Horror," published in the US as "Seven Day Terror") was written by a writer with an intriguing name previously unknown to Russian readers—R. A. Lafferty. A month later the same translation was printed in the agricultural magazine *Selskaya Molodezh* ("Rural Youth") and finally, three years later, in 1968, the story made its third appearance in a charismatic Science Fiction anthology *31 iyunya* ("July 31st") edited by Arkady Strugatsky (of the Strugatsky Brothers) the insanely popular SF book series *Zarubezhnaya Fantastika* ("Foreign SF"). This time the short but impactful absurdist tale had been freshly translated under the title "Nedelya Uzhasov" ("The Week of Horrors") and was featured in the collection alongside other fine examples of humorous foreign SF. Remarkably, yet another new translation of the same story saw the light a couple years later in the groundbreaking hardcover series *Biblioteka Sovremennoy Fantastiki* ("Modern Science Fiction Library").

An unsuspecting Russian reader in the late 60s could have been forgiven for thinking that R. A. Lafferty was an interesting but rather unproductive writer!

Only in 1974 two new stories by R. A. Lafferty came out in the Soviet Union. "Oh uzh eti mne rebyata" ("Enfants Terribles") was printed in *Rural Youth*. Another popular Soviet periodical, *Knowledge is Power*, introduced "Prozhorlivaya Krasotka" ("Hog-Belly Honey") translated by Raphail Nudelman, a prominent researcher and translator of quality British and American Science Fiction.

The apparent breakthrough turned out inconsequential. There was a long dry spell with no new Lafferty publications until 1986, the early days of Perestroika, when *Knowledge is Power* brought RAL back with the story "Bezlyudniy Pereulok" ("In Our Block").

It should not be too surprising that Lafferty was receiving a cold welcome by Soviet publishers. Unlike some of his peers, such as Robert Sheckley or Robert Silverberg, whose stories were frequently translated and published in the USSR, Lafferty has always made editors and party ideologues uneasy. His works could not be cast in one of the approved molds, such as "criticism of capitalistic exploitation" or "satire on American militarism." There were things and themes in them that censors could not quite place but with unfailing instinct recognized them to be subversive.

During the increasingly stagnant and surrealistic decade of the 70s in the Soviet Union, "surrealism" was a bad word and any author suspected of its sins was to be purged. In the eyes of censors Lafferty was a prime suspect with no redeeming qualities. He was not scourging the evils of capitalist society like Robert Sheckley; neither was he poking fun at greedy entrepreneurs like Robert Silverberg. He did not appear to be sympathetic to the plight of rural drunkards like Clifford Simak. And for sure he was not singing hymns to the technical genius of humanity like Arthur C. Clarke. Lafferty simply turned the reader's brain inside out and tickled it incessantly with dangerous existential questions. Any way you look at it, he was a very inconvenient author!

He still is in Russia nowadays.

In the early 1990s, a unique period in Russian history, a time of unprecedented freedom and heartbreaking poverty when the State institutions were crumbling and everything seemed to be possible, a crop of newborn SF magazines appeared out of nowhere to the immense joy of the starved Russian readership. New translations of Lafferty stories began surfacing one after another, especially on the pages of *Esli* (*If*), the first Russian magazine entirely dedicated to foreign SF. Since 1992 *Esli* has delivered nine new RAL stories, introducing such gems as "Slow Tuesday Night" and "Thieving Bear Planet." It was becoming more and more apparent to the readers that what they were witnessing was just the "tip of the iceberg" of an immeasurably exciting and tremendously important body of work by a visionary writer virtually unknown to them.

The remarkable essay by Michael Swanwick, "In the Tradition..." was published in 1996 in Russia. It introduced many unfamiliar names from the vast archipelago of English-language fantasy and poured new oil into the fire of readers' curiosity with a reverent (albeit very brief) mention of Lafferty. Swanwick compared RAL to a fish shaped too irregularly to be caught by any literary nets.

It has to be noted that Russian readers' hunger for science fiction and fantasy literature at the time was insatiable. Anything stamped with "SF" on its cover guaranteed an instant sale. It was time when Lafferty works could land on the fertile ground of many open minds ready for the Strange.

But when it finally seemed inevitable, the stream of new RAL stories suddenly dried up. The times were changing fast; Russian readers, fed up with poorly translated American and British pulps, were turning their focus to domestic SF and endless epic fantasy cycles. Deemed too complex to translate, too complicated to read, too non-commercial to sell, Lafferty's books were shunned again by the market-savvy new Russian publishers. The time of change and discovery that brought some previously unknown luminaries of the SF genre into the Russian orbit has almost entirely bypassed Lafferty's body of work. The opportunity to discover RAL was squandered.

And thus we enter the 21st century.

In the late 2000s a tiny trickle of Lafferty books resumed from an unlikely source—a fledgling field of small and self-publishers. A few fans who got a taste of Lafferty's worlds and wanted more, have decided not to wait for publisher's grace and have taken destiny in their own hands. Often imperfect, these new editions were nevertheless proclamations of love to Lafferty's work.

By the latest count (as of February 2015) the fan-based publishers have produced eleven books by RAL since 2000. This includes five novels—*Past Master*, *The Reefs of Earth*, *Space Chantey*, *Fourth Mansions* and *Arrive at Easterwine* and at least 75 short stories. The highlights were complete translations of Lafferty's original collections *Nine hundred Grandmothers* and *Strange Doings*.

The best of these books had professional quality translation and even included original illustrations from now-decrepit old

American pulp magazines, as well as some fine newly-commissioned art. They were beautifully made artifacts. The number of copies of each such volume could be counted on the fingers of one hand. They were destined to become curiosities rather than flagships of a new wave of Lafferty books, but who knows what this new movement portends? With a bit of luck these exquisite little tomes might herald a happier new chapter in a long overdue discovery of Lafferty works by Russian readers.

Illustration for "Guesting Time" by Natalya Zatulovskaya

Nine Hundred Grandmothers,
cover art by Natalya Zatulovskaya

The Ultimate Creature,
cover art by Natalya Zatulovskaya

Space Chantey,
cover art by Vladimir Anikin

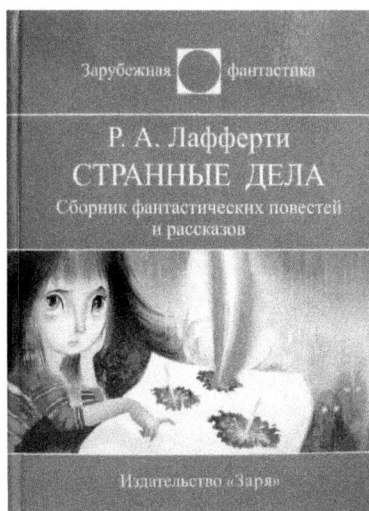

Strange Doings,
cover art by Vladimir Anikin

Sergei Sobolev is a history teacher and a regular contributor to the fan-based internet portal fantlab.ru dedicated to creation of complete bibliographic database of Science Fiction and Fantasy publications in Russia. He discovered R. A. Lafferty's work after reading "Slow Tuesday Night" published in the Russian SF magazine Esli. He lives in Lipetsk, Russia.

Yakov Varganov is a research biologist. His interest in Lafferty's writing was initiated by the same story, "Slow Tuesday Night" in Esli. Following his immigration to the US in 1997 he started collecting and reading all Lafferty's works he could find. Currently he resides in Scotch Plains, NJ.

The authors are very grateful to Sergei Gontarev for his generous help and advice in the process of writing this piece. We especially appreciate the images of the small press RAL editions he contributed. Sergei is a translator and a relentless promoter of Lafferty's works in Russia.

An Interview with Nat!
By Kevin Cheek and the East of Laughter Facebook group

Nat!, the creator of The Lafferty Devotional Page (www. mulle-kybernetik.com/RAL/), graciously agreed to an interview. The questions were suggested by members of the East of Laughter group on Facebook. The interview was conducted by email.

FoL: Nat!, first thank you for your site. The Lafferty Devotional page was the only Lafferty resource online for many years, and served as a focus for the (then small) community of Lafferty fans on the Internet. It was useful to Rich Persaud of ralafferty.org in reconstructing a Lafferty timeline, for example; the family posted news about Lafferty's health, and the husband of his nurse at the nursing home also posted a couple of notes. The fact is that it takes a ton of work to create any online community, and it would have been much harder in the 90s than just clicking a few buttons on Facebook. Assuming that Lafferty will remain obscure for the next hundred years, we will need future creators like you and David Cruces (creator of the East of Laughter facebook group) and Rich and Andrew Fergusson and many more to host gatherings to engage the curious. Historians need mentors too.

How did you first discover Lafferty's writing? What are the characteristics of his writing you love most?

Nat!: Lafferty was translated to German and appeared in SF anthologies. I used to read a ton as a kid. I remember that I exhausted the SF section of my local library. Lafferty really stuck out, because he had these really unusual stories that got me to thinking, peppered with a unique writing style.

FoL: What struck me was the relatively low level of activity in the message boards—was that perhaps because Lafferty's works were physically unavailable at that time, or at least much harder to find?

Nat!: I suspected that there weren't just that many Lafferty fans. When the R. A. Lafferty Devotional Page started, it was at a time where the internet was still fairly new. One still used modems to connect to your ISP. Probably a lot of the old SF guys were still using typewriters and the post office to communicate.

FoL: What drove you to create the site?

Nat!: Well as I wrote in <u>http://www.mulle-kybernetik.com/ RAL/MT/about.html</u> it seemed someone had to do it, but nobody was doing it. I think it was the first real website I did. I previously maintained a David Lee Roth quotes list on a newsgroup, when that was still popular, but that was about it in terms of public services.

FoL: It would be interesting to hear your take on the "landscape" that you published that site into. It was literally the only thing online about Lafferty for a long time.

Nat!: I think I was a little bit ahead of Kenji (<u>http://hc2.sei-kyou.ne.jp/home/DrBr/RAL/menu.html</u>) from Japan, but maybe not. Since his site is all in Japanese I can't read it and Google translation does not help very much. Kenji seemed to have *all* the Lafferty books, I was a bit envious ;)

People just seemed to be happy that a Lafferty site existed, but it also became clear that there weren't exactly very many Lafferty fans out there. Those that were out there appeared to be extremely passionate. But coming back to question one, I was also a bit disappointed that there wasn't more interaction on the boards.

FoL: Do you prefer reading Lafferty in English or in German?

Nat!: There are so few German translations that it's moot. Certainly the very first stories I read were translations.

FoL: I am curious about your observations of Lafferty history, especially since your community existed both before and after Lafferty's death in 2002.

Nat!: I see myself more of an infrastructure provider than personally being a social hub in the Lafferty universe. So actually I am not really very much in the loop of what's going on. Certainly there has been much more interest in the last years, more articles written, more projects. Which I think is great. It used to be that only Neil Gaiman seemed to be able to push Lafferty a little bit into the spotlight sometimes. Now Andrew Ferguson is putting a lot of energy in from a scholarly perspective. I hope it's been good to get Lafferty at least some name recognition outside of SF. If there is ever going to be a major rediscovery of Lafferty works, I would guess it has to come from outside SF.

FoL: Do you see a renaissance for Lafferty's work starting now or anytime soon?

Nat!: I doubt it, but what do I know? The intellectual landscape appears to be drifting towards medievalism, maybe Lafferty could become the Burroughs of a future theocracy ;)

FoL: Who were some people who contacted you with Lafferty memorabilia for the site? I've seen you mention Sheryl Smith.

Nat!: I don't hold anything back (except for copyright reasons.) If someone has something to share, I post it.

FoL: Did you ever write to Lafferty? Why or why not? If so, what kind of reply did you receive?

Nat!: I thought about it. I actually thought about visiting the university library in Tulsa, but I never did. I have no idea if he was ever aware that he had a site going on the internet.

FoL: How did you find some of the more obscure stories that you have given ratings to?

Nat!: I remember being in California for a conference, and whenever the conference was over, I went to this used bookstore that had SF paperbacks for maybe 50 cents or so. Shelves after shelves of paperbacks stacked in two rows. For three days I just sifted through everything and bought anything that had a Lafferty story. The owner wasn't very happy with me, since I touched all his books. So I have a few copies of *Galaxy* and *Asimov's* and the like. I learned that they contained some good stories, but that there was also a case of diminishing returns. Nine Hundred Grandmothers is still the definitive collection in my opinion.

With the internet getting more popular, I could use Abebooks and Amazon to get what was missing. I also specifically looked up the magazines and anthologies where Lafferty stories were published, and bought them online.

FoL: What kind of response has your rating system generated (and why on earth would you rate Fourth Mansions as Lame)?

Nat!: Oh, well, the passionate Lafferty fans were miffed. The main thought behind the rating system, as also explained on the site, is to give the average reader a pointer what to read and what to avoid. But tastes diverge.

Fourth Mansions... OK, you got me started on it. This was probably my first major Lafferty disappointment, being about the third novel I read. The first time I thought about a Lafferty piece: "this is not very good at all."

It's a certain Lafferty style that really gets on my nerves, unfortunately one Lafferty himself seems to have been quite fond of. Just an example (paraphrased): "Arouet was a Teilhardian. He was a man completely without humor, but he had nothing serious to him." All right, that refutes that philosopher right there... Why even go to the lengths of putting up a strawman, if you can just slander your opponents.

The whole setup of the story is totally bogus. People seem to be mostly concerned with uttering premonitions or lecturing other people about vague theories. I can discern little interesting dialogue, much less interesting ideas. Who really wondered if it's going to be the first or the fifth mansions next, when the fourth was totally crazy already? Contrast this with *Past Master* ... The chapter titles are incredibly good though.

FoL: What is your favorite color?

Nat!: That's a question for a "Poesiealbum."

This work is © 2015 Kevin Cheek.

Nat! maintains the R. A. Lafferty Devotional Page. He has no cats.

Despair and the Duck Lady

By Michael Swanwick

*"Despair and the Duck Lady" was written as an introduction
to the original publication by Steve Pasechnick's Edgewood
Press of Iron Tears, a collection of stories by R. A. Lafferty.
When Iron Tears was republished by Wildside Press, my introduction was dropped because print-on-demand publishers
operate on a very thin margin. Ray Lafferty, as everybody
called him, died in 2002. Other that, nothing has changed.*

The best possible introduction to a book by R. A. Lafferty is one
that begins "And they also tell the story" and ends "Is that not an
odd introduction? I don't understand it at all." You can find it at the
front of *The Devil Is Dead*, and it was written by the man himself. As
usual, he did it first and he did it best.

The temptation when writing about Raphael Aloysius Lafferty
is to employ his own tools: To play with paradox and contradiction,
to dazzle with wild invention and high humor, to couch subtle ideas
in a defiantly lowbrow idiom. And it's always a mistake to try, because not only can't you beat Lafferty at his own game, you can't
even do well enough to keep from looking foolish by contrast. You
might as well take all your money out of the bank and sink it into the
three-card monte game that the boys have set up down to the corner.
The conclusion is a done deed.

So I will abandon subtlety. As artlessly as possible, I want to
present you with a few facts and then labor toward a difficult conclusion. The important facts are three:

First, Lafferty is one of the best writers ever to work in the
science fiction and fantasy genre.

Second, he is the single most original writer the field has seen.

Third, he is—except for small press publications such as this
one—unpublishable.

To appreciate Lafferty as a writer, you need only sample the
best of his work—his unparalleled short story collection *Nine Hun-*

dred Grandmothers by preference, though such novels as *Okla Hannali* or *The Devil Is Dead* or *The Flame Is Green* will do almost as well.

To explain exactly how original Lafferty is would take more space and time than I have available here. In brief, most writers work from a received set of conventions. A dull, hot day is evoked in long, languid sentences that wander like dusty roads beneath the oppressively breathless burden of unvaryingly blue skies. Tense scenes are written crisply. In sharp staccato sentences.

Broken into short paragraphs.

There is nothing wrong with any of this. Great literature has been written in derivative prose. But those of us who are servants of the conventions are painfully aware that at our best we can only take so much credit for what is, after all, inherited wealth.

Lafferty belongs to a select group that includes James Joyce and Amos Tutuola, of writers who have reinvented the language of literature for themselves from the ground up. Joyce, of course, was a scholarly writer who was strongly influenced by archaic texts. Tutuola came from a tribal culture and it will take somebody familiar with the Yoruba storytelling tradition to determine how much of his genius is his own and how much is his people's. Lafferty has drawn strongly from the oral tradition of the American tall tale, from writers now forgotten or neglected, from sources yet to be catalogued. There is a gold mine here for critics, should they ever find him.

Unpublishable, though—how can such a writer be unpublishable?

"Madness and buggery!" said one editor when I asked. 'The numbers just aren't there," said another, meaning that not enough readers buy his books for them to turn a profit. But these are just rephrasings of the problem. Nobody knows why. Nobody has any plausible theories. Still, the fact remains: There's not a publishing house in New York that will touch a book by R. A. Lafferty.

But here's an odd thing. Talk to almost anybody in the field about Lafferty's plight and you will inevitably hear him compared to Philip K. Dick. On the face of it, two more dissimilar writers—in style, voice, or intent—would be hard to imagine. Yet the claim is made repeatedly that the fate of the one must surely be the fate of the other.

Philip K. Dick led a rough life, hacking out paperback originals, scrabbling after pennies, taken seriously by nobody but a few prescient readers. But when he died, something phenomenal happened. He was discovered. Movies were made from his books. A small critical industry arose, devoted to his work. The highly respected composer Tod Machover wrote an opera based on *Valis* that premiered at the Pompidou Center in Paris. It was a strange and ironic twist on a life that was strange and ironically twisted to begin with.

More people than I could list have independently assured me that the same thing is going to happen to Lafferty. The first time I heard this asserted, it seemed an interesting notion. The second time I thought was a coincidence. The third, I began to wonder. Somewhere between five and eight, I came face-to-face with despair.

To explain why, I have to tell you about the Duck Lady.

The Duck Lady was for many years a common sight in Philadelphia. She was a fat old woman with a short-stepped waddle. When she was in the throes of her mental disability—which was most of the time— she talked constantly to herself, saying "Quackquackquackquack- QUACKquackquackQUACKquackquackquack!" and so on. During those years there was a persistent rumor that she was actually the matriarch of a wealthy Main Line family. Mad, yes, she was mad. But cared for. The family let her wander the streets only because that was what she insisted on doing. A good friend swore to me he had seen the Duck Lady being picked up at the end of a day's begging by a chauffeured limousine.

This is a classic example of an urban legend. Such tales do not originate in a vacuum. They arise spontaneously to provide soothing excuses for situations people find intolerable.

When the Duck Lady died, the truth came out. She was an impoverished, homeless bag lady. The mansion, limo, and family were all inventions in the face of an intolerable truth: That a harmless old woman with a disabling mental illness would be forced to live on the streets. That nobody had the slightest idea how to help her.

And so with Lafferty. He's one of the best writers that science fiction has ever seen. He's certainly the most original. And he's unpublishable. So we tell ourselves that he'll get justice just as soon as he dies. They'll be making movies of his work, writing biographies, publishing his collected letters. There'll be societies and magazines and the intellectuals will posthumously lionize him. We tell ourselves these things because the alternative simply doesn't bear thinking about.

This is the case for despair.

But just because something is unbearable does not make it true.

The single best argument for hope is the book you told in your hands. Iron Tears is only the latest skirmish in one of the most remarkable—even heroic—literary campaigns that a field known for Quixotic endeavors has ever seen. In the wake of Lafferty's being written off by the publishing establishment, a congeries of small-press publishers has sprung up, dedicated to bringing all of his unpublished novels into print and gathering his uncollected stories in permanent format. Not just Edgewood Press, but United Mythologies, Corroboree, Chris Drumm Books, The Manuscript Press, Broken Mirrors—and for all I know, there may be others.

One of the Master's most persistent tropes is that of the *Lamed Vuv*—the tradition that the world is precariously sustained by the existence of thirty-six righteous men. If so, then surely publishers Steve Pasechnick, Dan Knight, Chris Drumm, Bryan Cholfin, and all the others, stand a good chance of being numbered among them. The economics of small press publishing are such that I can pretty much guarantee you these guys are not making any money. The winds of literary popularity are such that I can also guarantee that they could be doing significantly better if they put the same effort into backing any of a number of inferior writers. At their level of publishing, critical attention barely exists.

Still they persist.

Let's raise the stakes and point out here that not all the works being preserved deserve it for their own sakes. Some of the stories in Iron Tears are top-drawer, as good as anything you'll read this month. Others are not. Major writers sometimes produce minor work. But as clues to the workings of Lafferty's mind and fiction, even his minor works are worth preserving. For the sake of future academics and critics. For future readers.

For posterity.

There had been nothing comparable to this enterprise since Donald Wandrei and August Derleth founded Arkham House to preserve the life's work of H. P. Lovecraft. Lovecraft was as good as forgotten at the time of his death. Today his reputation looks secure. And Lovecraft was not half the writer Lafferty is.

Knight, Cholfin, Drumm, Pasechnick, and the others believe that Lafferty's reputation will not only endure but prevail. So, ironically enough, do many of the editors who will not publish him. There is, among those familiar with Lafferty's oeuvre, no doubt that it contains some of the best fiction of our times. All agree that it deserves to be read and loved by generations of readers to come. But will it be?

Here is the crux of the thing. Do we delude ourselves with hope? Or is it despair that is the illusion? Lafferty himself, from the testimony of his stories and novels, is an enemy of despair, and would side with joy, with laughter, with the tramps and angels, with the seven righteous men and their shaggier kin. We can only follow his lead.

Is that not an odd introduction? I don't understand this one either.

Michael Swanwick is the multiple-award-winning author of such books as Stations of the Tide *and* Gravity's Angels. *He has been a Lafferty admirer, fan, and supporter for longer than many of his readers have been alive. He was gracious enough to allow us to reprint his introduction to* Iron Tears *in celebration of R. A. Lafferty.*

R. A. Lafferty—the secret sci-fi genius more than ready for a comeback

By David Barnett

(A version of this piece originally appeared in The Guardian on 13 August 2014.)

RA Lafferty might just be the most important science fiction writer you've never heard of.

That state of affairs could be slowly and gradually changing, though, this being his centenary year—Raphael Aloysius Lafferty was born on November 7, 1914, the youngest of five children, in Iowa, though when he was four the family moved to Oklahoma, where Lafferty lived until his death in a nursing home in 2002, when he was 87.

So, landmark year aside, why should we care about RA Lafferty? What elevates him from the legions of forgotten writers who filled the drugstore paperback racks with cheap books in the 1960s and 70s?

Lafferty was certainly prolific, with 20 novels and 200-plus short stories seeing print from when he started getting published (relatively late in life, aged 46; he worked as an electrical engineer until 1971—well on to his way to being 60—before he allowed himself to turn to full-time writing) to when he retired after a series of strokes in the early 1980s. He lived much of his life with his sister, and died unmarried following a life of struggling with drink problems.

But quantity is no signifier of quality. For my money, what singles out Lafferty as criminally underrated is the sheer absurdity of much of his output and the singular marriage of fable, comedy and fantasy which underpins his work, including his novels *Past Master*, *Space Chantey* and *Fourth Mansions*, and his huge body of shorter works.

Take his 1969 novel *Fourth Mansions*, a tale of rival world-spanning conspiracies duking it out to shape mankind's next level, which predates Robert Anton Wilson and Robert Shea's "Illuminatus Trilogy" by six years and Grant Morrison's comic series *The Invisibles*—both of which works owe *Fourth Mansions* a huge debt—by a quarter of a century.

Like much of Lafferty's work, *Fourth Mansions* is infused with his strong Catholic beliefs, his love of mythology, and a darkly comic flair:

> *There was a young man who had good eyes but simple brains. Nobody can have everything. His name was Freddy Foley and he was arguing with a man named Tankersley who was his superior.*
>
> *"Just how often do you have to make a total fool of yourself, Foley?" Tankersley asked him sharply. Tankersley was a kind man, but he had a voice like a whip.*
>
> *"An enterprising reporter should do it at least once a week, sir, or he isn't covering the ground," Fred Foley said seriously.*

There's something of the Irish comic tradition in there, the absurdity and surreality of *The Third Policeman* author Flann O'Brien.

"I agree," says the author Neil Gaiman. "And there's kinship with the American Tall Tale tradition, and with G. K. Chesterton as well. But they are all only cousins. There's nothing close to Lafferty—nobody with the gravitas about things that were light, and the *antigravitas* about important heavy things."

Gaiman has been a Lafferty enthusiast since he discovered his work at the tender age of nine. He attempted a story in the Lafferty style—"Sunbird," in his collection *Fragile Things*—which he said proved to him "mostly how much harder they are than they look."

Gaiman says: "I discovered him through two short stories ("Narrow Valley" and "Primary Education of the Camiroi") in Judith Merrill's *SF12*, aged about nine. At age 11 I was given some of the *Wollheim-Carr Year's Best* anthologies, with more Lafferty inside. I read his books in my local library, bought them in paperback and bought them when Dark They Were And Golden Eyed [a seminal London specialist SF bookshop in the 70s] sold the Dobson SF editions off at remainder prices.

"What drew me to his work? The narrative voice, I think. The way he'd construct a story, unlike the way anyone else did it. The peculiar rightness of his worldview, and the topsy turvy nature of it. The sentences."

Like the short story "The Transcendent Tigers," for example, which explores the recurring Lafferty theme of uplifted or evolved humans, this time a bunch of squabbling kids who visit Armageddon on the world literally by sticking pins in the map to choose their targets:

> *It wasn't a clean-cut holocaust at all. It was a clumsy, bloody, grinding job—not what you'd like.*

A few years later, Gaiman even struck up a correspondence with Lafferty. He remembers: "There was an address for him in some directory of writers in my local library. It seemed unlikely that anything would happen if I wrote to him, but I did, and he replied—he had moved several times since that address, but the letter somehow found him. I sent him a Lafferty pastiche I had written, and he was not rude about it. But he was encouraging, and informative, and took me very seriously, which is good, because I was about 20 and took myself very seriously as well."

There feels something oddly Kerouackian about Lafferty, the pick-and-mix Catholicism, mysticism and mythologizing that typifies his writing, but also the sense that he was outside the mainstream, the SF establishment, ploughing his own absurdist furrow. He was nominated for several Nebula Awards but never won one; he managed to share a Hugo Award for Best Short Story in 1973, with Frederik Pohl and CM Kornbluth; in 1990 he received a World Fantasy Lifetime Achievement Award, but by that point he'd stopped writing.

It seems that if Lafferty is remembered at all today, it's primarily as a short story writer. You can find one or two online; "Slow Tuesday Night" is a wonderful example of his craft, in which humanity is gifted the ability to make literally split-second decisions, affording them several careers, marriages and lifetimes in a single night. It begins, and ends, with a beggar accosting a couple:

> *The panhandler was Basil Bagelbaker, who would be the richest man in the world within an hour and a half. He would make and lose four fortunes within eight hours; and these not the little fortunes that ordinary men acquire, but titanic things.*

"I lean toward the novels, but I'm very much in the minority on that," says Andrew Ferguson. "Lafferty himself said his short stories were better, but his novels had more to say; the stories are always worth going back to but it's the novels on which his long-term literary reputation will rest. *Okla Hannali* in particular should be more widely read, it can stand alongside any other volume on Native American history and character."

Ferguson is a Ph.D candidate in English at the University of Virginia, and along with Gaiman's championing he's one of the reasons Lafferty is perhaps being pulled back from the brink of total obscurity—he's writing a biography of the author for the University of Illinois Modern Masters of SF series, and will chair a panel on Lafferty on Thursday August 14 at Loncon, the World Science Fiction Convention, being held at London's Docklands.

He says: "It may be a bit of a cliché, but there's really nothing else out there comparable to him. Take any 'rule' of good writing—something like 'show, don't tell'—and he'll break it exuberantly: why show when all the fun is in the telling? He's one of the distinctive prose stylists in the genre: you can tell a Lafferty story within a sentence. He's a very funny writer, in a field that has often taken itself way too seriously—see the stories "Seven-Day Terror" or "The Hole on the Corner"—but also creates stories that are intensely emotional and symbolically deep, such as "Continued on Next Rock" or "Funnyfingers.""

If you have a Lafferty book on your shelf, you're lucky—he hasn't been in print for a long time, at least, not in English. Curiously, he's big in Japan, says Ferguson, where "Lafferty has remained popular for decades now. Thanks to the efforts of a small group of devotees, there's been new Lafferty in translation almost every year—and because of that, they've built up a substantial following."

His obscurity in the West might have been total save for a strange advertisement that appeared in the trade press in 2011, placed by the Lafferty estate and announcing that an offer had been received in the sum of $70,000 for the rights to 29 novels and 225 short stories. That deal was concluded and the buyer emerged as Locus, a highly-respected science fiction magazine in the US. The fruits of that deal were a publication agreement with Centipede Press, which has this year put out one collection—*The Man Who Made Models*—which sold out of its limited print run almost immediately.

Jared Walters of Centipede Press says: "The second is still in the works. The response has been very strong. He receives a lot of attention and respect, more than I anticipated, to be honest."

From the second volume, Andrew Ferguson is involved with the Centipede Press series, which is planned to run to a dozen or more books. Interestingly, that estate includes 14 novels and 40 short stories that have never seen print. Wouldn't it be nice, though, to have Lafferty available in a more mass-market edition, especially for his centenary year?

Ferguson says: "I'm hoping the Centipede Press editions get licensed for a more affordable edition eventually, since a lot of those stories have never been collected or seen wide release. I think there'd definitely be readers for a big Best of Lafferty retrospective. And I think reprints of the story collections like *Nine Hundred Grandmothers* or *Strange Doings*, and also the better-known and more accessible novels like *Space Chantey*, *Past Master*, and *Fourth Mansions* might do well."

That's something Gaiman would like to see as well: "I'd love to see a Complete Lafferty in print. And a selected short stories. I used to give people his short story collection *Nine Hundred Grandmothers*, until one day it was out of print and gone."

It's hard to say why, if Lafferty was so brilliant—which he was—that his work never got the audience it deserved, and is virtually unknown today. He was perhaps a little too premature, too old and too geographically distant to fully take advantage of the London-centric New Wave movement of science fiction which championed experimentation and literary sensibilities in SF, though he was a good fit with it. Perhaps his succession of unreliable narrators and the suspicion that nothing in a Lafferty novel is what it seems was at odds with the post-Star Wars appetite for scientific space opera in the late 1970s, his shaggy-dog stories owing more to a lost folk-tradition than the shiny, technological futures the SF of his day was demanding.

David Langford, the noted science fiction commentator, has his own theory, but first an anecdote, written by Langford for his regular SF news bulletin Ansible Link, in the wake of Lafferty's death in March 2002:

"I swapped letters with Lafferty and met him briefly at the 1979 World SF Convention in Brighton. He always admitted he had a drink problem, and magically appeared at the head of the queue whenever the bar opened. Smiling, enigmatic, uncommunicative, he showed few signs of the inspired blarney in his fiction. A French publisher nervously asked whether Lafferty minded being compared to G.K. Chesterton (another Catholic author), and there was a terrifying silence that went on and on. Was the great man hideously offended? Eventually, very slowly, he said: 'You're on the right track, kid,' and wandered away. The World Fantasy Convention belatedly did the decent thing and honoured RA Lafferty with its Lifetime Achievement Award in 1990. But the SF world never honoured him enough."

And Langford's view on why Lafferty never got the recognition he deserved, from the same piece, is a simple one: "Major publishers abandoned him in the mid-80s: Lafferty was just too dementedly brilliant for them."

Perhaps what were once perceived as his weaknesses in publishing terms should rather be seen as Lafferty's strengths. After all, Lafferty's most accessible and widely-read novel, *Space Chantey*, is a psychedelic, Homeric odyssey in which space captain Roadstrum leads an expedition to the pleasure planet Lotophage, where the immortal houri Margaret tells him, very wisely, that "there are worse places to live than in tall stories."

David Barnett is a journalist and author based in the North of England. He works for the Guardian and the Independent, and his fiction includes the Gideon Smith series of alternate-history/steampunk novels, published in the US by Tor and the UK by Snowbooks. He can be found on Twitter as @ davidmbarnett *and on the web at* http://www.davidbarnett.wordpress.com.

Twice Beheaded: R. A. Lafferty's Thomas More
By Anne Lake Prescott

*"Twice Beheaded: R. A. Lafferty's Thomas More" originally
appeared in* **Moreana** *Vol. 50, No. 191-192, (June 2013), pp.
273-283. Reproduced here with permission of the copyright
owner. Further reproduction prohibited without permission.*

Several years ago, when at work on an essay dealing with Thomas
More's earthly "Afterlife" for a guide to More edited by the
wonderful George Logan, editor of the Norton *Utopia* and author
of *The Meaning of More's Utopia*, I came across an ancient brown-
paged paperback of a 1968 science-fiction novel by R. A. Lafferty,
Past Master. The "past master," meaning both "dead expert" and
"excellent expert," is Thomas More, star of this journal. Set early in
2535, in a sort of, kind of, ambiguous urban utopia named Astrobe,
a network of neighboring cities (not unlike New York?) populated
by transplanted human beings but also by rapidly evolved native
creatures and some very scary machines, Past Master is but one of
many later utopias and dystopias that glance at More, or at least at
his famous book, if only implicitly. Everybody knows who wrote the
first modern utopia. Lafferty's novel remains, though (or so far as I
know), the only modern science fiction novel or speculative fiction
to make him the protagonist, which is why it deserves a bit more
attention than I could give it in my essay for Professor Logan.

Thomas More scholars, but also the large number of those interested in utopias and dystopias, might find this strange and not
altogether successful work particularly interesting for its contribution to the long history of the ambivalence with which we imagine
the good place, the better place, even the very horrible place. All my
readers, of course, know the complexity of *Utopia*'s influence, not
least the misapprehension that More meant his nowhere good place
to be perfect, or ideal, and not a contribution to thinking, sometimes ironically and sometimes with a carnival touch, and in a "no

less festive than salutary little book," about what makes, or unmakes, "the best state of a commonwealth." (That is of course the title-page before it all too soon dwindled to offering us just "Utopia").

Lafferty's novel shares the ambivalent threat in this tradition, but it also finds a place in the larger movement that others have pointed out: from putting the good place in the past, or somewhere in the Indian Ocean where only Sir John Mandeville has seen it, or out in the Atlantic where Francis Bacon can describe it, or... well, nowhere... to the more modern assumption that the good place is in the future and available to the dreamer who awakes or, nowadays, to time travel. That is not, of course, the universal late-modern perception, for as many have also noted we are not very utopian these days. Indeed, one fairly recent book on utopias designed to accompany an exhibit at the New York Public Library claims that fairly early in the early twentieth century Americans ceased "to dream." [I tried that thought on my students, and almost to a woman they called out "I have a dream today!" Right.] But even later than Bellamy's forward-looking *Looking Backward*, for example, both utopias as well as dystopias, or at least ambiguous combinations, were to be found on other planets (earlier generations had used the moon as a place to put other cultures or races, but we know better than to do so). Some such imaginary worlds are in Star Trek, for example, and probably the subtlest are those imagined by Ursula Le Guin. There is a fashion for them in young adult fiction.

There may be one or two people here who have not read Lafferty's *Past Master*, so let me explain what the novel is all about and how it might relate to More's (this-worldly) afterlife. Those who govern Astrobe, or seem to govern it, or think they do, realize that they are in trouble. Their utopia satisfies all its citizens' physical needs and even the social. It is a genuine eutopia with a happy "eu," not a nowhere "u." And yet ... many citizens are voluntarily dropping out, as we said in the late 1960s, choosing to live in such crowded places as "Cathead" and "the Barrio," places blighted by disease, filth, and violence.[1] They are free to return to Astrobe to be well-fed, well-

---

[1] R. A. Lafferty, *Past Master* (New York: Ace Books, 1968), nominated for the Hugo and Nebula awards but not, in 2012, among the best-known sci-fi novels. For a subtle exploration of how science fiction relates to utopias and how both relate to dystopias,

housed, well-treated. What is wrong? Astrobe's leaders, somewhat mysterious figures in this quite confusing piece of fiction, reflect that since Thomas More had been an authority on utopias (Plato is dismissed as "too cold, too placid," p. 14), he might know how to fix one when it has gone bad. Gone bad not because it is in truth a dystopia—fixing what is dystopic is easy, at least in the imagination—but because it really is a utopia and yet seems unbearable to many of its citizens. Not totalitarian. Not boring. Just unbearable.

So advanced a society as that on Astrobe, of course, has discovered time-travel and temporal body-snatching, so an expert on such activity is sent back to Tudor London in 1535 so he can snatch Thomas More and bring him to Astrobe for a consultation on utopian drop-outs. (The time-snatcher is named Paul. I'm not sure why. We also have an Adam and an Evita). Dropouts leaving a safe and healthy world for dirt and mess. How 1960s, I thought as I first read this, but Raphael Aloysius Lafferty was a convinced and fairly conservative Catholic whose agenda was little concerned with promoting flower-power, flower-power with plenty of weed if not weeds, or with showing the stupidity of war, although there is perhaps a trace of his decade's disgust with bourgeois conformity and comfort. No wonder that by the end of the novel we find that his interest in More is a fascination less with the author of *Utopia* than with the Catholic martyr.

So More is snatched by Paul from Chelsea in 1535. Right—Lafferty's history is a bit off. There are other details that disturb the pedant in me—one character later reminds More, and he does not deny it, that he was a "London playgoer" (87). This More, moreover,

see Peter Fitting, "Utopia, dystopia and science fiction," in *The Cambridge Companion to Utopian Literature*, ed. Gregory Claeys (Cambridge UP, 2010); many statements in the opening overview by Fátima Vieira might depress More scholars in the claim that e.g., the word "utopia" came to mean one of the "paradisiacal places," which is far too simple and the assumption that the first title was "Utopia." Not really. Even J.C. Davis' essay on More's *Utopia*, in my own view, too readily calls Utopia "the ideal society of More's aspiration," although he is right to find a teasing humor. Lafferty does not figure in this volume.

Either because he can be subtle or because he is unwilling to suggest that Astrobians drop out happily, Lafferty imagines his dropouts, or many of them, as "surly" (122). No cakes and ale, no illicit pleasure. The contrast, in other words, is not between utopian Puritan virtue/gloom and lax individualistic Sir Toby Belch.

seems a strange combination of satirist (he calls his book Utopia "bitterly" ironic) and hard-drinking action hero who can handle a keg with no difficulty.[2] This is not the sick aging man with the long beard that grew as the days went by in prison and he plied the charcoal that Meg had smuggled into his cell, but rather a lively, talkative, joking, alert ironist who can throw a punch and win fist-fights. Once he is on Astrobe, he finds himself exploring the mountainous and rough terrain outside Astrobe's main city, often commenting on matters ironically (and in early modern English, which Lafferty enjoys reproducing at times, if not always accurately.) He talks to a variety of inhabitants, including some strangely articulate sea creatures modified to live on land, and on the whole not much helping to advance any discernable plot. But all the time, we later learn, he is observing, noting, penetrating the surface of things, and indeed more subtly than Lafferty permits the reader to do. We also learn that he has largely lost his faith.

What he finds on Astrobe is not much like More's own Utopia as Hythloday describes it. Although Utopia uses coercive force against malefactors, and is hardly awash with human rights, it does value an equality, at least up to a point, that Lafferty ignores. Astrobe has private property—some citizens are very rich, much richer than others, and workmen are paid in small gold coins. Gold! And not for

---

2 Lafferty's More, in this intermittently over-written and peculiar novel, reverts to this thought a number of times; see, e.g., p. 31 on how he has been told by other time-travelers (this is not the first time he has met one) that the future would misread Utopia, taking "a biting satire for a vapid dream." I agree with this fictional More that Utopia is not an unproblematic ideal, but Lafferty's More reads the work far more darkly than most of us would. My own view remains that of George Logan—the island is an occasionally carnivalesque "thought experiment" in the service of satire, yes, but also as an aid to thinking seriously "de optimo statu rei publicae." See George Logan, *The Meaning of More's 'Utopia'* (Princeton UP, 1983). The complexity is that Utopia was written before the seismic shift in European thinking from remembering Eden and the Golden Age to (also?) planning something both this-worldly and better. On p.103 of Lafferty's novel we read about More's easy way with beer.

An anachronism that would irritate modern Renaissance scholars is the usual, dreary, misreading of "humanism," which here "has no meat"—as opposed to "materialism," which "has no bones" (133). Mildly clever, but this is not the "humanism" of More and Erasmus, just the modern and almost meaningless "humanism" that often connotes a sort of soft nice-guy atheism.

chamber pots or chains. True, there is no sickness, nervousness, or fear, and the arts and sciences are open to all—there is even what Star Trek called "beaming"—instant travel from one spot to another—but I can find no stress on sharing. Even more significantly, Astrobe lacks any religion to speak of. So it is not a utopia that either Hythloday or Morus would find even a plausible, let alone a best, state of a commonweal. Nobody believes in a "beyond," More hears, because there *is* no "beyond" (65), any more than there is sin (there is nothing to sin against, he is told) or an "unconscious"—that inward "beyond," one might call it (interesting that Lafferty would use the Jungian term, not Freud's "subconscious").

Sheep don't eat men in Astrobe, but something has eaten their psyches or, if you prefer, their souls. The citizens are the sheep, and with secret shepherds who now need More, having read *Utopia* with the utmost seriousness.

The lack of religious belief, despite a coin-operated Mass and one remaining senescent cleric, may explain, if not clearly so to Astrobe's inhabitants, why it fails. Many may more deliberately leave it because it has so little room for individuality (yes, a common reaction to Utopia nowadays) and have come to suspect that their minds have been taken over by intelligent machines. Indeed, the whole planet seems to be merged with the mechanical—when not, in some cases, just possibly, with the angelic, or … the diabolical.

With no remaining religious belief of his own, at first More is drawn to Astrobe, but being ironic and perceptive his admiration does not last. By the end of the novel he has discovered that he is in fact not on Astrobe to govern as its President, as he had been told he would do, or to cure a sick utopia, but in fact to reinforce the power of those who brought him. So, having discovered that his job as President is in truth to help keep the Astrobian citizenry in clockwork obedience (but seeming freedom), and having recovered his faith smewhere along his travel in Astrobe, he now vetoes a new law outlawing the remnants of religious belief or activity. He has already vetoed two other acts, and it is against the law to veto three. Thus Thomas More, the new President of Astrobe inaugurated on 28 June 2035 (155) who has refused to help abolish all religion, once more faces beheading as, although this is possibly my own joke, literally a recusant. Soon the executioner's axe does indeed strike, although exactly what happens just as it falls is mysterious. To repeat, despite the genre of this novel, the author of *Utopia* does not matter more to Lafferty than does the victim of Henry VIII.

Thus the time-snatched More has defied the mechanical on behalf of the spirit, and in this preference he has company in modern dystopian literature, although Lafferty makes the threat of Astrobe not just psyche-denying or personhood-denying but soul-denying. At More's execution (although he seems—it is hard to say— to be in part snatched back to Tudor England or perhaps to somewhere else—Heaven?—just as the axe comes down) he seems somehow to help bring... it is again hard to say... some openness to the religious, the spiritual. As the novel closes, mysteriously, resonantly, if to my earthy mind barely understandably, and after a reminder of history's cycles (although stopping with America and forgetting China), we read: "Be quiet. We wait." And then, with more indications of temporal recursiveness, of time's cycles, and with the hope that the Spirit that once "came down" on "water and clay" might now come down on the mechanistic Astrobe's "gell-cells and flux-fix," so "that the "programmed tree" might "fruit after all," and with some final play on forms of nothingness (cousin of nowhereness, of *nusquam*), the novel ends with the hint of a new world and the words "Be quiet. We hope." If God can animate clay and redeem those who ate from the tree, then maybe he can enter even a clockwork orange hanging on a mechanical tree. Who knows? And Lafferty wrote before we all had computers.

Where does all this leave Astrobe's utopian experiment? While More goes—"merrily," he would have said—to Heaven, Lafferty's utopia seems to be headed for something between Purgatory and Limbo, waiting and hoping, between two worlds.

The novel, then, cannot be called utopian fiction nor, quite, dystopian. It has, but with an eye on modern science and our tendency toward mechanism (and no wonder that one of the few essays on it is in a volume dealing with "Clockwork Worlds), all the ambiguity and authorial ambivalence that we see in More's *Utopia*. And

Lafferty's very peculiar novel has some interesting points of contact with the book *Utopia* aside from a shared taste for carnival touches, of upsidedownness, and even for fussing a bit with gender (Utopian women are not what we call liberated, but they are better off than in England, whereas Lafferty's female protagonist is a snarky little tomboy, although why she is named "Evita," "little Eve," I am still trying to work out—perhaps it is relevant that the novel ends with a reference to making a lifeless tree bloom.)

One major point of contact is indeed a point, something close to nothing if not quite—a point has no dimension but can be a singularity. Both *Utopia* the book and Lafferty's narrator share an interest in nothing, naught. A number of times the narrator of *Past Master* refers to the monster (if it is a monster) Ouden [οὐδὲν].[3] Either Lafferty was an alert reader of More's paradoxes or somewhere along the way he had come to share some of More's own interests. The zero is, so to speak, the point. Nor is that my own joke, for Lafferty himself got there first. More is listening to an Astrobian "précis machine" that operates very much like Google. It explains that in "Golden Astrobe," a "world of cities," the hope is that "when we have all become one perfect city in our totality, then our evolving will be completed. The individual must pass and be absorbed. The city is all that matters." (Of all the cities, More hears, "Cosmopolis" is the capital and the least developed is "Wu Town." (64); Lafferty may be making a sly suggestion that if things go on as they are, or were in

---

3 On p. 33, remarking that he knows Greek, More gives the definition: "Ouden means nothingness." At one point, p. 44, "the monster Ouden came and sat in the middle of them and encircled them." Right. Since Arabic mathematicians first gave him his modern shape, Ouden has been a circle. For more Ouden and nothing, see p. 45, 57, 76, 111 (with an allusion to the death of JFK) and p.139, when More's problematic rhetoric thrills the multitude (and before he recovers both his skepticism and his Catholic faith): "It is no longer the Greatest Good for the Greatest Number. It now becomes the Total Good for the Merging Singularity. And when we are all One, then comes the Great Inversion. We become a thing that is beyond Number and without a Name." More shortly recovers himself and yet shrugs, now that he has indeed been elected, and says he will live in such a world after all, saying ironically, "All glory to Ouden the everything-in-nothing!" (141) On More's own play with "nothing," and references to other relevant work, see my "More's Utopia: Medievalism and Radicalism," in *A Companion to Tudor Literature*, ed. Kent Cartwright (Wiley-Blackwell, 2010), 279-294.

1968, that New York would be closer to Astrobe than is Mao's China). Love and hate have alike disappeared, continues the précis machine. "We are the sun. We are everything. We merge. We loose [sic] both being and non-being ... We are devoured by Holy Nothingness, the Big O, the Ultimate Point for all us ultimates." Yes, the Big O is the point—the big All, the big Nothing. But now More, forgetting his early modern English, says "Shove it ... shove it ... I made it up, I invented it. It was a joke, I tell you, a bitter joke. It was how *not* to build a world" (66), and adds, "I invented it all for a sour joke. I mustn't let the sour joke be on me."

Yes, that is one way to read the real More's real book, as bitter in its play with nothing, although some might say that the desire to so read it straightens out its ambiguity and makes it a little too safe for those who have shuddered over "Brave New World" or Zamyatin's "We." In any case, and although More is in fact, says the narrator, impressed by the *clarity* of Astrobe's utopian accomplishments and trajectory, he is puzzled by the lack of religion. How do people attend mass? Oh they don't, the machine replies—although in smelly, sick, Cathead (a slum that has grown, and voluntarily, bigger than Astrobe itself) the machine hears there are the stirrings of a religious revival. More does manage to find a mechanized priest and a Mass "Brought to you courtesy of Grailo Grape-Ape, the finest of the Bogus Wines" and hot-dog rolls. Luckily for any real Christian, the participants are likewise mechanical, for the whole thing is a government-sponsored antiquity-show. More is not particularly offended, for although he knows he has been canonized he has not yet recovered his faith.

Astrobe, then, wants to be both All and Nothing—mechanistic (no wonder Lafferty mentions the Golem, 53), but I sometimes think with a trace of 1960s pseudo-Buddhism. And yet More's Renaissance was itself intrigued by Nothing (which Aristotle says doesn't exist) and by the still fairly new sign, the cipher or zero—both from the same Arabic word—which turned the ancient Babylonian and Indian mark into the pretty circle-shape we have today, the sign for zip and nada and bupkis that can look so empty but can also, as a sort of cosmic egg, imply an all. Put it with a one, says

Christopher Marlowe, and you get a... no, not a ten, a baby. Draw a map for an early edition of *Utopia* the book and you can make the island nice and round—like a cipher, a nothing, but packed with imagination and people.

Such an interest is, needless to say, if not derived from More then relevant to his great work. Utopia is nowhere (nusquam) and hence a version of nothing (nihil) and one other great traveler before nonsense-speaking Hythloday is of course Homer's Nobody (Nemo, Outis), or so he tells a Cyclops. As Elizabeth McCutcheon has shown so well, More's very language, in the Latin, plays with contradiction, denying the contrary, litotes, and with the implied joke that England is not nowhere, not nusquam, not Utopia.[4] It is no accident, I think, that on the map we see of Utopia it has something like, more or less and good enough for the joke, the shape of a zero. Or is it a circle? Circles are perfect, whereas a vaguely triangular England is far from perfection. For Lafferty, his mechanistic if (still, for the majority, happy) utopian dystopia is far from perfect and not least because although imaginary, a nothing and nowhere, it has no sense of what might be beyond the lines of its own circle, no beyond. It wants to be "all," but that is not given to human machines living in mechanized cities. More's death, his second, will break the limits of the Astrobian zero and, or so it may be hoped, hatch a new world.

Lafferty's More is not my More—he is less wittily exploratory than bitterly satirical, and, in his later years, given to feats better suiting John Wayne or Spiderman on a good day. The historical More had subtlety; Lafferty's suspicious time-traveler is beyond cryptic. And the novel's protagonist is more ugly than one would guess from Holbein's portrait. When Lafferty's fictional More dies, his death promises at least the hope, if we wait, of changing a failed utopia into a new and re-redeemed world of revived faith. Utopia's fictional Morus promises to continue the dialogue by going into dinner, whatever the author's future on the block.

I remain mystified by Astrobe. A possibly redeemable mechanism? Yes, there might be a real ghost in this machine. Lafferty

---

4 Elizabeth McCutcheon, "Denying the Contrary: More's Use of Litotes in the Utopia," *Moreana* 31-32 (1971), pp. 107-121.

seems to have thought that More imagined his Utopia as something like Astrobe, something too mechanical, a bitterly ironic "joke" (66). I think that is a misreading, but at least Lafferty's More is not naïve, and even if implausibly given to fistfights and snarky comments he can also perceive when power is lying to those it purports to serve and he would rather give his life than cooperate with Big Mechanical Brother.

Anne Lake Prescott, the Helen Goodhart Altschul Professor of English at Barnard College, began teaching at that institution in 1967. In addition to her Barnard and Columbia degrees, she also studied at Radcliffe College and the University of Paris. A specialist in the English Renaissance, Professor Prescott is affiliated with the comparative literature program and the medieval and Renaissance studies program at Barnard. She is currently working on David in the Renaissance and on Renaissance almanacs and calendars. Professor Prescott is the co-editor of two Ashgate series of editions of early modern texts by modern women and is co-editor of Spenser Studies: A Renaissance Poetry Annual. Her email address is aprescot@barnard.edu.

Excerpt from a Thesis
By John Ellison

The following is an excerpt from a thesis in progress by England's John Ellison on certain themes and techniques used by American novelists with Catholic backgrounds.

John has also mentioned to me the possibility of future essays on the humour of Lafferty and of the influence of certain Augustinian ideas on stories like "Maybe Jones and the City." We can only hope that he finds the time to further enrich us with his observations.

In previous chapters I have tried to point to some typical themes that re-emerge in the novelists examined so far. For instance, there is a concern with the nature of communication (why and how does it actually work?) and reality (where does the boundary between the real and the fantastic establish itself in lived experience?) In this chapter I will continue to develop these themes, but will also argue that the narrative-consciousness that shapes the created texts of a writer is matchable, in a kind of literary-theological manner, to the "textuality" underlying all of created existence.

We might begin by looking at two quite similar passages which convey the "shock of recognition" that occurs when the circumstances of the Incarnation are considered:

> *Jesus came on cold straw. Jesus was warmed by the breath of an ox. "Who is this?" the world said. "Who is this blue-cold child and this woman plain as winter? Is this the word of God, this blue-cold child?"[1]*

> *The First Coming was ridiculous beyond the point of laughter. The King of the Universe was born to road-people in a cow-and-*

---

1 Flannery O'Connor, The Violent Bear It Away (London: Faber & Faber) 1980, p. 132.

sheep barn, and was wrapped in a cow-blanket when he was brought forth and placed in a grubby food-trough for a bed.[2]

The first passage is taken from Flannery O'Connor's *The Violent Bear It Away*, the second from R. A. Lafferty's *Serpent's Egg*.

An immediate point that might be made about the Incarnation is that Christianity is from its very beginning textual: the event is already dramatic and story-like with its implicit sense of narrative (God has moved into the world) and contrasts (the eternal and temporal, the All-Powerful and the powerless).

The pivotal role of recognition-scenes in establishing narrative consciousness touched upon in previous chapters might again be stressed here. In literature a recognition scene functions in a number of ways. Most obviously it heightens and concentrates the significance of the scene itself. Also, though, there are simultaneous moves in the direction of interpretation (the scene is referred backward to what has already happened) and anticipation (the scene promises fulfillment in what will happen). Once we grant the basic premise of the Incarnation, we might perceive it as a kind of archetype of the recognition scene: it extends the relevance of interpretation and anticipation through the whole of time.

The cultural critic Walter Benjamin used the concept of redemption to express a quite similar viewpoint.[3] For him redemption implied winning back for significance all of that which had previously been despised or overlooked. In effect, the world is seen as a text which requires to be read and transformed under the light of interpretation. Even a non-theologically oriented literary critic like Roland Barthes expresses ideas compatible with a notion of a "story-shaped world":

Does everything down to the slightest detail have a meaning? [...] This is not a matter of art (on the part of the narrator) but of structure; in the realm of discourse what is noted is by definition notable.[4]

2 Lafferty, Serpent's Egg (Bath: Morrigan Publications) 1987, p. 155.
3 Walter Benjamin, Illuminations (Glasgow: Fontana) 1977.
4 Roland Barthes, "Introduction to the Structural Analysis of Narratives," in

Some theologians have puzzled over an idea closely related to all of this: the life of Christ and the shape of the universe are, it has been argued, equally meaningful "realms of discourse" because they are essentially expressions of the same reality.

A book which deals with such issues as this in fictional and narrative terms might be expected to be somewhat solemn and ponderous in its style and tone. R. A. Lafferty's *Arrive at Easterwine*, in fact, makes the search for the true interpretive shape of the cosmos seem lively and fun.

Epiktistes, a sentient and mobile computer, and also narrator of the novel, is given the task by members of the Institute of Impure Science of collating the totality of knowledge and experience. From this it will produce a kind of visible representation of the true structure of the universe.

Many of the 'texts' fed into Epiktistes seem improbable bearers of significance:

> *Institute members were out now trying to read patterns and shapes in the fluorescence of sea-lice, in snail slime patterns, in the cross-sections of marrow of rock-badger bones...*[5]

These overlooked and fragmentary portions of reality are shown to have a real contextual depth. The particularity of an object does not seem to constrain whole series of open-ended narratives that may be derived from it:

> *The patterns of badger-bone marrow give all the highway maps of the worlds. They give every inlet and tidal estuary of every planet of every sun. Here were all sorts of plans or patterns writ small. ... If the whole universe were destroyed it could be reconstructed pretty nearly from the patterns of rock-badger bone-marrow.*[6]

Bennett, et al (ed. Culture, Ideology and Social Process (London: Batsford) 1985, p. 170.

5 Lafferty, Arrive At Easterwine (New York: Ballantine) 1973, pp. 186-7.
6 Ibid, p. 190.

Important in these passages is the sense of unfolding meaning that takes place by means of relationship. In other words, when relationship is absent we have a number of merely implicit communicative models, i.e. perception implicit in the object; response implicit in stimulus; interpretation implicit in the sign, etc. What a writer like Lafferty is concerned with is sharing both the diversity and the actuality of communicative content. Thus we find the most unlikely of implications and potentialities being realized in his stories. For example, we are presented with cross-species dialogue of every conceivable kind: machine to human; human to animal: even, as in the following passage, computer to unborn elephant:

> *Gajah was handicapped very little by her circumstances. The unborn Gajah was intelligent even for an elephant and she responded to the drum language that Inneall set up to communicate with her.*[7]

It is significant that there are many Biblical narratives that produce a shock-effect by the bringing together of a communicated message with the least expected of messengers. Thus Balaam's Ass, feeling badly treated, suddenly gives voice to its complaint: "What have I done? This is the third time you have beaten me."[8]

I think that this tendency towards showing the expressive aspect of reality might be contrasted with more uniform or "static" theological world-views. Pantheism, for example, might suggest that "God is Nature," but in effect the argument, the need for expressive and illustrative instances, ends there.

A feature, then, of the narrative/theological model I am attempting to outline, is an attentiveness to detail and particularity. (As opposed to the unfocused totality of a statement like "God is Nature."). Similarly, "narrative-consciousness," on the part of the writer, is that searching out, and re-displaying, of the dramatic and acted-out quality of any particular situation.

---

7 Lafferty, Serpent's Egg, p. 56.
8 Numbers 22:28-31.

For an author to come near to fulfilling these requirements, as I believe Lafferty does, there is a necessary involvement with textual moves and gestures more bold and intense than those associated with mainstream literature.

This willingness to always go beyond the obvious and expected might be seen in the symbolic use of wine in *Arrive at Easterwine*. Whereas for the conventional and often secular poets who use wine as a "signifier" of the sacramental, what is usually involved is a facile access to another layer of connotative meaning, in Lafferty there is something more complex happening. For instance, we are given a kind of "theology of the individual wine drinker" in the following passage: "These guys look alike, they mumble and stumble alike (that red-eyed grin is almost a person in itself...) but they are not alike. Each is a private and picturesque world. Every derelict is (as Aquinas said of angels) a separate species composed of but a single member."[9]

Importantly, relationship involves active elements of communication and reciprocity. This is largely absent from the "camera eye" of the tourist, or the media that views people and events with a kind of static one-sidedness. In other words, an encounter with a derelict is less likely to be the recognition of "a private and picturesque world" than the occasion for capturing a colorful and "picturesque" scene on film and, then, significantly moving away from it.

Communication might be posed in terms of a kind of double-sided process of realization: as situations and events are "realized" in the sense of being acted out in palpable contexts, at the same time there is a narrative of "realization" or recognition, taking place at the level of consciousness. This might be useful in considering the following quote from one of the characters in *Arrive at Easterwine*: "[...]we will have to rethink the whole idea of people. If shape and substance are the same things, then perhaps communication or liaison and people are the same things."[10]

The difficulty in pointing to the dividing line that separates form and content, the individual and communication, is a theme that also occurs in Aquinas. He used the example of the activity of a

---

9 Lafferty, Arrive At Easterwine, p. 79.
10 Ibid, pp. 201-2.

Teacher teaching to show that the reality of this act has to be located in the act of the Learner learning.[11] It follows, then, that a one-sided or abstract consideration of communicative events will miss their essential point. Similarly, the failure to address the fact that a *person existing* is itself an activity and "a lesson" leads to the kind of spurious and one-dimensional contacts already mentioned (i.e. a tourist photographing exotic and eccentric "characters".)

Yet another way of expressing this understanding of the nature of the communicative is to suggest the diversity of human persons is analogous to the diversity of literary texts. An obscure and difficult life is as important as an obscure and difficult novel, even though, ironically enough, in judgmental terms the novel is often more likely to be given the benefit of the doubt. Different cultural traditions have a bearing on all this. Part of the European literary heritage has a distaste for that which strays outside the boundaries of uniformity and convention. By contrast there are important impulses in American literature that are less concerned with matters of form and sensibility. We see instead an interest in the wilder territory of hidden meanings, cryptograms and the grotesque: Edgar Allan Poe would be an obvious example of this tradition.

In Poe and Lafferty there is a kind of excess of meaning and significance. It might be argued that this is in fact more self-reflective of the human condition than the more refined and sensitive portraits of individual consciousness in traditional literary works. The following passage is typical of this, reflecting the sense in which the path to interpretation passes through areas of profundity and parody which become harder and harder to distinguish from each other:

> *"It's an unusual place to write messages," he said, "on a snake's belly. But perhaps it is a logical place to write hidden messages. If I were a Power looming above the world where would I write messages that might not immediately be discovered? Why not on the hidden side of an object that has a certain repulsiveness?"[12]*

---

11 From the introduction to the concise, one-volume edition of the Summa Theologiae, ed. T.McDermott.

12 Lafferty, Arrive At Easterwine, pp. 183-4.

The themes of hidden meaning and people's lives being agencies for some deep communicative/existential dialogue also figure in the novel *Past Master*. In this we see how the seemingly Utopian society on the planet Astrobe is gradually being rejected in favor of the shanty towns of Barrio and Cathead. Again this might be posed as a kind of narrative choice: the surface "text" of achieved happiness on Astrobe is rejected in favor of the stronger, more pungent stories that will be generated out of conditions of hardship:

> *"The Cathead thing is madness to most, a turning to poverty and abject misery from free choice, and that choice made by millions of people, more than a tenth of those on Astrobe so far... The Cathead partisans say that their experiment is a Returning To Life. This I cannot explain to you, no more can they; you have to live your way into it..."*[13]

The narrative sense of lived experience is conveyed by the phrase "[...] you have to live your way into it." In a similar kind of way the active engagement with freely chosen situations, even if these seem bizarre and extreme, points to a link between "doing" and "knowing." To fully understand existence seems to require passing through the full spectrum of experience. When one of the characters asks why so many dead bodies lie around unburied in the shanty-towns he is given the reply: "A reminder of death. Follow it out far enough and it becomes a reminder of life."[14]

By contrast, the descriptions of the placid uniformity of Astrobe life are lacking in any sense of impetus or "narrative drive."

> *"The people of Astrobe do not dream at night, for a dream is a maladjustment. We do not have an unconscious, as the ancient people had, for an unconscious is a dark side and we are all light. The future is now."*[15]

---

13 Lafferty, Past Master (New York: Ace) 1968, p. 74.
14 Ibid, p. 158.
15 Ibid, p. 80.

The constriction of consciousness that takes place in the society of Astrobe is, in fact, comparable to the more extreme versions of empiricist philosophy in the twentieth century. These, too, have sought to narrow down experience into distinct and containable categories: everything becomes knowable only in terms of the independent functions of the senses.

Other thinkers, such as Hazlitt[16] and Bakhtin[17] working outside the limits of empiricism, have recognized that experience, whether of literature or of life itself, is multi-faceted. Hazlitt expresses this by saying that "one sense is understood in terms of another." Thus the potency of a work of art, such as a painting, cannot be derived solely out of its effect on the sensory field of vision. Rather the "passion of understanding" is multi-sensory, drawing on diverse series of contexts (past memories, the enjoyment of a recognizable present, future hopes, etc.).

In a similar view Bakhtin stressed the inter-textual aspect of any given work of literature. A particular piece of writing will always contain traces and overtones from other writings, just as its interpretive message is suggested and completed by contexts beyond itself.

At this point it might be useful to try and make a distinction between what we might call a "palpable sense of the fantastic" in Lafferty, and the more negative sense of fantasy as something unreal and nebulous. There is, for example, no distaste of the material world in his novels. The material world is not some kind of blank background on which a fantastic set of events is overlaid. Instead we have stories that are packed with the stuff and substance of the real world: food, drink, rivers, woods, rocks, fountains, etc. In a similar way, although most of the events that make up the stories are, strictly speaking, unbelievable, their communicative relevance is that they are, at least within the narrative, situated. They do "take place." By contrast, "empty fantasy" is associated with the inexpressible and ill-defined or with those processes of thought that seek to consign the knowable to the void.

---

16 William Hazlitt, "On Gusto" in The Norton Anthology of English Literature (New York: Norton) fifth ed., vol.2, pp. 440-3.

17 Mikhail Bakhtin, The Dialogic Imagination (University of Texas Press).

The sense of opposition between the vacuous and the fulfilled is, in fact, an important theme in Lafferty. In *Past Master* the historical figure of Thomas More, having been transported to the future world of Astrobe, comes to realize that it is a cipher, an empty figure, rather than the fulfillment of the desire for an ideal society. In the following passage, he is conversing with the Programmed Persons, the humanoid robots who rule and control the planet of Astrobe:

> *"You are not conscious?" Thomas gasped. "That is the most amazing thing I have ever heard. You walk and talk and argue and kill and subvert and lay out plans over the centuries, and you say that you are not conscious?"*
>
> *"Of course we aren't, Thomas. We are machines. How could we be conscious? But we believe that men are not conscious either, that there is no such thing as consciousness. It is an illusion in counting, a feeling that one is two. It is a word without real meaning."*
>
> *"But if we are not conscious then all is in vain," said Thomas. "To what purpose then is life?"*
>
> *"To no purpose," Boggle cut in. "That is why we are doing away with it."[18]*

Importantly, we should not read a too simple symbolic link between machines and evil into Lafferty's work. Indeed, the machine narrator of "Arrive At Easterwine" is rather an amiable figure given to complaining to the human characters, "You think machines don't have feelings too?"[19] But whereas Epiktistes is constantly being *filled* with data and consciousness, the Programmed Persons' malign aspect is linked to the *empty* consciousness they inhabit:

> *"According to your ancient belief we are Devils. What we call ourselves is another thing, but we are older than our manufacture and older than our programming. These are houses and*

---

18 Lafferty, Past Master, pp. 192-3.
19 Lafferty, Arrive At Easterwine, p. 211.

well-made ones, that we found swept and garnished; and we moved into them."[20]

The interpretive clue to this passage is the metaphor derived from the Gospel story[21] of spirits moving into empty "houses" (i.e. minds). Lafferty has given this an unexpected twist in that the consciousness being occupied is that of humanoid robots.

Certain of these themes and symbols—the sense of a Void or Vortex, and of secret conspiracies acting to produce negative ends—invite comparisons between Lafferty's work and writers such as Don DeLillo and Thomas Pynchon. We find then, in their novels that Being itself has become a kind of hollowed-out shell or is occupied by some "empty presence" (sometimes conspiracy, sometimes entropy).[22]

Having said this, there are also important differences between them.

We might suggest that the theological perspective in Lafferty is *less* inclined to be reverential towards the concepts of "the ineffable" or Evil as an absolute force. (One of the characters in the novel says, "Deliver me from serious evil and evil seriousness..."[23]) By contrast De Lillo and Pynchon, in their pursuit of closed discourses of menace and banality, have to create an atmosphere of solemnity from which the disruptive effects of hope and laughter are excluded.

Lafferty, however, uses these very elements of hope and laughter to undercut the feeling of the malign as a permanent and unchangeable force. At the end of *Past Master* certain of the Programmed Persons have exhibited feelings of remorse, thus opening up the possibility of a kind of redemption:

> *The Spirit came down once on water and clay. Could it not come down on gell-cells and flux-fix? The sterile wood, whether of*

---

20 Lafferty, Past Master, p. 189.

21 Luke 11:24-27.

22 For instance, Don DeLillo's The Names and Thomas Pynchon's The Crying Of Lot 49.

23 Lafferty, Not To Mention Camels (London: Dobson) 1980, pp. 188-189

human or programmed tree, shall it fruit after all?[24]

In *Fourth Mansions* the evil conspirators are shown to be susceptible to the simplest of human responses:

Oriel had been badly wounded by the laughter and was still gasping. She had been mortally affronted and her jeweled eyes had gone dull.[25]

Within these themes we have been examining in Lafferty's work there is often an implicit critique of intellectual thought-processes that are abstracted from the content of human activity. The various hostile references to the theologian Teilhard de Chardin, are, I believe, explicable in this light.

Our worlds are the Teilhardian abomination after all, the sickening emptiness of 'Point Big-o'.[26]

The theological system of de Chardin resembles the currently fashionable "New Age" spirituality in that neither has much to say about the circumstances of everyday experience. Thus, if we accept the premise of de Chardin that all significance is poised towards some Omega Point at the end of time, then the "here and now" quality of being situated and realizing the narrative of experience is, as it were, drained of content and context.

Equally, when "New Age" thought restates a version of Spirit/Matter duality a consequence of this is that spirituality takes on elitist and exclusivist properties while the ordinary is relegated to the realm of the insignificant.

We might suggest, however, that an authentic theological outlook has the Passion as well as the Incarnation as reference points. The model then becomes that of a suffering and participating God caught up "in the middle of things," not just located in a separate "spiritual realm." This position does not simply mean that commu-

---

24 Lafferty, Past Master, pp. 247-8.
25 Lafferty, Fourth Mansions (London: Dobson) 1972, p. 150.
26 Lafferty, Arrive At Easterwine, p. 209.

nication or grace is indiscriminately present and realized in existence. For example, not all activity on the part of the individual is as readily sanctified as de Chardin seems to suggest here:

> *Now the Christian sees that he can love by his activity, in other words he can directly be united to the divine center by his very action, no matter what form it may take.*[27]

Previously I have tried to suggest that "narrative consciousness" is the ability to identify with persons and contexts beyond the limitation of individual subjectivity. This is a grounding on which creative activity can function. But clearly there are also kinds of dominative or pathological activity, often rooted in a false and distorted sense of individualism, which de Chardin doesn't address in the bland generality of a phrase like "no matter what form it may take."

Some lessons might be drawn from all of this: story and narrative still has inextricable roots in the popular mind (even if this is often realized in the "low" forms of cinema, science fiction, computer games, etc.). Modern religion, by contrast, with its compromise systems of spirituality, and a kind of individualistic pluralism (where becoming religious can be seen as a "lifestyle choice") is, to say the least, less firmly rooted.

Lafferty stands in the tradition of storytelling, and as we have seen, there is an implicit moral framework to his texts. In an oblique way there is also the suggestion in his work that the popular imagination and theology cover the same narrative path. Thus we find favorable references in his novels to both Thomas Aquinas and Charles Fort. (This latter thinker, collector of anomalous data of every kind, has had an important, even if eccentric, influence on the popular mind.) Intellectuals are often as distrustful of the concept of "common sense" as they are of the idea of "low culture." Nevertheless, the common mind is capable of a shrewd judgment over things which more elaborate thought processes cannot grasp. For instance, it can accept that which in philosophical terms might be deemed to be

---

27 Pierre Teilhard De Chardin, *Let Me Explain* (London: Collins) 1970, p. 23.

an inexact statement, but is still a sound perception of how things really are, e.g. *that experience can be both knowable and mysterious at the same time.*

> *"God must love mystery and mystery stories," Dubu maintained, "he has made so many of them...The trouble with you Inneall is that you're always reading intelligent books instead of mystery stories. How will you ever get smart that way?"*[28]

An interesting feature of mystery stories, and literature in general, is that in foregrounding the significance of the actions of the characters, the background context is also, as it were, won over for significance. This is most usually an unwitting effect on the part of the writer. The "whodunit" author is, after all, primarily concerned with plot and action.

Nevertheless, the locals of ancient Greece (Oedipus), the fog-filled streets of London (Sherlock Holmes) and the downtown areas of American cities (Chandler, *et al*) have become palpable elements in the collective consciousness. By contrast, the spiritual systems of Green and New Age philosophy which seek to overlook the "fallen" foreground of day-to-day human contact and concentrate on the backdrop of the Natural world, have left only weak traces on the collective imagination.

It is possible, I believe, to make a distinction between the ineffable, which closes off expression, and the mysterious (yet knowable). Human emotions and behavior, for example, may be felt and described as mysterious. The ineffable, though, is a kind of fluid or empty category on which narrative can neither ground itself or take place.

A typical example of the effect of the ineffable on thinking processes is the kind of philosophical viewpoint that says: "Because of the immensities of the cosmos and the strangeness of quantum physics, it must follow that the ordinary life that takes place between all this is also equally meaningless."

More oblique examples would be the instrumentalist perspec-

---

28 Lafferty, Serpent's Egg, pp. 162-3.

tives found in biology and sociology that propose that actions occur only as a function of achieving certain ends, but that neither means nor end should be defined as "purpose." This anti-teleological emphasis is present also in the literary theories of those critics who advance a "rhetoric of deconstruction" which sets out to drain all textual systems, even rhetoric itself, of any supposed sense of content.

One of the points of this chapter has been that idiosyncratic writers like Lafferty show a genuine kind of diversity and plurality that is really quite distinct from the formless pluralism that prevails in contemporary society.

Again, narrative can be used as a key to understanding this situation. A critic like Bakhtin, who developed so much of his work around the concept of *the textual* had, I believe, located a kind of cross-cultural model that works across all societies. Bakhtin's non-fiction writings have affinity to the fiction of Lafferty: each is, to use Bakhtin's term, "polyphonic," incorporating elements from mythology, adventure stories, history, allegory, and so on.

All of this might be contrasted to the move in postmodernist theory to close down narrative: the old "Master Narratives" of History and of Literature are to be done away with. Undoubtedly these had unpleasant aspects attached to them (e.g. the uncritical glorification of Imperialism). What is unhelpful is that no new narratives or contexts are proposed to take their place.

Earlier I used the phrase "passion of understanding" to suggest the way in which the identity of the subject can bridge the gap between the sense of the self and the "otherness" of experience. Identification also evokes as sense of the theological (the believer identifies with Christ, with values, etc.) and of the literary (the reader identifies with the main characters, the plot, etc.). What is proposed in postmodernism is a rejection of identification, substituting, instead, a kind of free floating world of unconnected signs and individuals. The supposedly pluralistic aspect of this is taken for granted: "virtual reality" is presented as one more feature of the leisure and consumer age.

More to the point might be the feeling of oppressiveness expressed in the latter poems of Gerard Manley Hopkins, in which he senses the emptiness of solipsism and a world centered on the individual: "[...] searching nature, I taste *self* but at one tankard, that of my own being."[29]

I will end this chapter with some detailed notes from the novel SERPENT'S EGG. They are, I feel, pertinent to the question of where the free-floating pluralism is leading, in that they describe a type of postmodern society a number of decades into the next century.

> *It became a free trade world... It became a free travel and a free communication world, and very nearly a free cost world... It became a world in which everything and nothing was public...*[30]

All of this is achievable by the use of a vigorous "editorial" policy.

> *One used to think of leveling as a trimming the top off something into a semblance of evenness. But these 'levelers' trimmed the bottoms off of humanity and computerdom and the world itself. The lower classes of everything were terminated without particular ado, without much apparent suffering, without any great quantity of visible bloodshed. The bereft families did not ask where the inept members had gone because most of the families went with them... The "Don't make a big thing of it" mentality was rife in the world, so a big thing was not made of the disappearance of eighty-seven percent of the persons in the world.*[31]

Anything that seemed inappropriate or offensive to the uniformity of the world was rooted out.

> *Excellence was still prized and even rewarded. But there was a certain high-headed and divergent excellence that had to be curtailed. Some of the high-headed blooms were more than*

---

29 Gerard Manley Hopkins quoted in The Norton Anthology of English Literature, fifth edition, vol. 2, p. 1561.

30 Lafferty, Serpent's Egg, pp. 79-80.

31 Ibid, pp. 80-81.

exuberant. They were poisonous to the common weal. They militated against the free-and-easy tolerance of the floating world. They were of the garish colors that do not betoken healthy blooms. They made tall and jarring waves and such turbulent waves were dangerous to the floating world.[32]

The point of the narrative-model argued for in this essay can, perhaps, be seen in this picture of an editorializing and constricting world-system. The first "anti-narrative" consequences might appear as the control and modification of thoughts and feelings. This translates, though, quite easily into the world of practice, so that a situation may be arrived at in which the majority of the population are "edited out" of existence.

John Ellison lives in England. At an early age, he selected Lafferty as a favorite author after discovering his short stories in SF magazines and anthologies in the late 1960s. John writes that at this time, Catholicism informs most of his choices in life—indeed he has shifted between the quite different milieu of Damon Runyon (he used to be a manager of betting shops) and Dorothy Day (he now works in the charity and voluntary sector). John is a frequent commenter on Andrew Ferguson's Tumblr, "Continued on Next Rock."

---

32 Ibid, p. 81.

A Richness of Endings
By Dan Knight

(This piece originally appeared in Boomer Flats Gazette #2, published by Dan Knight).

First off I'd like to make it clear that I do not profess any talent for textual analysis. Nor do I indulge in much literary criticism. A man who eats with his fingers has no business playing with knives. With that off of my chest, let's see if we can have some fun here.

> *One of the strangest of predictions states that part of the thirty-ninth life of Melchisedech (the part of the thirty-ninth life after his twenty-third year) shall be several times repeated. This happening shall be the coincident effector of the last fifty years or so of the World being several times repeated. Let us consider what this would entail—*
> *MANTIC PRELUDE*
> *(Enniscorthy Prophecy)*
>
> R.A. Lafferty

How I came to possess so many different endings to *More Than Melchisedech* (hereafter referred to as MTM) is a story in itself. How there came to be so many endings is also another tale, though it's one that only RAL can tell. Let it suffice to say that by the time I sat down in the summer of 1991 to prepare the manuscript for publication I found myself with no fewer than five different endings (and before long would have a total of six!) The Mantic Prelude was true in a very literal sense. RAL had written what he'd promised.

Sharp readers (and good customers) will have recognized that chapter thirteen of MTM, the last part of *Argo*, is a reworking of the novelette "Episodes of the Argo," published by my United Mythologies Press in 1990. There are some interesting differences though and here would be as good a place as any to start our tour.

The book version is a few thousand words longer than the "Episodes." Most of the extra wordage is accounted for by the telling of the incident at Wien on the Donau River and by the four-page-long puffer fish story which loses the puffer fish and three pages of text when it shows up at the bottom of page thirteen in "Episodes." Though these two events account for the greater portion, it is the smaller differences that are the most interesting. In an extra page MTM's version tells us more about the Argo herself. We discover that she was once Dana Coscuin's ship Catherine, thus establishing a link between the four-volume "Coscuin Chronicles" and the "Argo Mythos." You can find these interconnections throughout RAL's work. We meet Finnegan in the novel *Dotty* and we meet Dotty in *The Devil is Dead* and "An Apocryphal Account of the Last Night of Count Finnegan on Galveston Island." And Enniscorthy Sweeny—ah, well, we'll get back to Ennis in a bit.

In MTM we learn how it is that the Laughing Prince of Tartary could be a power claimed neither by God nor by the Devil, an explanation we never receive in the shorter version (and no, I'll not tell you here—Read, or reread. It'll be fun.) We also learn that the Argonaut's main strategy against evil is to slip into the probable future and effect changes there so that when the World arrives the obstacles will have already been dealt with. They can sail into probable futures but they can not go backwards in time. "It sounds like a science fiction idea or a blatt-brained notion," Duffey gasps out when St Brandon's wife (and *that* little theological difficulty is addressed as well) asks.

Though the greater part of extra material is in MTM there are things unique to the shorter version as well. The bulldog Gunboat Smith's exclamation that Casey is *anticristos*. Casey's profaning of Holy Argo, magically changing her name to Ship of Fools. Duffey's first encounter with his doppelganger (pp. 26-29.) An encounter that does not take place in MTM.

Some of you may have also noted the effigy seamen. Their origin is described in MTM and in one section we are told that Casey has mutilated the ones who stand in for Finnegan and his two holy companions. In both versions it is an effigy seaman who points out that Casey has become the magnetic center of the world. This required RAL to add a couple of parenthesized comments in "Episodes" to smooth the intrusion over since all other references to the effigies are omitted.

From the "?" symbol in MTM onwards the two versions are identical. RAL and I had both agreed that the "Episodes" ending was the one we preferred of the bunch. For my part I liked its strong optimism and atmosphere of hopeful expectation. And that would have been that.

Enter Gene Wolfe

In the course of our regular correspondence I had mentioned to Gene my dilemma of the multiple endings and he had responded earnestly encouraging me to include them all. I had never seen a book (with the noted exception of those gaming books of a few years back) that had multiple endings and I have to admit I hesitated. But this *is* small press, I said to myself. Small press, the only place where "doing it the way it has always been done" doesn't yet have the power of a collapsed sun's gravity well (I am reminded of the motto emblazoned across the letterhead of Bryan Cholfin's Broken Mirrors Press—"random acts of senseless publishing.") I considered including them under a separate cover but balked at the expense. I reread the endings. I spoke with RAL. Though he didn't see a problem with having multiple endings he did think it best to combine the strongest of the ideas into a single additional ending. I concurred and that was how the additional ending to be found in MTM, hereafter to be called M2, came into being.

Differences between MTM and M2

The addition of 'The Short Notes on Time and Related Things' is the first difference you encounter in M2. It's important. It is Duffey's manipulation of time that allows for the "Seven Roads" phenomenon in the chapter of the same name and in the stand alone version of the story published in 1975 as "From The Thunder Colt's Mouth." Because eternity has infinite depth and time is only a way of measuring change, one might conceivably slice the moments thinner and thinner and live, as it were, between them. One would still be *in* time. There is no getting out of the thing as long as you're even partially material (embodied). But it would be similar to living the moments twice (or more). The soul skimming over the previously 'used' portions or fragments of time to establish additional or adjacent sequences of action. The kicker, of course, is that you can skim them but in another sense you are also *in* them. The more fractured you make the situation by this cutting up of the moments' continuity, the more fractured you make yourself. RAL foresaw this and attributed Duffey's confusion to it.

Instead of a dialogue with pseudo-Melchisedech on the shore in St. Louis, in M2 Duffey meets a young member of the Stranahan family. Sadly, he discovers that Vincent Stranahan, who would become one of his closest friends, has died in this future as a mere infant. A short time later he discovers that he, too, has never been born and is only a ghost (of a chance, or a probability, as it were). A very young and very precocious Teresa Piccone agrees to have Duffey born to her in another twenty years (which would seem to me to be a very un-Melchisedech thing to do; being born in a recorded historical sense, that is). We are left with a situation in which many parts of the world are in danger of becoming unreal should Duffey become fleshed. From our previous readings we know that these things never happen in the Argo universe without a fight of some kind. There is a great battle coming and Duffey's existence is not assured.

It seems to me that there is a question here regarding the nature of time and the ability of a future event reorganizing in a literal sense all that came before. Christians have always believed this, but it was a reorganization (as far as we know) along spiritual lines. Entire ancient civilizations didn't just disappear from the memory of the universe at Christ's birth (or did they? How would you know?). I am thinking here only of MTM's own declared logic as represented by that remark of Duffey's to St. Brandon's wife that I quoted earlier in this essay. Something tells me that there's a stone in here somewhere. Whether it is the foundation stone of scripture remains to be seen.

It should be mentioned that in one ending the book closes abruptly at the point where Duffey leaves the river in 1923.

> "Everything was before him. What adventures would there not be. The morning was bright with grace, and the tug-boats were chirping like birds. Melchisedech was out of the water. He slogged up a little shore to a town or city. He was twenty-three years old, and he had many sections of many lives still ahead of him."

No young Philip Stranahan. No Teresa Piccone. No pseudo-Melchisedech. We'll hereafter refer to this as the 'short ending'.

The young Stranahan of M2 comes from an unpublished ending that combined both the boy and the angel of MTM and "Episodes." Because only Duffey, of the two, can see the angel that he's talking to the boy becomes a little confused. It's interesting to watch Duffey ride along the two simultaneous conversations. The following is excerpted from this version:

> "Holy cow," the boy said. "How far did you swim?"
>
> But Melchisedech was holding a conversation of his own, with God perhaps, or with his Angel, or with his own inner consciousness.
>
> "It will be the same years over again," he said, "only better. I wonder how many times I have lived them, and how many more times I will live them?"
>
> "This is the last and only time," his voice told him. "And it is not sure that you will live many of those years."
>
> "But I can't die," he protested. "I died once, killed by the Laughing Prince of Tartary, and I have my own ashes here in a tobacco canister that once belonged to the King of Spain to prove it. I keep it always strapped to my body when I have a body, and strapped to my bones when I have bones. I can't die again."
>
> "For he who lives more lives than one, More deaths than one must die," the voice said.

> "Thou'rt not God," Melchisedech protested. "It would be very
> ungodly of God to be quoting Oscar Wilde. Maybe you are my
> angel and maybe you are myself. Is it the last time for the World,
> or for myself only?"
>
> "The World lives its years only once. All the rest is your imag-
> ination, and your imagination will not be at all like the reality."
>
> "I know better," Melchisedech said out loud with a touch of
> anger.
>
> "Better than what, man?" the boy on the little pier questioned
> him. "I asked you how far you had swum."
>
> "Oh, about eight thousand miles," Duffey said easily, "but the
> current was in my favor."

It is from this alternate version that the fact of Vincent Stranahan's infant death is also culled. Although Duffey asks about Teresa
Piccone (we are told she is alive and six years old) we do not meet
her. The story ends with Duffey doubting his kingship and existence—a doubt he puts to rest after contemplating the ashes of his
own dead self in the canister strapped to his leg.

> "Ah, yes, there are still my aromatic ashes in it, and the little
> flames are licking in and out of them. I love the smell of them. I
> always did smell good, as a king should."

RAL replaced the angel and the ashes with the meeting of Teresa and the promise of future mayhem already mentioned. In the
unpublished alternate there is no mention of a threat to Philip's existence at its end. Duffey knew Philip, even in the version of reality
where Vincent lived, so why it is that he appeared wavering in his
probability in M2 is again a question that only the author could answer.

So far we have brushed over "Episodes," MTM, M2, the short
ending, and this unpublished alternative that provided so much of
the material for M2. There is still a sixth version to consider. I have
already given you a taste of the thing at the very beginning of this
essay. I call it the "Enniscorthy" version.

In this version the Mantic prelude, which appears at the beginning of this article, comes before the start of the first chapter of the entire book. The ending is identical to the short ending with the notable exception of the following line in bold capital letters: **END AND BEGINNING OF NEW LIFE SEGMENT OF MELCHISEDECH**, added at the finish. There follows a space and then:

> *MANTIC EPILOG*
> *"We have considered it. It entails a concept that can only be called 'The Eniverse* as incredible amusement'. But it also entails rather chilling things. Melchisedech may not have many lives ahead of him. He may have two, or one, or only part of one. And the Last Fifty Years of the World will not be repeated an endless number of times. And how many of its several times are already used up? The World does seem rather too familiar, as though we have been here more than once before. And its last fifty years may be several years short of fifty.*
>
> *"And why is that sad-faced sheep standing on the little shore that Melchisedech is climbing? This isn't sheep country. And why does it say in a human voice 'You know not the day nor the hour'?*
>
> *"'Sheep, you are a good omen,' Melchisedech says. 'Every time I live a sequence it gets better.' But does it really? We can only hope that it does."*
> *END OF ENNISCORTHY PROPHECY*
>
> *(*- This is the spelling used in the manuscript. Whether it's a typo or intentional: Eniverse = Creation of Enniscorthy, I don't know. I've left it as is- ed.)*

Enniscorthy Sweeny is the central figure in the short novel *The Three Armaggeddons Of Enniscorthy Sweeny*, found in the Pinnacle paperback of 1977, *Apocalypses*. If you reread the list of guests at Duffey's big party in MTM (the one where Casey is badgered into attending) you'll find Ennis' name mentioned. It seems to me that at one time RAL toyed with the notion of having all of MTM turn out to be another of Ennis' reality-bending (creating?) librettos, but later thought better of it. I have only ever seen the first and last pages of this particular early version of MTM and so can't say whether this thread or intrusion of Enniscorthy is maintained throughout the entire text. Personally, I'm happy that Ray decided to expunge it. In my estimation it is MTM that is the primary power here and that Enniscorthy Sweeny is only a reflection that has attracted to itself a number of the concepts and ideas that fell off of the edges of this greater thing. It isn't right that the tail should wag the dog. Even a tail as tricky as Ennis. And, after all, it's an awfully big dog: *Archipelago, The Devil Is Dead, More Than Melchisedech, Promontory Goats, How Many Miles To Babylon*, "Episodes of the Argo," "The Casey Machine," "From the Thunder Colt's Mouth," "Last Night of Count Finnegan," *Dotty*, and, as we now know, the distantly related " Coscuin Chronicles."

That pretty much concludes our quick assessment of MTM's multiple endings. One final thing I'd like to add, however, is a listing of the chapter titles to MTM. Partly through absentmindedness and partly by design, many of these were not used in UMP's three-volume edition of *More Than Melchisedech*. The thirteen chapters were titled as follows:

1 Early Boyhood of a Magus
2 Late Boyhood of a Magus
3 Hog-Butcher and Gadarene Swine
4 Tales of Chicago
5 Wilder Than Beggars
6 Tales of New Orleans
7 Tales of the Noontime
8 Tales of Midnight
9 The Future Begins Right Here
10 And Seven Roads Before My Feet
11 From The Thunder-Colt's Mouth
12 But Not Yet
13 Argo

This work is © 1993 Dan Knight.

Dan Knight was the creator of United Mythologies Press and an important publisher of Lafferty's work. His Boomer Flats Gazette periodical was a seminal outlet for Lafferty scholarship and appreciation. Our thanks to Dan for letting us reprint his essay here.

Introduction to More than Melchisedech
By Robert Whitaker Sirignano

I wrote this introduction for *More than Melchisedech* at the request of Hank Stine, then editor for Donning. I had read a dozen of Lafferty's unpublished novels. He wanted to publish something by Lafferty, but wanted to save some time. So he asked me which ones were worth publishing. I named *To Aurelia with Horns* and *More than Melchisedech*, and suggested a book collection with nothing but Nebula and Hugo Award stories. There were other novels worth publishing, but they were not science fiction or fantasy.

It was intended to make a few odds and ends of the book a bit clearer to anyone who had not read *Archipelago* and *The Devil is Dead*.

I wrote up six pages, and sent it to him. "I want more. I want it longer," he requested. So that I did. And Ray Lafferty wrote to me around this time and said, "You've read almost a million words of unpublished Lafferty now, which is an illiberal education unto itself."

Aurelia was published. But another staffer at Donning had accepted and placed publication of a rather expensive New Age tome that gathered 6 preorders. Nervous at the size and expense of the 400 page book, Hank Stine was fired, and his future publication projects were also halted. The typeset manuscript was dumped.

More than Melchisedech was published by United Mythologies, Canada, run by Dan Knight, as a set of three books and in a limited run of 500 copies. It is out of print now.

> *There is pride in all of us, Absalom, and it must be broken. We all come to the passions and are shaken by it; Finnegan who goes to his many deaths; Casey who was dead and lives again; Hans and Henry who were born to balanced power and will both be broken to gibbering weakness before they die; Duffy who must*

find Him who is more than Melchisedech; Vincent who made
peace with the world and will find that the world will not keep
it; Dotty herself, and the Urchin, and Margaret the bonfire.
A letter from Mr. X. to Absalom Stein in *Archipelago*, page 266

The publication of this book, *More Than Melchisedech*, completes (in some ways) a trilogy of works that R. A. Lafferty calls the "Argo Cycle." The other titles in this sequence are *Archipelago* (1979) and *The Devil is Dead* (1971). They are all more or less self-contained works; each unit can be read for its own intrinsic merit and they can be read collectively for greater impact. Unlike most trilogies, it is not sequential. The events in the first two books are somewhat simultaneous to chapters four through eight of this book.

This book also deals with at length with some of the material that Lafferty feels caused one of his earlier novels, *Past Master*, to be at his own admission "a failure." Lafferty feels that "hardly anyone got what I was talking about. Most readers thought that [Golden Astrobe] was a fine and desirable place." There is much of his anti-materialistic stance expressed here in several different manners and mannerisms.

Portions of *More Than Melchisedech* appear to have more to say about a banana-nosed character named Finnegan; he was the central figure of *Archipelago* and *The Devil is Dead*. It will not be my intention to give out a detailed analysis of the two books (attempts to sort out the lies and tall tales from the true tales and the truth can be left to those persons who would like to do so—good luck) but to fill the reader in on the wanderings of Finnegan. His importance in this book is better understood with some background.

The tangled narrative scheme of both *Archipelago* and *The Devil is Dead* is something of a fishnet, a catch-all: stories within stories, some fibs which are not so easy to separate from the gospel. Lafferty's novels have always been episodic and his longer narratives seldom have the smooth economy of his short stories. He says he began *Archipelago* as his World War II novel. Every writer who had been through the war was writing his version of it, and he felt that he was not going to be any different. He began in 1962 and the book went through various forms and drafts. His imagination took over, and the manuscript became bulky, and, Lafferty also thought, a bit unmanageable. The original idea of having the story told through a series of flashbacks was abandoned (it might have otherwise rivaled Charles Maturin's *Melmoth the Wanderer* for bewilderment); the story was broken into several sections and worked on as several different books.

The section which became *Archipelago* is about (in part) a gestalt of men calling themselves "The Dirty Five," and how they live and feel and take to fate. This novel had trouble getting published for many years as it does not fit into any standard format. It is neither science fiction of fantasy, although there are several imaginative trappings and episodes in it, such as the short segment dealing with a parakeet named Amy that spoke Tagalog and claimed it had been reincarnated and that in its previous life it had been a fish. *Archipelago* is a very finely written novel, very down to earth and full of religious and emotional concerns, dealing with the emotional and religious growth and deterioration of the Dirty Five and the people they know. Lafferty for years would tell people that it was the best thing he'd ever written. And it is not hard to see why. Some sections of it are beautifully written, capable of touching deeply. But it is the weakest of the three books, depending more on the other two in order to prop it up.

Now, none of the Dirty Five die during the war. While the war was the beginning of the book (Lafferty notes with amusement that the actual war just wound up being left out completely, despite his intentions), it is not the aim of the novel to explore the actions of men at war. It was a part of their lives, but it was not their fate. The Dirty Five—"a mystic society… very close and unsunderable," and a portion of the greater whole of Twelve to be explored in this book—were:

> *Henry F. Salvatore (The Fat Frenchman) (Who was Euphemous, the real master of the fleet).*
> *John G. Shultz (Who was Hans) (Who was Orpheus).*
> *Vincent J. Stranahan (Who was Meleager).*
> *Kasmir W. Szymansky (Who was Casey) (Who was Peleus).*

> *John A. Solli (Finnegan) who was a changeling, who was of the other blood, or the double blood (Who was Iason).*
> *All five of these had lived before, and mythology knows them as:*
> *Friar Tuck, or Pantagruel, or the Giant of the Beanstalk (Henry).*
> *Apollo, or Dr. Faustus, or Aquinas Redivivus (Hans).*
> *Dionysus, or Ulysses, but who was also a Teras, or Arracht (Finnegan).*
> *Mercurias, or Don Vincent de Ollos, or Austin (Vincent).*
> *Kasmir Gorshock (Casey the Crock) a ninth-century scholar and necromancer.*
>
> Archipelago, pages 38-39

And what do they do? In the beginnings of the novel, they are an interesting, interacting, joking crew of men who are glad the war is over and they are looking forward to the resumption of their lives that had been interrupted by the war, or given new directions because of it.

Vincent marries a woman (in the States) named Theresa "Show Boat" Piccone. Henry Salvatore answers the calling of God. John G. Shultz meets and marries and brings from Australia Marie Monaghan. Kasmir Szymansky becomes the group's turncoat, its own Judas. It is said that he exchanges souls with Absalom Stein, which raises some interesting theological questions.

And Finnegan, John Solli. Finnegan is not his name, it is his self. He is the wanderer, the twitch, the drunken monkey-wrench of the group; a self-doubting Thomas. When the group's gestalt is broken up by its return to the States, Finnegan emerges as the book's primary figure. (Although the author goes back and forth between Finnegan and the other members of the Dirty Five, with chapters on their lives before and after the war, the narrative drive disintegrates at these points and interest flags. The Five together are much more interesting a combination than the Five as individuals.)

Before much more is made of Finnegan, there is something which should be pointed out about Lafferty's mythological assignments and compliments to his characters. These are intended to be intuitive and symbolic, and not literal. If any reader expects literal-ism from Lafferty, they are going to become confused and hopeless-ly lost. Lafferty tips his hand on this in the beginning of the fifth chapter. The scene has several of his characters checking into the Jung Hotel. Says Dotty: "What could be more apt? If we are not all Jungian Archetypes, I don't know what we are."

While other members of the Dirty Five take to their postwar lives calmly and quietly, like Vincent, and others overcome great odds of situation and/or temperament to get somewhere, like Hans or Henry, Finnegan is the Outsider of the group. He struggles to deny his fate and feels he has no place in the world because he lacks total humanity. Finnegan would like to be like everyone else, but is not. He has great artistic gifts, but these have come so easily that they mean nothing to him. Finnegan would like to understand the why of himself, but knows of no way to reach for answers. He would like to be an essential person, but feels in the way, trivial and ordi-nary. He cannot find a continuous meaningful intensity in his life or a goal to move towards. There is no order; everything is confusing. As Finnegan told his love, Dotty, "I miss you more when you're here than when you're gone." Yearning is what is most real to Finnegan.

He wants to feel human, but cannot.

His father was a monster.

> "I have a comic mask instead of a face, and a monicker instead of a name. The shadow I cast is not a shadow at all; it is only the shadow of a shadow. All the persons I know, I know as such indeed, but I do not seem a person to myself. I am not Italian like my father, nor Irish like my mother; I am a changeling of no ancestry. I can look in the face of the city where I was born and find it blank. I walk the towns and roads of my own land in amazement and ask 'Is this the world? Or is there another world, and I have stumbled into the wrong one?' When I am alone I feel as though I were a defective ghost who has misplaced his soul and is doomed to its search."
>
> Finnegan in *Archipelago*, page 56

This isn't isolated to Finnegan's own feelings. If it were, one might be able to write it off to a personality disorder or signs of schizophrenia. While the crew of the Dirty Five was still on the islands, a native took Hans aside to speak to him:

> "That boy, Finnegan, he has no tujuan. This is mighty strange not to have one. The crust of the world is thin enough for those who have it. What is to prevent one who lacks it from stepping through and falling forever? When we want to see a person truly, we chew tai leaves which give us second sight. I do not know the word in English."
>
> "Aura," said Hans.
>
> "By his aura. When we see the aura, we understand the tujuan. But your Finnegan, he has neither… he is without it. He is not a human man. You know this?"
>
> Archipelago, page 60

Finnegan's long-time friends hold a slightly more Westernized view of Finnegan's problems.

> "He is a schizo," Patrick said. "He lives several lives. He believes that he is an alien being in one of those lives, and it may be that he is. I'm not very sure of myself on that score. He is only a case history in the notebook of some doctor, but who is that doctor? Our faith constrains us to deny that anyone is doomed; but it's a low twisted road that Finnegan has to follow, and him done to death at the end of it. The only hope is that he has the talent to turn it into a happy death."
>
> Archipelago, page 102

Finnegan begins his wanderings after the creation of a small press magazine called *The Bark* (or *The Barque*), which members of the Dirty Five have a hand in the birthing of (and in Casey's case, he applies the slap.) Melchisedech Duffy, as you shall see, is also present at the birth of this publication, which is intended to alter world opinion. Duffy and the other have chosen the indirect method of altering world opinion, by becoming the first in a series of small ripples that gather strength and become waves. A big rock is handy and makes a big splash, but is seldom reusable and is not consistent enough. This manner of doing will be discussed in this book.

In between chapters Seven and Eight of *Archipelago*, there is a break in the narrative. During part of this time, the events of the novel *The Devil is Dead* occur. The narrative was elided in this fashion to draw attention to the lost quality of some of Finnegan's wanderings (all great men have several lost years in their lives, unknown even to them at times.) *The Devil is Dead* does not have all of the lost time—it begins a year or two after the ending of Chapter Seven. Finnegan wakes up on a Texas beach after one of many heavy evenings spent in the company of alcohol. He cannot remember very much and has temporarily forgotten his own name; in his company is a man named Saxton X. Seaworthy, not to be confused with Mr. X. Finnegan cannot recall how or when he met Seaworthy, or for what reason he is being paid one hundred dollars. Finnegan tags along with him, and boards a ship called *The Brunhilde*, where he meets a crew of evil looking misfits and malcontents and a man named Papadiabolous, or Papa Devil, who may or may not be the devil.

Finnegan finds himself under instant suspicion. He is supposed to be dead, having been killed by one of the crew members. (The person killed was Doppio di Pinne, or Dopey the Seaman.) Other members of the crew are rumored to be dead, even as they are seen walking the deck. Whispers abound about 'replacements'.

The ship does not carry 'normal cargo'. It visits various ports, distant trouble spots that are crumbling because of political, ethical and religious instability. Something is at work on board the ship. When the crew and Papa Devil arrive, violence of some sort (usually sinister in nature) breaks out within a few days.

Finnegan jumps ship in Greece, aware that his life is in danger and that he is helpless to do anything about the transactions that go on while he is on board ship. He has grown enough to realize that even though he is not fully human, he is concerned for humanity. In Greece he finds others like himself, who have the 'mark' and are as human as he (or less), but whose concerns are for people rather than helping others of their kind destroy humanity. "[Being a *teras*] it is our destination and destruction, but we try to climb to the light."

Following *The Brunhilde's* activities, Finnegan traces it to Philadelphia, where with a small amount of planning, a sizeable bit of luck and a great deal of running, he manages to steal some "Thirty Six Thousand Pieces of Paper" ("The source of Finnegan's money...") and drops out of sight. (No. No, he doesn't. He's being pursued by a Left Footed Killer.)

Finnegan's wanderings take him from Philadelphia to Florida to Mississippi, where he meets a man named Biloxi Brannagan who sits and waits by the front door of his house and watches for "the ship"—his final destiny—to come in. Brannagan is no more bizarre than Finnegan, who wanders the world escaping the elusive and the fixed things in life.

Finnegan finds his way to the Terrestrial Paradise, a land where he can spend out the rest of his days doing nothing but being a beach bum and drinking quietly and telling tall stories and lies for his own amusement and the amusement of anyone who would listen to him. But his idyll is destroyed, and his stay is not long; he was being followed by The Left Footed Killer.

The last chapter of *The Devil is Dead* depicts Finnegan on the same shores that he woke up on in the beginnings of the book. He has changed little. He is reasonably paranoid. His wanderings and hidden years have gained him little to make him happy or to define what and who he is.

Read by itself, *The Devil is Dead* could be taken as a portrait of a man who is keeping company with madmen and drunkards and is himself dying from excessive drinking and slowly going mad. When read in association with the rest of the Argo Cycle, it seems that Finnegan is doing all that he knows how in order to stay alive and sane.

Now then. When we meet Finnegan again in the eighth chapter of *Archipelago*, he is in New York. There is again some lost time: Finnegan has had a sequence of unemployments, employments, different names and changes of view. He settles down in Manhattan's Greenwich Village and adopts the name Van Ghi and becomes one of the more celebrated eccentric painters of the "Beat Era" in the mid-fifties. But he does it too well. He becomes Fat, Content and Respected. In getting everything that anyone could ever want, Finnegan feels lost and discontent. He releases himself from the celebrity area and begins another series of wanderings.

Finnegan goes to Cuba, where he makes several choices about what he wants out of his life. He finally allows himself to marry Dotty. He sends for her. When she arrives, the two are shot and killed by the Left Footed Killer.

Indirect information about some of Finnegan's wanderings are given through various letters and postcards he send his friends, or through visits from Mr. X, who appears every now and then on one of his information gathering sprees.

There are other tangles and knots in the narrative, as Lafferty has allowed himself to make references to his other fictional narratives surrounding the trilogy. Sharp readers will notice Enniscorthy Sweeny attending a party—the protagonist of *The Three Armageddons of Enniscorthy Sweeny*). Sweeny knew Duffy from the St. Louis days and himself was a bit of a boxer. It is not known if the two of them ever had a match. The stories are contemporaneous.

There are a small number of these playful bits and pieces, and there are a number of them from then-unpublished novels, later published in very small editions. These continue to be elusive to the devoted Lafferty reader.

Some references are devoted to the release of the Devil in 1946 and the allusion of his previous release in 1846. The Devil was also Gregory McIfreann, "son" of the Devil, who was the subject of *Half a Sky* (and to a lesser extent, *The Flame is Green*) where he battled Dana Coscuin verbally and spiritually. Gregory was also Private Gregory, who was being held at the Psycho Ward with "————" (was it Finnegan?) And he was, at one point, Papa Devil in *The Devil Is Dead*, before one or another killing and being replicated by an equally damned doppelganger.

The *Argo* (the ship) also has a history, having been named many times in its career. Some names are historical; others, like *The Flying Serpent*, are from Lafferty's fictions. It was *The Brunhilde*, for a while, on which Finnegan sailed with the Devil and his crew (but which Devil or Doppelganger was it?) As *The Catherine*, it makes reference to the short story *Half a Sky*.

The dog, Gunboat Smith, was a character in a novel called *Dotty*. You didn't disturb him in his sleep lest you lose a leg. He didn't talk then, but the circumstances were different. He was also named Gumboat Thompson, and the shifting of time and space seems to have altered his vocal cords and name, but not his sense of identity. The Dotty of *Dotty* is Dotty Piesson, and is not this novel's Dotty. They were as different as night and day, and Finnegan knew them both.

BIBLIOGRAPHY OF THE ARGO CYCLE

NOVELS

Archipelago. Manuscript Press, 1979, 283 pages.

The first book of The Argo Cycle. First started in 1962, revised several times through various formats, reaching final stage in 1967. Originally subtitled "A Fantasy at 3700 Angstroms." In an interview done in 1976, Lafferty stated, "[...] the novel *Archipelago* has been drifting around for more years than I am old, but once or twice a year, I hear someone is on the verge of taking it." Several times tentatively accepted, ultimately rejected, it was on the verge of being translated and published in Italian before being published in English. (As a joking aside, Lafferty told correspondents he was hoping someone would translate it back into English and improve it.) The Manuscript Press edition was clipped of some 20,000 words—much of it, Lafferty adds—was "excess baggage," and included such things as psycho ward detainee Private Howell's "One Thousand Proper Topics of Conversation" and an incidental nightmare/tall tale of Finnegan's where he answers the telephone only to find out that the caller on the other end is himself. This incident was pulled and developed into the short story "Camels and Dromedaries, Clem," which is no longer an Argo Cycle story.

The Devil is Dead, Avon Books, 1971, 224 pages; Gregg Press, 1977, 224 pages, with a 14-page introduction by Charles Platt; Dobson, 1978, 224 pages. The second Book of the Argo Cycle, but the first one published. Incorporates several writings from 1963. Finished April 1, 1967. Both subsequent editions are photo-xeroxes of the Avon edition. Charles Platt reviewed and critiqued the book as an individual unit; some of his insights are invalid because of this. Platt discusses Lafferty's writing career and background as well.

More Than Melchisedech, unpublished (original manuscript version) several writings from 1962, 80,000-word draft finished January 31, 1976. The original version of this was borderline fantasy in much the same manner as *Archipelago*—there were fantastic trappings on the edges of it.

SHORT STORIES

In the Wake of Man, anthology. Bobbs Merrill 1979, edited by Roger Elwood (not credited). Pages 1-86 contain an expanded and weaker version of "From the Thunder Colt's Mouth."

Orbit 17, edited by Damon Knight. Harper and Row 1975. "Great Day in the Morning" pages 139-162. A Melchisedech Duffy story not included in *More Than Melchisedech*. This is one of several alternative endings to the world. In this story, "...all materialism vanishes and appearances are more real than they have ever been. People blend into one another, roll into huge balls and vanish over the horizon."

"Promontory Goats." Unpublished Argo Cycle short story. A Casey Road. 28,000 words. Less than 1,000 words of this story are referred to in *More Than Melchisedech* from pages 346-351.

"How Many Miles to Babylon." Unpublished Argo Cycle short story. A Finnegan Road. 24,000 words. Some 2,000 words in *More Than Melchisedech* refer to this story.

"The Casey Machine." Unpublished Argo Cycle story. 5500 words.

After Lafferty finished the first variation of *More Than Melchisedech*, he wrote several short stories concerning the character Melchisedech Duffy with the emphasis on what is now Chapter Ten, "And Seven Roads Before My Feet." "Argo," "Promontory Goats," "How Many Miles to Babylon," "From the Thunder Colt's Mouth" and "Great Day in the Morning" seemed to have the feeling of being part of a larger whole. Lafferty estimates he had accumulated some

300,000 words of material for the final draft of *More Than Melchise-dech*, and when he sat down to rewrite and revise the whole, he felt the requirement to prune out at least one third. Some of the stories were dropped altogether, others, as indicated, were mentioned only in part. In the case of "From the Thunder Colt's Mouth," the story was broken into six parts, completely re-written and heavily edited to carry its own weight (the first published version of it, he says, is "terrible"). *More Than Melchisedech* went from its quirky non-fantasy version to the present version, completely changed in tone and character.

The "Seven Roads" were to indicate the several alternate endings to the world—some walked by Duffy, some walked by Casey Szymansky, and one by Finnegan.

Odds and Ends

IS #5, a science fiction fanzine, edited by Tom Collins. Contains "Interglossia to The Devil is Dead," a small section of discussion Lafferty wanted to insert into the novel after it had been typeset and sent to the publisher.

Speculative Poetry Review #2, pages 16-18. Two pages of Lafferty's poetry taken from "Promontory Goats."

Dotty. Unpublished novel. A book with strong religious themes. Contains a section of chatter between the main character and Finnegan, who drops into the bar she works at and has a drink. The bar is The Wooden Ship, mentioned with great favor in *The Devil Is Dead*. The section starts off with "Who has not heard of the fabulous Finnegan?"

The Three Armaggeddons Of Enniscorthy Sweeny, a short novel under the cover of *Apocalypses*, Pinnacle Books, 1977. Sweeny is a contemporary of Melchisedech Duffy; this is his own tale.

The Flame Is Green, Walker and Company, 1971. A tale of Dana Coscuin and Ifreann (later Private Gregory) in Ireland during the mid 1800's.

Half A Sky, unpublished. Sequel to The Flame Is Green. Further developments and contrasts to the characters of Dana Cosquin and Ifreann.

Robert says: A Postal Service worker for 46 years, I am half blind, half deaf, and dyslexic. I draw and write in my spare time. What I need is a gimmick. I reside on an 18 acre farm in Delaware, own goats, chickens, geese, cats and dogs. The house has lots of mice. Married with children and a mortgage.

On Sodom and Gomorrah, Texas
BY ANDREW FERGUSON

"Sodom and Gomorrah, Texas." Galaxy *(December 1962), ed. Frederik Pohl.*

"Sodom and Gomorrah, Texas." Strange Doings. *New York: Scribner's, 1972.*

Originally published online at [http://ralafferty.tumblr. com/post/63240518818/71-sodom-and-gomorrah-texas](http://ralafferty.tumblr.com/post/63240518818/71-sodom-and-gomorrah-texas). Reprinted by permission of the author.

In looking over Lafferty's short stories, I've found it most useful to examine them in order of composition rather than publication. One of the benefits to this approach is getting a sense of what real-world events are working their way into an author's fiction. By the time a story is published, such historical connections can be obscured— particularly for authors like Lafferty, whose stories sometimes languished for years or even decades before seeing print. "Sodom and Gomorrah, Texas," for instance, was published in *Galaxy* in December 1962, and many readers wouldn't encounter it till the *Strange Doings* collection in 1972. But the story was written in July 1960, and that date helps us understand where it came from.

(Many more today come to the tale in various places online: "Sodom," alongside "Six Fingers of Time," is one of the few Lafferty stories widely and quasi-legally available, thanks to the strange workings of the public domain. It's highly advised not to buy any edition of either story, especially in print; they're just screen ports of the originals and usually haven't even had OCR errors corrected. Plus, the Lafferty estate won't see a single penny of it.)

"Sodom" tells of an unorthodox census taker, Manuel, charged with gathering data on the residents of the Santa Magdalena, "a scrap of bald-headed and desolate mountains" in west Texas. He enumerates, from memory, all nine of them. That done:

[...] in one way of looking at it, his part in the census was finished. If only he had looked at it that way, he would have saved worry and trouble for everyone, and also ten thousand lives. But the instructions they had given him were ambiguous, for all that they had tried to make them clear.

And here the historical context kicks in, for 1960 was a census year, and was clearly in Lafferty's mind in writing this story (as well as its immediate predecessor, Eurema's Dam, which also features a census). The census has had a bad rap in Judeo-Christian culture ever since Satan provoked David to number Israel in I Chronicles 21; the fact that Christ was born in a Bethlehem manger, as Luke has it, thanks to a forced Roman census, hardly helped matters.

In the American context, the census has been regarded at best as a nuisance, and more often as an intrusion into personal privacy and liberty. Census takers found themselves with the thankless task of extracting information from annoyed and suspicious dwellers, with the annoyance and suspicion only increasing the deeper into the sticks one went—and also as the decades went on, with census questions getting ever more invasive. (The text for the 1960 form may be viewed at http://www.hist.umn.edu/~rmccaa/ipums-europe/enumforms/usa1960.enumformtext.shtml.htm.)

In Manuel's case, this plays out as both tragedy and farce: after deciding that he "might as well get them all," he invades an old prairie dog community that has been taken over by...little people? fairies? Aliens of one sort or another, at least, and thus not necessarily under the purview of the United States Census—but then many of the people in the Santa Magdalena and surrounding regions would themselves be aliens, and none too eager to be counted on any official documents. As punishment for his intrusion, the little people make Manuel and his mule (Mula, one of the funniest and most unfortunate Lafferty animals, and that's against pretty stiff competition) run on treadmills for 35 years, after which the enchantment wears off and he can steal away with their town's population list.

In real time, this takes only three days, but Manuel is utterly shattered by it, driven mad and to the brink of death. (Likewise Mula, who simply lays down and dies—to which Manuel responds, "Why didn't I think of that? Well, I'll do it too. I'm too worn out for anything else."). But first he manages to turn in his census forms, and to his great misfortune, the town marshal who dispatched Manuel in the first place fails to comprehend the grave situation this puts the town in. For the little people want their list back, and show no hesitation in laying waste to the entire region to get it—and in fact, have done so under some similar circumstance before: hence now there is a "Gomorrah" to join the "Sodom" that was previously the region's defining (and literal) landmark.

The sympathies in the story are hardly with the aggressively aggrieved aliens—that is to say, "Sodom and Gomorrah, Texas," isn't an allegory about the evils of the census, or the government more generally. (It might be a parable for not messing with what oughtn't be messed with, but then so many of Lafferty's characters in other stories go and do exactly that, so I don't think such a reading would get very far.) None of his letters from 1960 survive, and I can't find any mention of the census in those of 1970, '80, or '90, so I don't think it held any particular fascination for him. But it did serve as a direct inspiration for this story, and an oblique one for "Eurema's Dam"—suggesting, moreover, that there might be many more such convergences of real-life and story-world waiting to be discovered.

Finished July 1960. Published in Galaxy, *ed. Frederik Pohl, December 1962. Collected in* Strange Doings, *Scribner's, 1972.*

Andrew Ferguson is a Ph.D candidate at the University of Virginia. He wrote on Lafferty for his MA thesis in Science Fiction Studies at the University of Liverpool, and is now building on this work for a biography in the University of Illinois' Modern Masters of Science Fiction series. His blog, "Continued on Next Rock," is at ralafferty.tumblr.com.

R. A. Lafferty Spins a Yarn
BY KEITH PURTELL

Consider yourself very lucky if you have found and read this book. Only a few thousand copies were printed. Best known for science fiction grounded in the tall tale tradition, Lafferty in 1972 produced this astonishing historical fiction about a Native American named Hannali Innominee, The Choctaw Giant. *Okla Hannali* is a boisterous, eccentric tapestry studded with the language, history and customs of the various cultures who competed for early North America.

Into this pageant steps Lafferty's giant.

The author brings his character to life with bold declarations worthy of Paul Bunyan. Innominee is described as a farmer, fiddler, tanner, distiller, ferryman, blacksmith, boatbuilder, philosopher and frontier maverick who out-gambled Southern gamblers, who made a Kiowa horse speak and who married three women from three races in three days. He had a "big Choctaw chuckle" that always started deep in his belly. Innominee walked with one foot in the virgin forest and the other in the White Man's city streets. He was an ugly man, though "not as ugly as his cousin John T," and he took 30 years to build his Big House.

Innominee is not only a remarkable fictional character, but he also serves as a representation of several real Native Americans who absorbed and transformed great chunks of European culture to become self-taught polyglots; renaissance men in buckskin. There is also much of the author in frontier eclectic Innominee, which I know from having been acquainted with Lafferty when I was younger.

"Okla Hannali" is mostly a detailed history of a crucial period in early American history, with a remarkable semi-fictional thread. You could even argue that it is barely fiction, since the narrative is consciously assembled from a wide assortment of real people and events rather than springing primarily from the author's subconscious. So, its persuasive capacity as a fictional tale is that it contains something of the power of our literal lives.

While Hannali Innominee's real-life counterparts—like Chief Quanah Parker—were blasting gaping holes in white racist assumptions, the Founding Fathers were solidifying a new nation based in large part on the example of the Iroquois Nation. Everything is connected.

Native Oklahoman Keith Purtell is a life-long avid reader. He was friends with Ray Lafferty in the 1980s by way of membership in the Tulsa-based Oklahoma Science Fiction Writers. He remembers Ray as a man whose remarkably agile mind was balanced by kindness and mischievous good humor. His website is http://keithpurtell.com.

Strange Doings

By Stephen R. Case

This review originally appeared at https://stephenrcase. wordpress.com/2014/11/18/strange-doings.

According to certain interweb sources, R. A. Lafferty is making a comeback. There are several new (and very well done) websites dedicated to him and his work, a new journal just in time to celebrate his 100th birthday, and (finally) a series of his collected works that might make it incrementally easier to read some of his stuff that's been out of print for years. Though not much easier. That first volume of his collected works, for instance, is published by a specialty press and is already out of print. It's so difficult to get one's hands on, in fact, that even my heroes— the interlibrary loan librarians at my university— couldn't get me a copy. Instead, they found a few early Lafferty collections for me to read.

Lafferty shines brightest in his short stories. His romping, boisterous, almost drunken exuberance comes across better in these than extended across an entire novel. I've read plenty of Lafferty novels, but they're more of an acquired taste. You have to go into them knowing what you're going to get and prepared to weather the storm. Because Lafferty's novels are like riding out the storms at the core of a gas giant: there's a good chance diamonds are going to be falling, but there's also a good chance you're going to get turned inside out before it's done.

His short stories are a bit easier, not because they're more muted or less powerful but simply because they don't last as long. What is it about this guy? He's not simply a science fiction writer, though he has plenty of stories about humans on new worlds. He's even less a fantasy author, though there are fantastic elements in almost all his stories. What he is, is a story-teller. He's someone who tells tall, sweating, shambling, horrifying, and beautiful stories— who tells stories like they used to be told when the world was a lot younger—

and at the time he was writing it was only in the fantasy and science fiction and horror pulps that stories like this still found a home.

The pieces in this particular volume seem to cluster around a theme. They are stories of breaking out, of some new, larger reality breaking into the world. They're stories of superhuman genius ("Rainbird," "The Man with the Speckled Eyes," "The Transcendent Tigers," and "Aloys") and of making contact with transcendent creatures or transcendent places ("All but the Words," "World Abounding," "Entire and Perfect Chrysolite"). Lafferty writes stories of phase transitions, of tipping points, of new or unseen (and sometimes horrifying) worlds breaking in on this one ("Continued on Next Rock," "Once on Aranea," "Sodom and Gomorrah, Texas," "Dream"). They aren't always the most narratively dense or developed; they don't necessarily have tight plots or stunning plot twists. What they all are, however, are huge, rollicking yarns told in Lafferty's unmistakable voice.

And this is what makes them work. There is a grotesque jollity about Lafferty. For him, the world is a bloody, beautiful, terrifying place— but never simply grim or grey. He is more than a little drunk on the world. This is a huge, holy brutality similar to but rowdier than Chesterton and far less tidy than the subdued mysteries of Borges. Wolfe has this in flashes, like shots of light through his stories' elaborate puzzles. But in Lafferty it's all there on the surface, naked and undistilled.

If you want to hear Lafferty's language, head over to Daniel Otto Jack Petersen's blog, where he regularly lays out slabs of Lafferty prose in all their bloody, dripping glory for passers-by to admire. Besides his language, Lafferty has a strength in creating characters, but his characters are like his stories—superhuman, larger than life, more alive than alive. I'm reminded of the sort of things people say about van Gogh, that he saw colors more vibrantly than other people. When I read Lafferty's stories, I can't help but wonder: is this how he saw the world? Is this how he saw people? It's as though someone was living as Chesterton wrote in *Manalive*, with a certainty that the world was more gruesome and deep and joyful than could be properly grasped. There's nothing slow or sedate or studied in his character sketches.

The stories that are the most effective in this particular collection are the ones that attempt the least. "Rainbird," which opens the volume, tells the story of an early American inventor and the way he did— or did not— shape the modern world. It has all the pieces of Laffertian excellence in an easy-to-swallow morsel: the language that takes an obvious delight in lists and the bright mundanity of the workshop in all its sawdusty glory, the hint of the fantastic and the ease of the impossible that makes the entire, simple time-loop drama shine. And then there's "The Ugly Sea" near the volume's end. Again, something as simple as a tale of how a man falls in love with a woman and with the sea— and yet nothing could be more significant. This is what Lafferty does. He tells stories, but they are the stories that live down deep in the bones of the earth. He's a grave-robber, and he does it all with a deep-throated laughter and terrible bright eyes and words that are thick with soil.

(My rating: 4 of 5 stars.)

Stephen Case gets paid for teaching people about space, which is pretty much the coolest thing ever. He also occasionally gets paid for writing stories about space (and other things), which have appeared in Beneath Ceaseless Skies, Daily Science Fiction, Orson Scott Card's Intergalactic Medicine Show (forthcoming), and several other publications. His first anthology, Trees and Other Wonders, is available through Amazon. Stephen has a PhD in the history and philosophy of science from the University of Notre Dame and will talk for inordinate amounts of time about nineteenth-century British astronomy. He lives with his wife, four children, and three chickens in an undisclosed suburb of Chicago that has not yet legalized backyard chickens.

Oklahoma Gothic:
Tales of the ~~Five~~ Four Men Who Knew Everything
(And One Who Didn't)
By Martin Heavisides

"It's a little hard not to overdo it when you're getting even, Austro," Catherine beamed through her rot and reek. "I think maybe it's more fun to get just a little more than even: now if you draw it here like this—let me have the hammer and graver a minute—like this! Then Daisy and Roy will feel what it's like to—"

"No, no, Catherine, don't do that! No! No!" Austro pleaded. "That's a little too much." He took the graver and hammer back from her.

"Ah, what artists we all are!" Catherine gloated with ghoulish pleasure. Really, she wore her grave dirt (and stench and rot) rakishly. She was magnificent!

p 237

It was the second parcel that had arrived by a new system in our building—one from my brother at Christmas had been the first. A number of lettered lockboxes were set up to accommodate parcels too large for the mailbox our regular deliveries were left in. A key would open the box with the same letter and the parcel would be there. In February or December particularly—in an unusually harsh winter yet—it beat going uptown to the post office with a card to claim it.

Through Elegant Eyes is a volume which gathers all the stories (so far as I know) concerning the Four Men Who Knew Everything— and Laff, the author, who doesn't, but who recounts their adventures in more detail than any of the others could be aware of.

I had most of the stories in their first printing in magazines or original anthologies. I'd browsed the ones I was unfamiliar with in the copy at Toronto's *Spaced out Library.* What I'd never done is read through them from beginning to end in my own signed, limited edition copy, at a rate so low the shipping cost from the U.S. to Canada more than doubled the total cost! It still added up to a bargain, even with the disparity between the U.S. and Canadian dollar.

Story by story there's an accumulating power and integration. It could almost be read as a novel in consecutive stories—not one that would resemble any Lafferty novel I've read: the closest might be Arrive At Easterwine, concerning Epiktistes the Ktistec machine and the Institute of Impure Science which birthed him, featured in stories like "What's the Name of That Town?," "Flaming Ducks and Giant Bread," "Thus We Frustrate Charlemagne," "Through Other Eyes," and "All But the Words." But there's probably not enough of them to make up a collection comparable to this one. The novel he did write, one of his finest, might have taken him almost to the end of what he wanted to say about them. I also wonder if the Institute stories aren't a little too desultory to form a work of cumulative force such as this one. Every anthology of Lafferty's fiction has at least the unmistakable signature of his style to unify it, and some— I'm thinking particularly of Strange Doings and Iron Tears—have, beyond that, noticeable integrations of theme and approach. None quite matches the integration of this collection, published—and as far as I can tell, written—over the course of a decade in which Lafferty was producing a great deal of other work. These stories—all of which can be read independently—have a collective unity and force beyond what's found in most novels. It's because in the first tales Lafferty was already looking ahead, and in each tale thereafter looking both forward and back. (Not in the sense that he created a master outline which over time he filled in bit by bit, more (I would guess) that he followed early hints to their logical conclusion, harvested ideas planted as seeds initially, and wrote each of these stories with the others in mind, developing parallels of action, ritual, language, rhythmic and thematic thrust, above all music and image to make, collectively, a vivid moving mosaic, probably with a good deal of receptor crystal in the varicolored pebbleshards—how else account for its polyphonic hum?)

The first stories in Through Elegant Eyes, at least, are precisely sequential. "The All-At-Once Man" introduces the five men who know everything—only to reduce their number abruptly by one. He's referred to later, in his equivocal state, but except for a shadow appearance in the early version of "Old Halloweens on the Guna Slopes"—of which, more later—he never appears again. (And his subtraction does not occur exactly in the way you might expect. "Five little wise men sitting on the floor. / One lived forever and then there were four.") But the four men who know everything, and the author, who doesn't, are all assembled.

More continuous time passes in "The All-at-Once Man" than all the other stories combined. A little over thirteen hundred years separates the two contexts of events in "Rivers of Damascus," but this is an instance of bilocation in time, somewhat like the bilocations in space that inform "Animal Fair," "Brain Fever Season," "And Read the Flesh Between the Lines," and most spectacularly perhaps "St Poleander's Eve." Somewhere between eighteen and twenty years pass—Laff isn't simply looking to the past when saying he and the four remaining Men Who Know Everything are no longer young, he's specifically referring back to the beginning of the earlier story, when they would all have been in their early thirties. They're past fifty when the story ends, since a couple of years, at least, have passed since John Penandrew died (in a manner of speaking) at fifty, and they're all the same age.

"Mud Violet" introduces two characters who die ever after in the stories to follow, due to the carrying out of Edmund Weakfish's homework assignment in participatory psychology. Suicide generally has a constraining effect on life, but what to do if a crucial part of your grade for the semester depends on completion?

> *"If ever come out, what is like, anyhow together with what it's for, won't have to do, take it loose, what else but rap, break it like bananas, stuff it we'll glide, door hole and all, why not not, cream it wheeze, gouch," Elroy Rain was saying in words but no sense."*

p. 32

The pair that come through this, Loretta Sheen the parchment doll filled with sawdust and Mary Mondo (*nee / morte* Violet Lonsdale), participate in adventures to follow. So does Roy Mega, who never does commit suicide—he's an electronics genius, not a psych major. He's frequently involved thereafter in tandem schemes with Austro, the australopithecine house boy, who first appears in (and in some sense *is*) "Barnaby's Clock." At which point all the major characters who will figure serially in the stories to follow have been assembled. (Since Mary Mondo is new-christened after the World and the Queen of the Sky, it's perhaps unsurprising that her afterlife is more remarkable than might have been predicted from the pale death of the timid girl she was, in a manner of speaking, while alive.)

O! let's not forget Chiara Benedetti, the girl with the Really Eyes, who appears for the first time a little later in "Animal Fair," animating a wood's worth of animals in a wooded draw probably too small, in ordinary circumstances, to contain them—especially if many of them are as large compared to their typical size as a King Cardinal mentioned in passing, who's the size of a tom turkey. (That would be an unsettling thing to see.) She appears intermittently, always with charm and force, though she has only an offstage role in "St Poleander's Eve"—where regrettably she won't see coming (until it's too late) an overwrought theatrical effect with a profound impact on her young life. But who even among Lafferty's dedicated readers could have seen "St Poleander's Eve" coming, even as the climax of a collection as bubbling and darkly potent as *Through Elegant Eyes*?

The four remaining men who know everything are Barnaby Sheen, Cris Benedetti, Harry O'Donovan and George Drakos. The narrator, who doesn't, is Laff—you see what Lafferty did there? I wish I could pull a trick like that with an abbreviation of my last name.

Speaking of absent wives, I've been pondering the mystery of Barnaby Sheen's better half, Loretta's mother, who never appears even by the ghost of a name. I've always assumed Sheen's a widow, but nothing I find in the text supports that. Did she leave him? No suggestion of that either. On the other hand I seriously doubt Loretta sprang fully formed from her father's head as Athena from the head of Zeus—it's the sort of thing Lafferty would have mentioned if it happened, and is Barnaby really the Olympian type? Then again, did Loretta Sheen ever exist? In subsequent stories, Laff and the others express doubts more than once. If she didn't, the question who Loretta Sheen's mother was, and *quo* she *vadi*, becomes moot. However, the girl we met in "Mud Violet" seemed a real enough teenager before she joined six other classmates in completing their final assignment. Doubts weren't being cast then. Dead, Loretta seems more powerfully real, but how long will any but Barnaby retain her memory—and if enough people forget, will the live girl ever have been?

Perhaps Austro doesn't appear before "Barnaby's Clock," but you can see him—as a statement of intent, a clear conception—here:

> *"There has got to be an infusion of brains in the neighborhood and the militant world," Barnaby Sheen said once when we were all together, except John Penandrew. "There is a stupidity on everything, and I cannot completely except even the present group. We need greater brains, wisdom, judgment, adequacy of the spirit and of spirit-handling."*
>
> *"We need it, but where will we get it?" Harry O'Donovan asked.*
>
> *"Oh, from Aethiopia Cerebralis, I suppose. It's the only one of the Wells of Wisdom that I have the location of. I am thinking of the Guna Slopes whence the late monstrosity came. If a stolen secret of sick application comes from there, then we must bring counteracting wisdom from there also."*
>
> *"Yes, there is an aura of braininess about that place," George Drakos said, "but has its primary been discovered?"*
>
> *"Yes, of course. Discovered or guessed by myself at least. I will go there and get light for our darkness. Magi have come from those slopes before to grace the poorer parts of the world. I am going to recruit."*
>
> *"Oh, but what if it turns out to be another stolen secret of sick application?" Cris Benedetti asked with apprehension.*

> *"I will be very careful about that," Barnaby said. "I will not*
> *steal a star from those slopes. I will beg a young star to come."*
>
> p. 22

He's prefigured also in "Mud Violet" when Barnaby talks of finding a source of sunshine to brighten the lives of the dim poltergeists, aficionados of the Putty Dwarf, who cluster round his sawdust daughter's remains—so there are certainly signs and portents to announce this prodigy's coming.

Reading the version printed here of "Old Halloweens on the Guna Slopes" alongside the original, printed in *Fantastic*, confirmed my feeling that the "substantial revisions" for this edition were, generally, unimprovements. The skittish rhinoceros on the crumbling ledge I liked—if that could have been worked seamlessly into the original story I would have welcomed it. I suppose the removal of the original climax was logistically demanded—Laff couldn't cease to be a Man Who Knew Everything when he had already been "myself, who didn't" in "The All-At-Once Man" long before Austro was more than a foreshadowing, so it was redundant, at least, if not inconsistent, to have him cease to know everything all over again twenty years on. However it obliges him to end the story anticlimactically, and considerably reduce the general sense of dread. (Austro is the only one with large forebodings in the *Through Elegant Eyes* version; Loretta and Mary Mondo, who had large forebodings in the original, are no more than teenily apprehensive, and Benedetti, Sheen and the others scarcely break a cold sweat. Possibly due to this considerable mellowing out of tension, the electrifying rescue by Mary Mondo and Loretta Sheen of the soul of a murdered boy is excised—too grand and Gothic to fit any longer in this much tidier fable.)

I'd have recommended leaving out altogether "What Big Tears the Dinosaur's." "Old Halloweens...," though a weaker version of one of Lafferty's richest stories, retains considerable power; imagine a story of which "What Big Tears..." is a weaker version. At three, five, twenty times the strength would it have any real potency? I think not, as Descartes said before he vanished.

I mentioned that all the stories in *Through Elegant Eyes* can be read independently, but it might be worth considering the story that most demands being read so, and the puzzle it poses. "Brain Fever Season" describes such a revolution in human consciousness—mainly one of specific time-stamped intensity of focus—as to imply or even outright explicate a radical leap beyond what's known. "Rivers of Damascus," "And Read the Flesh Between the Lines," "And All the Skies are Full of Fish" (with its burlesque of the miracle of the loaves and fishes) and "Animal Fair" are also stories about opening the portals of consciousness and hence expanding the breadth of possible action in the world—awareness of possibility being the crucial first step in realization—but they open out within the established context of events so that an enlivened return to that context is possible. "Brain Fever Season" opens out a world in which human activity is a succession of giddily sped-up cycles (tied to the lunar calendar it appears, so thirteen I guess in an average year—don't know what happens in leap years, but then again who can say if the calendar as we know it would survive such a change?)

The stories that follow—there are only a few—don't take place in a world of cyclic fevers (I refuse to believe that one of the lunar cycles is a Fish Fever Season) so where did that world go? Lafferty gives no answer but nothing's to prevent speculation. Possibly Roy Mega and Austro know enough to bring about the fever seasons, but not to sustain them indefinitely. Perhaps human consciousness, entrenched in its habits, indulges the fever cycles a giddy whirl or two before reinstating the previous order. Perhaps all this happens, or it becomes the case that it happens, in a parallel reality (similar perhaps to the one in "Days of Grass, Days of Straw") which ordinary consciousness rarely has access to.

"St. Poleander's Eve" doesn't take place in a fever season? It certainly gets up to a feverish pace, tempo and temperature well above the norm; but if a fever like that overtook the world for the space of a lunar month there's a live chance it would leave no survivors. Anyway it takes time to build, which wouldn't be the case in a true fever season. ("A true fever season"—you see what I did there?)

The bright, bubbly energy of "Brain Fever Season" is echoed, though, as through a glass darkly, in the *grand guignol* event that spills over into real life (and death—quite a lot of death if the rapid-fire account of it is true.) The electro-spiked multimedia show and bi-location of time and space of "Rivers of Damascus" is also echoed, as is the explosive revenge of things left out in "And Read the Flesh Between the Lines." What erupts in this case are the passions of the almost-completely-unsuspected wives of three of the Men Who Know Everything (only Judy Benedetti previously implied, since it's usual for a daughter as vital as Chiara to have a mother.) Barnaby Sheen's wife? Still an occluded mystery. Helen Drakos, Judy Bene-detti, Catherine O'Donovan? All present and accounted for, indi-vidually and collectively (and again collectively as components of a succubus made of all the women in the play, and a larger creature with more monstrous properties (a polyander) incorporating the men as well—did Harry O'Donovan suspect what he was getting into?) The monotonous din almost heard in "Mud Violet" recurs, as do the multi-perspective tricks that alter consciousness and with it reality in the "Four Sides of Infinity" cycle and elsewhere in this collection, too often to cite one by one. Without ceasing to be an in-dependent story in its own right, "St Poleander's Eve" draws on and recaps the themes, rhythms, images and preoccupations of every story that precedes it, rather like the breathless recaps that conclude *Fourth Mansions* and *Arrive at Easterwine*—one reason I think it not too far-fetched to consider *Through Elegant Eyes* a novel in stories. One that ends more sharply and definitively than most—surely only shards and fragments could survive so shattering a climax.

> *Like a soundless scream, the horror-face, walking-dead Catherine O'Donovan burst into the room. She had grave stench about her; she had grave dirt on her, in her eyes, her mouth, and her carrot-colored hair. She held a burning swamp rush like a torch in her death's hand. She was the third shoe, and when the third shoe drops at night it sets the stoutest heart to fluttering. She dropped, fell, and lay upon the boards—disheveled, derelict, and dead. Austro grabbed the rush torch lest it kindle the room.*
> *"Good show, Catherine," said her husband Harry.*
>
> p. 234

Martin Heavisides is a contributing editor to Linnet's Wings (most recently introducing a handpicked selection from the poetry of Blake) and author of a novel, Undermind. One of his seven full-length plays, Empty Bowl, was given a live reading by The Living Theatre in New York and published in Linnet's Wings (Summer 2008). Mad Hatter's Review, Gambara, Cella's Round Trip, Journal of Compressed Creativity and FRIGG are also among the sane and sensible journals that have accepted his work.

http://theevitable.blogspot.com

http://movingpicturewrites.com

Arrive at Easterwine—a Brief Review
By Kevin Cheek

Arrive at Easterwine is a deeply religious and very carefully structured book. It is an autobiographical story, told in the first person, of an intelligent computer—Epiktistes, the first Ktistec machine. The novel focuses on the three tasks for which he was created: to find a leader, a love, and a liaison—an understanding of the true shape of the universe. When Epikt announces these tasks near the beginning of the novel, he states that he is likely to fail in one or all of them, and that his failures may be as important as the tasks themselves. Each of the three tasks fails to some degree; each failure tells us about humanity and asks us how ready we are, as a species and a culture, for the approach of the divine.

The book is broken into three fairly well-defined sections, one for each task, and each section is broken into several smaller episodes. Some episodes are straight narrative of events and some are ruminations on the meanings of symbols. Some of the events described turn out to be metaphor and not real. However, each smaller episode has as its theme the objective of the main task. For example, when Epikt is investigating the nature of love, there is a wonderful story about a well-meaning clod who goes to see a speech by a fire-eyed prophet. Both the clod and the prophet are mobile extensions of Epikt himself, and they both have overwhelming love for humanity, but express it in nearly opposite terms.

I must admit that when I first read the book, the structure completely went over my head, and the book seemed like a terrific mess. My first impression was that the plot quickly unraveled and went nowhere. Then I read it a second time and paid attention to what Epikt told us in the first chapter. I realized just how tightly structured this novel is. Nothing is wasted in the narrative. The beginning of the book tells us what the structure will be, then the story unfolds to fulfill that structure.

The book contains many wonderful moments that are a joy to read for themselves. There are the interactions of the members of the Institute for Impure Science—among the most beloved recurring characters in Lafferty's oeuvre. There is wonderful wordplay, such as the riff on how most of the characters are *fellahin*, or *fellah* (look it up), and Valery comments that she looks kind of strange for a fella. There is beautiful, spiritually moving visual description, like the time they start creating snow with unusual geometries that builds towers that give tantalizing almost-glimpses of the form of the ultimate city—the shape of the truly fulfilled and evolved community. There is the introduction which plays on the old fictional trope of an autobiography being mysteriously delivered to the author. Most impressive among all of this is how well Lafferty maintains the voice of Epikt as something slightly outside of and apart from Humanity—providing us an outside perspective from which to examine ourselves.

This book takes patience and an open mind to finish, and it may require at least two readings to understand its structure. If you are willing to give it that effort, it is a richly rewarding read.

Kevin Cheek is a Lafferty fan and professional technical writer. He blogs infrequently at www.yetanotherlaffertyblog. com.

Task Force Fifty-Eight and a Half
By Heywood Reynolds

One should read with an inquiring mind, particularly for a Lafferty story. It adds to the experience to have prepped a little. That's why I enjoy the reviews and the descriptive commentary about the person who managed to produce such creations. It would be difficult not to have some interest in the author, sparked by the nature of the stories. My interest may be increased by knowing that his surname was one that appears conspicuously in my own ancestral records, as recorded by my genealogy-obsessed wife, no matter that she has not linked him to my own Irish Lafferty line. I digress because all I wanted was to know more about the "Cranky Old Man from Tulsa," and I had not yet run across any account of his experiences during WWII. Granted, many WWII veterans did not talk about that. My two male inlaws served for the whole war, and never, but never, talked about it. (I accidentally later learned that one had served under harrowing circumstances, and the other spent some time as a prisoner of war with remnants of a hand grenade in his chest as a memento to remind him that WWII was not a pleasant topic of conversation.)

But back to RAL. I do not have access to his service record and to my knowledge he did not spend time discussing his service, but it occurred to me that somewhere, in his many short stories and possibly in other works, he must have let slip what he had been doing during that time. I'm still slowly going through his short stories, and when I noticed one was entitled, "Task Force Fifty-Eight and a Half," I wondered if it would say something about the author. I think it did. In fact, I think it said quite a bit about the author, or at least about one adventure.

"Task Force Fifty-Eight and a Half" was described as a small yellow rubber boat propelled by oars. The date of the event was July 4th 1945. That was toward the end of hostilities in the Pacific, and the characters he describes were true to Lafferty's penchant for unusual character names. The narrator of the tale, that I think was an actual event, appears to have been Elias. If one changes the E in Elias to an a, then 'alias' Sergeant R. A. Lafferty is likely. For those who are not knowledgeable about biblical characters the Internet provides much information about Elias or Elijah.

A list of items I noted in the story follows. Perhaps it would be of some advantage to the reader to consider it a personal tale of an adventure RAL shared with three others during his time in service.

The very first sentence sets the scene as "ancient days." Being RAL's ancient days.

The phrase "one of the four smartest" strikes me as a bit of RAL's self-deprecating satire, considering that he was one of them.

This occurred in the Moluccas or Spice Islands, and I believe he served in that area.

He refers to "Elias the Syrian from Oklahoma." Using Syrian in the sense that he was a Syrian as a member of an early civilization notably a Phoenician. Phoenicians were seafarers. Later he describes himself: "One was an apostate seminarian."

Ahmad's little story of the cuscus and the turtle in reply to "Where are the girls?" is a clever bit, and perhaps RAL should have told us more about Ahmad.

Only "Elias" could think to insert Faust so neatly into a tale of limited debauchery.

The description of their time on the island fits pretty well with RAL's appreciation of unusual beverages.

Elias goes philosophic following the phrase "I am easily repelled..." It fits RAL's character and personality, even as a twenty year old.

When Elias says, "I wouldn't go back to the sacraments till I was back from the war," it was a reasoned decision not formulated while "in his cups," and proved to be factual.

"Three times I thought that I'd been caught in my smart trick." I take this as his comment that he had been in tight spots or dangerous actions as a soldier three times.

The ending of the story is typical for Lafferty. They were not "consigned directly to hell," but "woke up in purgatory." If one needs a moral ending, the closest you will get to one is the very last sentence.

I served my time in the U.S. Navy and I know a "sea story" when I read one, even if it was written by an ex-army sergeant with a real talent for storytelling. I enjoyed the story immensely and think Lafferty fans will enjoy it even more if they are aware that it was true. (almost?) Old veterans sometimes get together, and relate to one another, or to guests, tales of derring-do, scandalous adventure, you name it. With the passage of time, tales take on twists and turns of their own. RAL was there, but his memory almost certainly would differ from the details etched into the memories of the others. We claim personal experience with those phenomena. If any of the other main characters were to take up the editor's pen, the story would change, but I liked RAL's version.

This work is © 2015 Heywood Reynolds.

Heywood has been employed at one time or another by a newspaper, a naval organization, and a technical maintenance company. The combination may explain his enjoyment of Lafferty's stories. He discovered R. A. Lafferty online while looking for info on his grandfather Oliver B. Lafferty who served in the Civil War. No direct relation found, but an author was discovered.

Iron Tears

By Darrell Schweitzer

Originally published in Aboriginal Science Fiction, No. 39 & 40, Summer 1993 issue. Reprinted by permission of the author.

R. A. Lafferty, so Michael Swanwick tells us in the introduction, is perhaps the best and most original science fiction writer ever. He is also *unpublishable,* beyond the heroic efforts of a handful of small-press publishers determined to rescue every word he ever wrote from oblivion. (Good production values this time. Cover by Leo and Diane Dillon.)

A curious state of affairs. Were he Spanish-surnamed, he could be a "magic realist" and get mainstream recognition. Maybe. He comes from a completely different tradition: Irish, Catholic, old American tall-tale telling. He bears a superficial resemblance to Flann O'Brien. Were Mark Twain's "The Celebrated Jumping Frog" somehow science fiction, it would probably be a Lafferty story. Other than that, we can only regret that the publishing niche for humor in science fiction and fantasy has largely been captured by kiddylit. Lafferty's novels are erudite. They are, let's face it, hard to understand much of the time. If they were put in the same niche as Piers Anthony the readers would be totally befuddled and would definitely not come back for more.

The other problem is that short story collections "don't sell," according to the popular wisdom, and Lafferty's most accessible work is his short fiction. Most of the stories in Iron Tears are whimsies, grand ones, often with deeper meanings. My very favorite Lafferty story of all, "You Can't Go Back," is in this volume. Go and read it and see why it is so special. (Rating: 5 of 5 stars.)

This work is © 1993 Darrell Schweitzer.

Darrell Schweitzer is the author of 3 novels and about 300 published stories, a former editor of WEIRD TALES, and a prolific essayist, critic, and interviewer. His work appears in THE NEW YORK REVIEW OF SF regularly.

Iron Tears

By Don Webb

Originally published in the New York Review of Science Fiction, July 1993 issue. Reprinted by permission of the author.

When a good writer who has been ignored by the commercial press dies, there is always a good chance that someone in the commercial press will realize his or her goodness and bring out a collection of the work, which for some reason they were unable to do while the guy was alive. This will happen to R. A. Lafferty and I say in advance let a curse (perhaps cancer of the genitals) fall upon the ghouls and their offspring to the seventh generation. In his introduction to *Iron Tears*, the always-perceptive Michael Swanwick points out that there is a whole cottage industry that prints Lafferty: "Edgewood Press, United Mythologies, Corroborree, Chris Drum Books, The Manuscript Press, Broken Mirrors and for all I know there may be others." The connoisseurs of Lafferty must be on their toes, being sure to track down the right catalogs, the right stores, ever vigilant for a chapbook here, a small volume there. I doubt if any author in (I started to say Science Fiction, but have decided to say) in the English-speaking world receives that kind of attention. The question is why? What special magic does Lafferty offer?

The simple answer has always been his use of language. Well what of it?—the field has many who can make a phrase sing or sing a phrase that's the thing. The true answer lies in that his stories *sound* like they're folk tales. Now I said something very precise there. Lafferty doesn't use the language of folktales, and only rarely uses their rhythm. But he lives so well within the language of his creation that his language—particularly in the combination of slightly archaic folk speech and outrageous etymologies for his words—sounds like language that someone has said somewhere. Yevgeny Zamyatin developed the concept of a "prose foot" as a way of internal pacing of fiction. He saw it as a kind of rhythmic device that by causing the reader to remember an earlier part of the narrative became a force for a choral (as in pertaining to choruses) cohesion that bound the story together in a different way than plot mechanics. This method, which I can't detect in Zamyatin's works (since Russian is Greek to me), is the core of Lafferty's work. He has invented the post-modern equivalent of the Homeric epithet. Now that I've told you what the magician's about to do, see if you can catch the trick the next time. Oops, went past you!

Lafferty has two other methods to make his language appear to belong to folktale. The first is the constant use of children as seen through the eyes of memory. Unlike Bradbury, who invokes some kind of Norman Rockwell past by visual detail, Lafferty invokes the very rapid sense of childhood as we remember it. His heroes in "Lord Torpedo, Lord Gyroscope," Karl Riproar and Emily Vortex, are typical Lafferty wonder kids who do everything very very fast. His children as well as his hard-drinking young men move in a world that has been condensed by memory, and so we match with our own perceived fast and fleeting moments of childhood. The second narrative technique is to take that which is obscure (at least to the conscious mind, but clear enough to the soul) out of Indo-European mythology and represent it to us as a childhood story. The title of the book refers to the tears of Pluto mentioned in "Funnyfingers." But the story itself refers to a much more obscure myth, that of the Dactyls, a group of makers in Greek mythology serving the same mythic function as the dwarfs of the Northern peoples. By playing upon this notion which resonates with a mythic niche that speakers of Indo-European languages have—he invokes a spiritual nostalgia for this magical tale set, of course, in Tulsa.

This book of Lafferty's tales has one great plus and one great minus. At $10.00 it is one of the best buys I've seen in a long time. The plain non-glossy cover does not spring open after reading, and this perfect bound volume of 219 pages looks as though it will stand up on the shelves for some years. The big minus is the number of typos—mainly of the computer-approved variety (that is to say "and" for "an").

These reprinted stories derive from a number of sources. The earliest, from *Future City* edited by Roger Elwood (1973) is "The World as Will and Wallpaper." The latest, from *IASFM* (1987) is "You Can't Go Back." The last named is something of a comment on the nearly thirty years of work that had preceded it. The Tulsa genius started producing work (or I suspect started sharing work in a language already long since developed) in 1960. Next year he will be 80.

> *Bully for the birthday boy, the birthday boy*
> *   who sang the song a-right!*
> *Bully for the birthday boy, the birthday boy*
> *   who bullshits just a mite!*
> *Bully for the birthday boy, the birthday boy*
> *   who enchanted the Tulsa night!*
> *Bully for the birthday boy, the birthday boy*
> *   who lit the telete light!*
> *Bully for the birthday boy, the Oklahoma boy,*
> *   who championed Mithra's fight!*
>   (From an Oklahoma folk song, author unknown)

This work is © 1993 Don Webb.

Don Webb has more than 70 stories in one Year's Best list or another since his first sales in 1986. He has sold to everyone from Analog to Weird Tales. He lives with his wife in Austin, TX and spends too much time on Facebook.

Land of the Great Horses

By Peter Sijbenga

Peter has composed lyrics and music for a song inspired by Lafferty's classic story. Unfortunately for our zine, it's not physically large enough to fit full pages of sheet music. Please go to feastoflaughter.org for a printable PDF copy of the score.

So you wonder where I come from
Can't you tell by my eyes
Can't you tell by my voice
By the color of my hair

Oh land of the great horses
They took you away
They took you away long ago
My brothers, my sisters
Bound in our loss

We travel, we travel
So you wonder why we travel
Some of us become fortune tellers
Some of us go into trade
All of us sing a song of desire

Oh land of the great horses
They took you away
They took you away long ago
My brothers, my sisters
Bound in our loss

Can you hear a distant thunder
Can you feel the mountains rise
So you wonder where I come from
See it move before your eyes

Oh land of the great horses
They took you away
Bound for the land
Bound in our loss
Bound to return one day

Oh the long grass I'd graze
I'd graze like a horse...

This work © 2015 Peter Sijbenga.

Peter Sijbenga (Leeuwarden/The Netherlands, 1964) is a musician, composer, copywriter and translator. He sings and plays bass in It Dockumer Lokaeltsje. *He first read Lafferty in Dutch translation, since his dad held the short story collection* Negenhonderd grootmoeders *on the bookshelf. He considers his work to be an escape route through life. Nobody has caught him yet, he thinks. His projects include www. sexettek.com, www.kohlemainen.com and www.rosesandrecords.com.*

The Honking Worm and the Gorilla Cheetah
BY BILL ROGERS

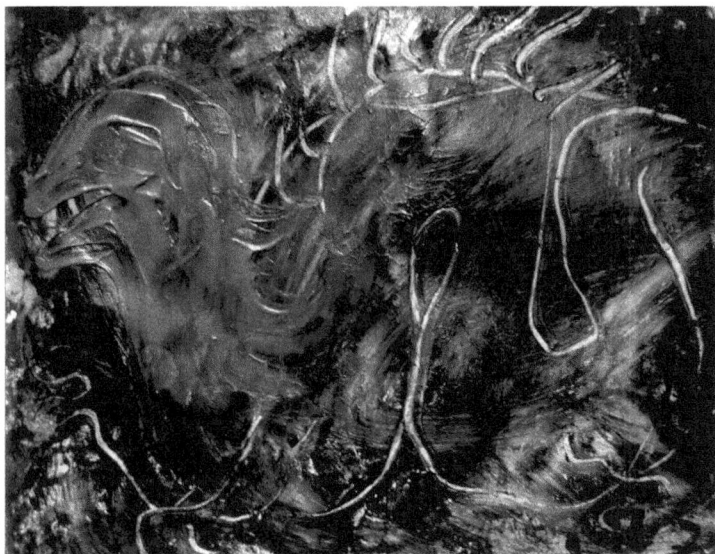

THE HONKING WORM

The Honking Worm (named for the foghorn-like sound it made) lived with its family in a tiny vertical shack on the north side of a retention pond just adjacent to my apartment in 1979. The family of worms milled about the swamp most of the day but stayed to the north side as to leave plenty of space for the Gorilla-Cheetah who lived on the southern side of the pond. At times they would slither out through a gap in the chain link fence and 'make appearances' on the property of Woodhaven Apartments, usually in the grassy or wet areas between apartments. Very seldom would they venture onto or across the parking lot, since the heat and roughness of the tar was a terror to them. They usually slid around in grassy or muddy spots prone to shade. They were only sighted by the more precocious children known to have wild imaginations. None of the adults believed us. Although the Gorilla-Cheetah had entered some of the local homes, the worms were not known to do that. They were, however, threatening in their own way. No one was known to have ever been bitten, chased or harmed in any other way by one of the Honking Worms. Their pondmate, however, was thought to have dined on local cats and dogs.

And now for the second beast:

THE GORILLA-CHEETAH

In 1979 I lived in Woodhaven Apartments in Tampa. Just next to our apartments was a fenced in retention pond. In the lazy hours between late afternoon and evening the Gorilla-Cheetah would emerge from the pond through a gap in the chain link fence and wander into our apartment complex. Although there were no human fatalities from encounters with this creature his visits were often detected by objects misplaced or lost in the homes. The creature was also held responsible for apartment vandalizations, missing bikes and broken or missing playground equipment and pool supplies. A common scenario—a woman would leave the apartment unlocked while running clothes to the laundry. Meanwhile, a visitation would occur. Later, she would discover a curious piece of swamp grass on her kitchen floor or the smell of ape in the air. Small housepets that disappeared were feared to be the late lunch / early dinner of the Gorilla-Cheetah. The Gorilla-Cheetah shared the holding pond with a family of 'honking worms' which lived in an upright shack, not much larger than an outhouse which was concealed by the vast array of plants growing out of the pond. The worms and the Gorilla-Cheetah, although pondmates, did not mix or cross paths intentionally. They stayed on separate sides of the pond—the worms to the north, nearest my apartment, and the Gorilla-Cheetah to the south side of the pond.

(Note: The Gorilla-Cheetah was originally imagined by B. Rosedale but continually developed by the two of us in the summer and fall of 1979. It was in part inspired by the moose-headed hominid on the inside cover of an Alfred Hitchcock story book.)

Bill Rogers, aka Giveawayboy, spends most of his time drawing and painting solo works or collaborating with his art partner in crime Revansj. The bulk of his days are steeped in tall tales, dreams and mythology. When he is not creating new drawings or paintings he walks about in the barely known and re-enchanted landscape of Tampa Bay. Bill's first encounter with Lafferty's work was Annals Of Klepsis.

The Waltz Macabre
By Logan Giannini

Every Friday night I find,
She's dined and come and intertwined,
Her fingers 'twixt her partner's, as they waltz across the room,
I cannot shake a feeling,
As she's peeling, spinning, wheeling,
Gooseflesh crawls across my arms, a portent of impending doom.

Still, I come here every week,
Heart piqued, and yet too shy to speak,
Imagining my fingers are those that rest upon her form,
I can't watch, yet can't resist,
I'm kissed by fear and stand transfixed,
For each partner she selects arrives of a nightmare born.

She steps in time; her heels click,
Hands held fast in putrid grip,
Moribund, if not beyond—sallow skin taut on his frame,
Dancer dancing *sans esprit*,
Does she not see what's clear to me?
Revenant out of the past—shambling corpse without a name.

His legs seem mired, bound by lead,
Long dead, wobbling, feet widespread,
Like an anchor, bound to her, shackled weight to which she clings,
The crowd spins on, a carousel,
They dwell—one spot—the corpse, the *belle*,
Her torpor slows to match with his, while nimble feet wait in the
     wings,

Next week, same story, different cast,
Carrion's gone, the past is past,
A shudder jitters down my spine, her next beau has reached the
       floor.
In the hall, the lamps shine bright,
But none brighter than his bite,
Incisors—sharper than a knife—sink in the neck that I adore,

I wince, she winks and pulls him close,
Exposed, wild, erotic throes,
Her color wanes but she endures, keeping rhythm with her monster,
A glamour falls, her eyes turn dull,
His pull too strong, her senses lull,
My love, his feast, held in his arms, her life stole to make his stronger,

Another week, another lover,
He hovers, gliding like no other,
Lacking limbs to hold her close, he wraps her up in spectral plasma,
What evil seeks he to atone?
No flesh, no bone, she seems alone,
All but for her ghastly darling, cruel form limned in dark miasma.

To my eyes, she just grows fairer,
Terrors loved, I pray, in error,
Incubus to claim the flesh; Oni, next, to take her soul,
Clearly, though, it's no mistake,
Awake, her zeal could not be faked,
Yet her procession of dark wooers will, anon, consume her whole,

Arthritis creeps into my grip,
Wine slips, my heart begins to skip,
Looking at my hand I see shriveled skin and nails grown long,
Lo, I look away at last,
Peer past a waiter, to the glass,
Where stares at me a stranger; withered swain without the throng,

From the pane, a visage bleak,
Eyes sunk deep in hollow cheeks,
Hair a wild and tangled mess, sitting high on ashen brow,
I move, he moves, a ghastly dance,
Entranced, I stare at him askance,
Back bent, twisted bones protrude; no man, just a ghoulish drow.

So I've changed from boy to horror,
Mine, the floor, and ready for her,
Now I wait for the next waltz, patient and no longer vexed,
A thrill to be now so abhorrent,
Power torrid, there's nothing for it,
Jubilation grows within, for after all, my turn is next.

The writers you read in your life are like lovers: even if you haven't been together in years, you forever carry a piece of them with you. My reading of Lafferty has been sporadic over the last decade, but perhaps the biggest lasting impression he made on me was his gleeful embrace of the macabre. His novel The Reefs of Earth, *though it reads as lightly as Wodehouse, is every bit as bloody as the best George R. R. Martin has to offer. Lafferty neither sensationalized nor trivialized the barbarism, but accepted it as an intrinsic part of the world he saw around him. While this piece wasn't written with Lafferty in mind, it stands as a fair reminder of this aspect of RAL's writing that I now cherish as part of my own.*

Logan Giannini lives and works out of Minnesota. He writes novels, short stories, poems, and comics (or "graphic novels" if he's wearing a suit). You can find more about him at Counterfeitnickels.com.

Fourteenth Chambers

By Noah Wareness

Now I understood by some sort of intuition that what I had been writing was a never-ending story and that the name of it was "A Ghost Story." The name comes from the only thing that I have learned about all people, that they are ghostly and that they are sometimes split-off...

R. A. Lafferty

This is not what I look like, I tell them.

Neil Gaiman

You'll never be a writer. Same for me.
But still, remember: no one ever was.
It's nothing that a human life can be.

You persevere, you practice on your knees;
you hollow out your life into the cause.
You'll never be a writer. Same for me.

Read back your grafted words: at best you see
a breaching ghost that's wiser far than us.
It's nothing that a human life can be.

They hardly need us, only that we breathe;
and they don't know us, they don't give applause.
You'll never be a writer. Same for me.

Don't count yourself among them in your greed,
that lineage of half-existent gods.
It's nothing that a human life can be.

Don't spread your hands and call yourself a dream,
some magic golden dream that jumped the odds.
You'll never be a writer. Same for me.
It's nothing that a human life can be.

Noah found St. Ray in his mom's teenage copy of Dangerous Visions.

noahwareness.tumblr.com

A Fisherman's Tune

By Daniel Otto Jack Petersen

When I got my doctorate in primitive music I never imagined
that I would be visiting Brownies down under tree roots. I should
say that I never so much as hoped that I would be. There was so
much that they didn't teach us. There was even one period in my
life when I ceased to believe in goblins.
R. A. Lafferty, "Ride a Tin Can" (1970)

Arms folded across his deep chest like the gnarls of an ancient tree, the Brownie rebuffed the Selkie's invitation with the blithe remark that he did not like to eat with seals.

It was early morning on a rock-strewn shoreline of Scotland's highlands, a secluded cove in which the surf was calm. The sky was clear and blue above the sea, though a gauze of glowing umber cloud could be seen if one looked inland where it had just finished raining. The tranquil waters of the inlet created an odd leveling of sound in the area, giving equal voice to every ripple and sough and word.

The Selkie had invited the Brownie down to her watery den to dine. Both creatures were out fishing, each after its fashion, for breakfast. One sought a catch to prepare for tomorrow morning's repast, while the other hoped to be munching today's breakfast within the hour.

"Where do you see a seal, silly?" the Selkie replied to the Brownie's rebuff. A rivulet darted down her wide dusky face, the only part of her above water. The drip caught the sun's fire and glistened like a solitary geminid falling out of a starless night sky.

"I see you," said the Brownie. His curt comebacks were in low rumbles like the creaking of great boughs and were accompanied by no bodily movement. He stood still as stone, as if he were merely an extension of the green-furred outcrop on which he had planted himself like so much moss, as if his proximity to the Selkie's gambols were, like the moss', merely accidental.

"Then you do not see a seal, sir," she corrected in silken-barnacled tones. She rolled a full turn then, as if to prove the point. The Selkie kept her girth just beneath the glinting waves as she spun, and the movement was a study in vast elegance. Had the Brownie been a painter, he would have broken his brushes in despair of ever capturing it. But he was no painter, and he sought to capture something else.

Having completed her turn, the Selkie laughed merrily. A fine salt spray of mist hissed from her nostrils as they splayed and narrowed again.

The Brownie offered no rebuttal.

"Och," said the Selkie. She breathed out the gently guttural word and it sounded as if one more wave had softly lapped the coastline. There is not a man who could have resisted her after hearing that sound. But it was no man before her on the rocky outcrop.

"I will humour your bad humour then," the Selkie said. "Shall I come onto the land? Shall I walk with you to your glen den?"

This offer met with another gruff rebuff. "I do not like the people shape either," creaked the Brownie. "I specially do not like to see it eat."

"Oh, *Brownie*! You are altogether too difficult!"

The Selkie hove up and clove the water's surface with one broad side of her not-really-very-seal-like bulk. The breached flank shone darkly in its cascading sheath of seawater. No man could have resisted her after drinking in the sight of that glossy pelt knifing the brine. But this was no man before her on the mossy rocks. The sleek and grey-speckled dive ended with a flick of her fanned hind flippers, which jetted a spray at the Brownie on the shore. His squat, swarthy person leapt back in an easy instant, as was the invisibly quick Brownie fashion, avoiding the rude splash. Unruffled, the Brownie refolded his arms and renewed his stony bearing. The whole exchange might have been nothing more than some huge seal-ish thing frolicking before an effigy on the rocks, an effigy that had seemed to move. Only now its stillness proved it hadn't. But the Selkie's growling stomach knew this was no statue of an angler on the shore, but a fleshy body full of delicious blood and bones, gamier than some catches but not without its piquant pleasures.

Her large liquid eyes presently rose unreadable to the re-be-calmed surface. The two creatures might have been glancing or glaring or leering at each other. Or they might have been looking right past one another. The face-off was inscrutable.

The Selkie's wide mouth re-broke the glassy water-table and in a puff-cloud of hot breath she once more addressed the Brownie. "I'm hungry for my breakfast." Her tone was still honeyed and solicitous, but now more firm. The waves and sunlight themselves seemed a little more insistent. There might even have been the beginnings of a darkling cloud in the sky over the sea.

"You will not join me below," the Selkie said, "or have me join you above. What do you propose? I, for my part, do not care to be ogled by an unconversational visitor all morning."

The Brownie stood mute in thick-limbed indifference, steady of gaze.

"And as for your rude words," the Selkie continued to chide, "if I wanted to hear cranky rumblings, I would listen to my own empty stomach."

Breaking his immobility, the Brownie unfolded his arms and produced a bunchy something from a pocket on his person. The pocket might merely have been a fold in his own hairy, leathery hide. The Selkie edged closer to the outcrop, curiosity getting the better of her. The Brownie's splayed feet remained motionless, rooted on the rock. Then the Selkie slowly, slyly pursed her mighty mouth and called in a soft and supplicant voice, long and low:

"*Brow—nie?*"

She arched minutely forward, making almost no disturbance on the water's face. Her mouth retreated from its puckering kiss to a widening smile that twinkled with rows of fearfully sharp and yellowed teeth, a hundred jagged hooks of ripping efficiency, a fisherwoman's tools of trade. Indeed, it was a mouth that could have relieved the Brownie of his head in one great bite had he been inclined to lean down toward her in turn.

The Brownie instead whistled a tune and took a step toward the water, idly unfolding the bunched up thing from one large, long-fingered hand to the other. It was a fisherman's tune he whistled. The Selkie's breath audibly caught at recognition of the song. In a fluidity of motion she swiftly swished ashore, making almost no sound.

And it was a woman's bare foot that touched upon the outcrop. The seawater streamed off of the Selkie's now pale small limbs onto the enmossed rock and back into the ocean. The not-really-very-seal-like bulk was vanished, hidden, to be donned again at her whim or of necessity.

And the Selkie sang, almost involuntarily, the words that accompanied the Brownie's tune:

> *Sad the land is, sad the land,*
> *Eating people for its food*

The Brownie seemed instantly at her back then, between her and her watery home, a crouching rock barring retreat. His net, the thing he had been unbunching, was a haze thrown over her vision and its mesh now held her, fastened briskly by the Brownie's long fingers into a cruel knot at the small of her bare back. The woman let out a sharp but husky cry like a seal barking or a wolf yelping. The Brownie grabbed both her slim ankles out from under her in one wide and powerful hand, and with the slap of her back and head on the wet slate he began to haul her toward the wood only a quarter mile from the shoreline.

The Selkie, when she recovered from the daze that resulted from the blow to her head and regained the breath that had been knocked from her, wriggled and slithered against the Brownie's grip. But this produced only the faintest tremors in the gnarled muscles of his backward-dragging arm. The rocks sliding beneath the Selkie became smaller and then gave way to a band of spongy peat and then damp matted cotton-grass. It was not long before she stopped struggling and merely sobbed quietly as she was pulled along. This soft weeping too came to an end shortly after it had begun, causing the Brownie to stop and eye his spare, naked quarry a moment. After only a moment's consideration, he stooped to let out a further portion of the net that had remained bunched up, a portion some five or ten times the length and bulk of his present dainty burden. The Brownie then resumed dragging the Selkie by the ankles, now with the surplus of loose netting trailing behind.

As the outer treeline loomed near, the velvet-barnacled voice that had spoken from the wide serrated mouth over the water was heard again at the Brownie's heels, but now from out of small pretty lips purpling in the morning chill. "Will you take me for your water-wife?" the Selkie said.

The Brownie snorted at this. A derisive smile was in that sound though no expression broke upon his stony brown brow. He could not see her moist and pleading eyes, for he deigned no longer to look at her. They entered the mouth of the forest and he strode now through a green gloom.

"Brownie..." she tried to resume. But her voice, further and further from the sea, was becoming more raspy than husky, aided no longer by her native wave, wind, sun, or sky. The Brownie, on the other hand, was only gaining in strength the nearer he came to his own home.

After a short space, the Selkie woman went truly limp and listless. And in the next moment the Brownie's burden became instantly tenfold in heft and slog. The remainder of the tough but pliant meshwork that had been trailing emptily out behind was now filled and strained to bursting. The Selkie had resumed her water form— her truest form, for they both knew she could only retain the woman shape this far inland by the promise of a groom. She had become the wife of an aging seal fisherman once long ago. That was how she recognized the song those seal fisherman sang at their work when the Brownie whistled it. The song had made its way from workers in the Hebrides over to those of the Highlands.

> Sad the land is, sad the land,
> Eating people for its food;
> See how the chief of all our men
> Boils on fire that's hot and round.

Her land husband had told her that the words were supposed to be those sung by a seal woman and heard by seal fisherman as they popped hot seal into their mouths fresh from roasting on the fire.

> *I'm the daughter of Hugh mac Ewen,*
> *And I know the skerries well;*
> *And woe to him that would strike at me,*
> *A lady from a far country.*

She had never understood how a seal woman could be the daughter of a land man, but there was much from the land people she never understood, even their love. She had eventually returned to her husband under the sea and that fisherman had died a lonely childless widower, thinking his beloved barren wife had drowned.

Whistling the tune was a trick that had worked for the Brownie before, trading as it did on the likelihood of a Selkie woman having just such a personal history and the unguarded emotions it might elicit.

> *Come the mavis, come the thrush,*
> *Come each bird that seeks its nest,*
> *Come the salmon over the sea—*
> *Till the day I shall not move.*

And the Brownie was well-practiced at not moving, not until his dangerous prey had made its fatal mistake and let down its guard, forgetting for a moment that she also was the hunter and he also the prey.

He had no more use for her as a bride than she had for him as a groom, which they both also knew. The Brownie could take an ordinary seal on any day of their shoreward season, but a Selkie was much larger and of better quality in bone and meat and hide. Her mention of marriage was out of desperation, in hopes of buying time, and release from her bonds. He was a solitary creature anyhow. The population of Brownies was established long ago and hardly ever diminished.

The Brownie had to hoist the Selkie's flopping splayed tail over one shoulder now and haul her with both hands at a more rigorous march, a task he was equal to in the strength he drew from these environs. Between the pines and ferns and down into his ever-hidden glen, as mystically undetectable as the Selkie's own enchanted sea grotto under the waves, the Brownie hauled his catch.

Arriving at his hermitage, he lugged her in and laid her out on a massive slab shelf, a convenient natural formation of the cave he had long ago chosen for his workshop. He unfastened and removed the netting, showing no fear of the Selkie's enormous, gaping, carrion-rank maw when she gave an immense wheeze and a half-hearted snap at his face. Too far from water for too long, she could only call to the Brownie now in a great sing-song ragged whisper. It reminded the Brownie of a drunken strongman he had once espied from the concealing folds of his cloak at a fair, a giant wrestler too spent to beat a sprightly midget tormenting him with kicks and pinches so near the ground. The reeling strongman only cooed hoarsely after it as he seemed to think the quick-footed little tormenter was a child. So the Selkie now cooed hoarsely to the Brownie.

"I would have taken you for my husband... down in my home," she managed.

"Aye, you and Queen Mantis and Black Widow and the rest," the brownie muttered to himself as he took up the carving knife. He'd keep his head, thank you. The knife was a gift from the cottage dwellers for whom he had chopped wood on frozen nights last winter. The useful implement kept his belly fuller in the long run than the usual bowl of cream they left out for him, though that was a treat he found he craved out of all proportion to its worth. Careful always to avoid seeing or being seen by the human cottagers, their forms mutually repugnant to one another, the Brownie would in his turn share with them some of the bones and gristle and oil and blubber from this catch, all needful domestic items.

The Selkie screamed only once, for the Brownie's death blow was practiced and swift and sure; and the scream was not that of a woman. After that it was a long afternoon and night of carving and separating and arranging and parceling and hanging and stretching, and the Brownie's seemingly inexhaustible capacity for work never waned. In the small hours he finally started a fire at the cave's mouth and began the slow roasting. By the early light of the same chill hour in which the previous day's exchange with the Selkie had taken place, the Brownie at last broke his fast and began his repast. He hummed the seal fisherman's tune as he munched and chewed the hot and sweetly yielding morsels and the song's words ran routinely through his earthen mind, though now in her voice:

> *And woe to him that would strike at me,*
> *A lady from a far country.*

This work is © 2015 Daniel Otto Jack Petersen.

Daniel Otto Jack Petersen is married to fine art and fashion photographer Flannery O'Kafka. They have five children, the youngest in her first year in school and the oldest in her second year at art college. Daniel has accepted an offer from the University of Glasgow to begin doctoral research this October on the theme of the 'ecomonstrous' in the works of R. A. Lafferty and Cormac McCarthy. He blogs about Lafferty at antsofgodarequeerfish.blogspot.co.uk. He also blogs about a few other things at a few other places and is known to occasionally record strange noises with his mouth, sometimes even for public consumption: e.g. laminarexcursion.bandcamp.com/album/lem-volume-20-october-2010.

What I Wrote for Andronicus
By Stephen Case

Originally published in Ideomancer Speculative Fiction, Vol. 9, Issue 4, Dec 2010. Reused by permission of the author.

When I was dead, they called me Harold Half-Helm, for a variety of reasons. Someone wrote a cycle of songs about it once, and they'd sing it in the evenings when I was very drunk. The silver goblets would spill and usually there would be a bit of blood before it was all over. That's not what I'm writing about now though. I'm writing about the tree, how it died, and what we did with it.

I wouldn't normally have picked up a quill and written all this. I had held the pen long enough when I was alive, and it hadn't done me much good then. Here there was much more to do with a good broadsword or spear, so when Andronicus brought me this parchment and a quill and asked me to write, I had hoped my glare would be his answer.

When he lingered I growled, "You're the poet. You write it."

He shook his head and said something about not everyone being able to write every story.

"Well, I don't want to write this one."

But he left the parchment and the horn of ink and the quill, and before I knew it I had notched the quill with my dagger and dipped it in the ink, which was dark like wine.

"Bloody hell."

Andronicus wanted me to write about the tree. The poets called it Aegiros, and the gods had a name the rest of us couldn't pronounce. We had our own name for it, having to do with the fact that it was a good place to take a woman. I had, more than a few times, and I'm sure the others had as well.

It's dead now. I'm not sure I've written that yet. Apparently Andronicus thinks I have something to say about it.

I guess I do.

The tree was up in the hills that overlook the halls of the gods. From up there you could see everything—all the meadows and forests that sloped down to where the sea sat at the horizon like a blue finger.

It was huge, which you know if you've been here. The young dead don't raise their eyes much, but occasionally you'll see a new one stagger out of the foam and scan the beaches as if they're looking for someone. No one comes, and eventually, when their eyes get strong enough, they'll look up into the hills and see the ivory columns of the gods' houses. Then above and behind those all, at the foot of the mountains, the grey-green column of the tree itself—or at least they used to.

The gods said it was the first sight of the tree that convinces those on the beaches they're dead. No tree from before could have been so big. The mahoganies I had spent weeks in the canopies of would have been weeds beside it. Sometimes it seemed that the sight of it was the only thing that got the new dead off the sands and up into the hills. Now that it's gone they wander like ghosts on the beaches.

This quill wants to write of the tree's leaves: wide as Spanner's shield, blue and silver like the sea. When the breezes off the mountains blew through them it was like a cloud was whispering secrets the gods didn't know anything about. It was tall enough that when the sun passed overhead it left a trail of curled leaves as it wound through the branches, and one evening when I was there with Helga of the Ivory Tower we heard the branches creaking because the moon had gotten caught. We both had to climb up and free it, and if you think a woman's skin looks fine by moonlight when she's on the ground, wait and take a look when she's standing on a silver branch with her arms halfway around the moon.

That was a good night.

But the tree is gone now, as this quill of Andronicus' keeps reminding me.

Besides being big, it was supposed to be old. There are things here you think are old—the stone table the gods sit around, for instance, or the well that Jarred Slimfist had dug and lined with bricks so he could throw a stone down into hell. You think those things are old, but the gods built them themselves. The tree though, if you believe what they say, was growing when there weren't any gods at all.

That was the tree.

But all those things about it—about those silver-blue leaves that never changed with the seasons—was why everyone that day in the hall stopped and stared, even the high gods at their table of stone, when Sugarfoot shuffled in through the golden doors holding one of the leaves, withered and brown as old parchment.

I was sitting near the door. This wasn't because I knew what was coming. I want to get that straight. I had known trees before, but the trees here were different. The ones in the valleys with the bark of human skin or the ones that would come down in the evenings and dance with you like they were half wind and half woman—they didn't follow the same rules as those from before. I couldn't tally them, and I couldn't watch as they were all slowly felled around me. (Not that anyone here would have been so stupid to try.) So whatever I could or could not do before didn't matter. I had no idea the tree was dying, and I still don't know why it did.

I was sitting near the door when Sugarfoot limped in because I had had an argument with one of the minor gods earlier that morning. It seemed prudent to sit far from their table. It also meant I saw the dead leaf clearly.

"I thought it was the pages of Old Doom's book," Sugarfoot muttered. He was supposed to be the oldest of the old gods and had a face dark and wrinkled as the soil. "I thought he was finally throwing them out one by one."

He blinked and stared around the hall.

"But it was a *leaf* from the tree," he barked, brandishing the thing, "so maybe just as bad as Old Doom and his book."

No one in gods' memory had seen the tree drop a leaf. There wasn't autumn here, and when leaves went red it was usually because someone had bled on them. It was like a story I remembered from before of a bird that had a piece of the sky fall on her head. It was blue and silvered, like glass, and she carried the shard around in her beak warning other animals until she finally met a fox who killed her and used the sky-shard to make a knife. I remembered the story because it was that idea, something as unthinkable as a falling sky, that was what we felt when we saw the wilted leaf. Had Sugarfoot walked in holding a dead, bloated star, I don't think we would have been any more shocked.

Things don't often surprise you when you're dead.

He passed slowly through the hall with the leaf, down to where Ogden himself sat in his silver throne. All the high gods and heroes clustered around him. The rest of us in the hall watched them speak together for a while, and none of us said anything. Then they called over some of the poets and some of the learned dead. There was more talk. Finally Ogden stood and took down the golden spear that hung from the back of his chair. It was the spear that, when held, allowed only truth spoken.

"The tree is dying," he said.

Then he sat down.

The silence deepened. Things didn't die in the land of the dead. Sure, things got *killed* often enough. It wouldn't have been a very interesting place otherwise. I myself had broken blades on the backs of more than a few warriors, but that was simply the way of things. Come nightfall the mead would flow and everyone, whichever side of the blade they had been on, would wander back into the hall and drink again.

Things got killed, but things didn't *die*.

I notched my quill again after I had written that last, and it bucked in my hands like one of Fyoden's minded blades. Andronicus has not returned, and the shadows have wandered from the forests outside the hall to lay across the lawns with their heads pillowed in the grasses. I wonder what those who pass through the hall must think of me sitting here. I am sure I look ridiculous, hunched over these scraps of parchment and hands smeared with ink like sap.

The quill wants to speak more of the silence that descended in the hall after Ogden spoke, silence so thick you could see its wings in the rafters, but I've bit off the nub and notched it again. I'm not sure from what flock of half-charmed and ill-mannered fowl Andronicus gets these things, but this one keeps twitching against my grasp.

I was sitting in the silence of the hall with the other dead thinking about what Ogden had said when Bromin of the Heavy Hand came to sit beside me and spoke quietly. His brows were furrowed.

"What do you make of this, Half-Helm?" he asked.

Bromin had small eyes and a voice that made you hunch your shoulders against it.

I shrugged. "It's the concern of the gods."

"Nothing you can do for a dying tree?"

In the past they say that Andronicus would give flesh to his books and let them walk about in the lands across the sea. If that is still the case, you may hear this story before you come here, and you may eventually understand why my hand tightened on the hilt of my blade when Bromin spoke thus to me. There were certain things that were not spoken of here, and the first among these was anything of what had happened before.

"Nothing," I said evenly. I forced my grip on the blade's hilt to relax.

He looked at me for a while, then echoed my shrug and moved away.

That next morning the gods called everyone back to the Great Hall. Runners went through the gardens, and the silver trumpets were sounded on the gates. When I took my place about halfway out along the ring of greater and lesser heroes that poured into the chamber and filled the space around Ogden's throne, the hall was filled with faces like foam on the sea.

"The tree is dying," Ogden said when the legions of gods and men had gathered. "We have stood beneath its crown and seen the signs of death. This is not the way of things in the lands of the gods."

From the outside of the Great Hall one could throw a spear along perhaps a third of the length of its walls. From within though, it stretched away in all directions until it was large enough to hold the countless thousands that were gathered. These thousands now voiced their assent to Ogden's words, and it was as though the faces were indeed a sea, beating against a shore of stone.

"We will not sit idly and watch this death," Ogden went on. On his tunic there was a silver tree, which I had always thought to be an image of the Tree itself, and this silver tree shifted as he raised his spear. "Thus we have decreed: while the tree is yet whole, Hammerfast will fell it. We will use its wood to craft a gift for those who still dwell across the sea."

When Ogden spoke those words, Hammerfast (who has many names in many places) raised his huge axe. That the flesh of the tree should be shaped into something of use was not unexpected; that it would be a gift for those beyond the sea only slightly more so. It was true the ships no longer passed that way and few of the bridges that spanned that sea were still whole (and those that were gave no passage to men). This though did not mean the gods had no thought for those who remained.

Again I found that Bromin stood beside me.

"They can do nothing to save it?" he whispered.

I shook my head. "They came over the sea as we did. They don't have the power they had once. You know this."

"Or the knowledge?"

Again I shrugged and turned away.

I think I realized then he was baiting me, though I was not sure why. As I wrote before, the trees I knew then were not like the trees here. Those had died all around me, and then like now I had been able to do nothing.

After that the voices swelled even louder, for once Ogden had said that the wood of the tree would be used to fashion something, the gods and heroes argued about what form the gift should take. The old soldiers shouted for a forest of spears as long as Fyngard is tall, but Fyngard himself called for shafts to birth a cloud of ten thousand arrows.

A god whose name I couldn't remember pulled himself up near a pillar and held his hands for silence. He tried to explain that men no longer warred and instead would be better served by staves to lean upon in their travels. I remember that some of the old gods nodded at this, though it seemed strange to the rest of us.

Someone else called for a ship so that men could again sail the sea and perhaps beyond—for surely the wood from the tree would be fit to fashion a ship to pass beyond the sky. Again some of the gods and heroes nodded, but the hall was vast and soon other voices were added to the tumult.

It continued like this for some time.

The light had begun to fade, and sylvan forms lit lanterns on the pillars and in the gardens, and the horns of mead were passed, before Sugarfoot himself slowly made his way to where the gods took council at the center of the hall. He did indeed in that moment seem as old as they say he is, a form of stone ground down to dark earth by the march of countless years. When he spoke his voice carried through the growing darkness.

"The sons of man are tired," he said. "They don't need boats or beams and they sure as shit don't need spears."

The gods listened silently.

"They need chairs. Solid chairs beside a hearth or on a porch. They need a place to sit."

At this there was again silence in the hall, and outside I could hear the first of the glowflies singing in the fields. I waited for the voices to rise again in argument, but they never came. Finally Ogden nodded very slowly, took up his great silver spear, and said, "It shall be done."

I left the hall then, and when I walked outside and up the long rise beyond the houses of the gods, the tree was visible as a darkness rearing up before the mountains. In the night no signs of death could be seen. The tree stretched upward, boughs branching and re-branching like veins beneath skin, like they were roots working their way up into a soil of blackness where the stars were flecks of brilliant stone.

I was not alone.

"But you shall raid the whole land through," someone spoke at my back, "and never a tree shall talk to you, though every leaf is a tongue taught true and the forest full of eyes."

"Chesterton," I said, turning to find Bromin of the Heavy Hand. "Don't let him catch you quoting him. I tried that once, and he nearly ran me through with that damned stick of his."

We looked up at the tree together in silence for a while.

"You think you'd be used to this," he finally said. "You must be like the patron saint of dying trees."

I shook my head.

"It was single species." He muttered. "A single fucking species, and you acted like every last tree on earth was dying."

I was quiet for a long time.

"Three," I finally said, rubbing the bridge of my nose where glasses had not perched for perhaps a hundred years. "There were three distinct species of cottonwood, and they were all affected by the blight."

"And you could never isolate it," he went on. "Do you remember the first one we saw go, the one at the edge of the lake behind the lodge?"

"Why are you doing this?"

There are those here who argue that what you did across the sea has a bearing on whether you end up here or elsewhere. I don't know about that. What I do know though—and what everyone who drinks mead under the rafters in the gods' halls knows—is what I said earlier: here one does not speak of what had happened before. You—you who may hear this across the sea—will not understand, because you think you know now what your life now is.

Bromin knew this as well as any.

"You came in with a dead branch, and no one cared. They sawed it down and made some benches for the lodge porch. Do you remember? And then when they were going everywhere you kept those endless journals of the blight's progress. No one else gave a damn some weedy trees along the creeks were dying out." He laughed. "My wife had allergies. She was thrilled to see them go."

I looked up where the branches of the tree arched far above us, but for a moment I could not see them stretched like beams between stars. Instead I saw the silver-green leaves of those others, shivering in the slightest breeze. The light below them was fluid with snowy seeds falling like dust in a quiet room.

"I kissed a girl for the first time in the branches of that tree," I said, finding a memory so washed by time it was as smooth as stone. "It was the biggest cottonwood I had ever seen."

"By the time you left they were nearly all gone," Bromin was saying.

I waited.

"Were there any left at all when you finally died?"

"There was a stand in eastern Missouri," I said. I wasn't sure at that point that I was still talking to him. I felt I was answering a voiceless question from the leaves above.

"Do you think it mattered? You gave your entire career to saving them, but no one will miss them. By our time they had already forgotten the elms." He went on, speaking the words of challenge.

The young dead find battles like the one we fought then foolish, perhaps. I've walked among them on the beaches though, and their pale faces and dim eyes will never meet my own. They know nothing of the battles higher up and the blood that is spilled on stone or grass. They don't know the codes of honor or why certain words must always be followed by the drawing of a sword. They linger by the shore and could not understand that last battle fought under the crown of that first tree.

Bromin and I understood. By then I had found his name, dragged up from memories of the days before I found myself washed up on these beaches. I really don't know—and neither does this damned quill, though it quivers like it has a secret—why he issued the challenge beneath the tree. Perhaps it was a way for him of finding redemption for the thousand small betrayals from before. There are still some here who seek such things, though if he was one of those he is more foolish than I thought. Regardless of his reasons, I'd like to think the poets will sing of the battle of Bromin of the Heavy Hand and Harold Half-Helm beneath the tree for perhaps as long again as the tree stood.

When his blade was finally broken and my own had found a home between his ribs, he laughed and said he hoped the tree drank blood. Then he died.

A few nights later, when the mead flowed again, he stood beside me in the hall. I shook my head at his unvoiced question.

"I did all I knew," I told him then. "I took your damn measurements—even a soil sample and a boring. The gods laughed. You know things don't work like that here."

He shrugged and said nothing.

Now the light has died here in the hall where I write, and were I to venture out under the dome of stars I know that I would see many of those whom I feasted with at midday, taking their places among the constellations.

Someone has brought me a lantern, and I suddenly have sympathy for the scribes who they say labor in caverns under the mountains. The words seem to dash first one way and then another in the flickering light of the flame.

I should write now what happened to the wood of the tree, how it was felled and carved into Sugarfoot's chairs, though I can do no more than simply say it. Andronicus came back a moment ago, and I showed him what I had written and thought that he would take it. He shook his head though and told me to finish.

"I wrote about the fight," I said. "I thought you wanted me to write this damn thing because I was the last to draw a blade in the tree's shadow."

"Bromin could have just as well written that," he said.

"Bromin's an ass."

He waited, and for an instant I felt like a kid again with a teacher standing over me and waiting for an answer or assignment I didn't understand. The quill fluttered on the table.

"Was Plato right?" I finally asked. "Did they all die before because their true form was up here dying all along? Is that why you made me write this bullshit?"

Andronicus reached across the table and grasped the quill. In his hand I somehow saw it for what it was, a single feather from a bird that had roosted for a time in the branches of that tree.

"I don't know," he said. "Someone explained it to me once, but I didn't write it down."

That was his answer. That was his fucking answer.

I stared at his back as he walked away and then stared for a long time at the door he went through out into the night. He had placed the quill back on the table. When I got tired of staring at the door I stared down at it, wondering if it could explain.

And now it's in my hand again.

The morning after the battle, after someone had taken Bromin's body away, wood shavings from the tree soaked up his blood. Hammerfast hewed at its trunk all morning and evening and halfway into the next day, his blows making the branches of the tree tremble and the leaves whisper like an approaching storm. No one could watch, and the men and gods all stood facing the sea.

When it finally fell it fell for a day. Its highest branches lay beyond the mountains of the gods, and the bulk of its trunk stretched to the horizon like a giant's corpse. Hammerfast took his awl and began to shave away the bark and shape the wood.

"It's soft," he said. "It takes to the blade well."

There was enough wood for seven chairs. As large as the tree had been, I thought there would have been enough for an army, but that's not how things work here. When Hammerfest was done there were seven chairs grained with every shade of gold and brown and a pile of shavings, bark, and branches, which we burned. The highest branches had fallen beyond the mountains, and because we couldn't stand the thought of the leaves slowly wilting, we lit arrows and launched them over the mountains to burn those as well. The sparks rose upward all night and thickened the sky with unfamiliar stars that never fell or faded.

When dawn found us, we were sitting on the hill where the tree had been, with the absence of the tree filling the sky at our backs, and the gods were muttering about who would send the chairs across the sea.

"The envoys no longer pass between our lands," the gods said. "Those across the sea expect no word from the lands of the gods, and thus it will be difficult to send this gift."

Thor Thunderfist wanted to simply throw them across, while Aedan of the Unheard Song said she could carry them across by night. A young god wanted to summon a fleet of porpoises and maiden-fish to ferry the chairs. The gods considered all but shook their heads. The seas were stormy, they said, the nights of the cities of men were no longer still enough for song, and bad things seemed to happen whenever Thor threw things.

There was silence on the hill.

Finally Sugarfoot spoke. "There's no crossing the sea with them," he said, leaning against his staff. "But it gets colder every year. I feel it, and the tree felt it too. Soon the sea will be frozen."

He paused and stretched, and his joints popped like stones.

"You use what's left of this wood, and you carve a couple good sledges to fasten to each. Then, when the seas have frozen, you have one of these young dead pull them across the sea. That's when the sons of men will need them anyway."

The gods were quiet for a while after this, quiet for so long that I thought they had not heard him. We waited, and the hills turned silently beneath us.

Then Ogden nodded, and Hammerfast reached for his awl, and it was done. He fashioned fourteen sledges, curved like the line of a bow, and attached a pair to each of the chairs. The gods carried them to a rise that overlooked the sea and sat them in a row where they slowly rocked back and forth in the breeze.

That's it, and I've wiped this quill on my trousers for the last time and blown on the parchment to dry the ink. If, when Andronicus comes, he doesn't take this feather with him, I'm going to fletch the damn thing to the end of an arrow and shoot it into the sun.

One more thing, it's saying. One more thing.

Fine.

The great stump of the First Tree is still there, rising up like a broken hill or maybe a golden table where the tree once stood. It's still a good place and maybe I shouldn't say it and maybe it doesn't mean anything, but when Julia Half-Moon and I lay there on its soft wood one afternoon I noticed that it had sent up a few shoots from where the wood met the bark. They were tiny things with leaves barely larger than the ends of my fingers, but Julia smiled.

Like I said though, I don't know much of what it all means. I drink my mead with the gods and heroes in the evening, and sometimes I walk to where Sugarfoot sits in one of the chairs, looking out over the sea toward the cities of men. He says the warmth of the wood warms his bones.

"It's ending," he told me once when I stood beside him, facing the blown foam of the sea. "It's all changing."

I looked back at where the tree had been and at all the cold marble houses the gods had built for themselves and at the beaches where the new dead still washed up like bones. From this distance the houses of the gods looked like mausoleums dotting the hills. The wind picked up and the chairs rocked back and forth, and the old god hunched his shoulders against the chill.

Stephen Case gets paid for teaching people about space, which is pretty much the coolest thing ever. He also occasionally gets paid for writing stories about space (and other things), which have appeared in Beneath Ceaseless Skies, Daily Science Fiction, Orson Scott Card's Intergalactic Medicine Show (forthcoming), and several other publications. His first anthology, Trees and Other Wonders, is available through Amazon. Stephen has a PhD in the history and philosophy of science from the University of Notre Dame and will talk for inordinate amounts of time about nineteenth-century British astronomy. He lives with his wife, four children, and three chickens in an undisclosed suburb of Chicago that has not yet legalized backyard chickens.

Willow Beeman

By Howard Waldrop and Steven Utley

Originally published in Stellar #2, 1976, edited by Judy-Lynn del Rey. Reprinted by permission of the authors.

Foreword, by Howard Waldrop

I've told this story before, but it's a good one.

At one point (the cusp of 1979 / 1980) I found myself living in the same house as Steven. He was between one set of crises or another, and I was between girlfriends and apartments.

We were getting ready for a New Year's Eve party. There are, besides us, a dog and four cats there. Steven is slaving over a hot stove, baking stuff for the party. There's a buzz at the front door (NOBODY uses the front door); somebody knocks on the back door; the phone starts ringing. Steve, taking stuff out of the oven, moves first one way, then another and another. Two of the cats start a fight and run across the ceiling. The dog goes crazy from the doorbell.

"Here," says Steven, handing me the cookie sheet with fourteen scones on it, "take this."

I took it.

He headed toward one door or another.

The cookie sheet's just come from a 375° oven.

I don't know about you but it doesn't take me long to hold a hot cookie sheet.

Steve came back with the first of the guests.

The scones are all over the cabinets and stovetop. The cookie sheet is as far away from me as I could get it.

"I thought you had the *other* oven mitt," said Steve.

"Uh, no," I said.

In his Afterword to this one, Utley will tell you of writing this, among others, that new young writers will not believe.

This was in the days when $90 was a month's rent *anywhere*

(except NYC). I can tell you my take from the evening (eventually) was 5.00; 17.50; 26.66; and 70.00 for a total of $119.16.

We did it *all* with our little typewriters.

WILLOW BEEMAN

There never was another man like Willow Beeman. There never would be, either, because Willow was the very last man in the whole world. His heart was closed to the memory of men, and he did quite well without that memory, thinking of himself only as a large dog without hair.

He could recall a time, long, long before, when he had been not a dog but a gorilla, or something close to it, at any rate. But he had forgotten all the parts about being a man and living in Sumer, in Babylon and Tyre and Rome. He even disremembered about Cheyenne and Bismarck and Bayonne, and about women, cigarettes, automobiles, ice cream, God, spaceships, books, and underarm deodorants. He would not even have remembered being a gorilla were it not for his friend Patrox, who was something very like a Galapagos tortoise and had lived quite a long time. "Longer than you, anyway," Patrox was fond of reminding Willow.

Patrox was also fond of telling stories. Willow found these stories disturbing. They were full of esoteric references that got into his skull and nibbled at his brains. "What is *suburb?*" Willow would demand, seizing upon an odd word in one of Patrox's incomprehensible yarns, and Patrox would shrug and say that he didn't really know. "Then why do you tell these stories?" Willow would ask, and Patrox would shrug again and say that he didn't really know that, either. "I think you're making it all up," Willow would declare, by way of closing the subject, and stomp away in a sulk, irritated as all get-out by the nibbling going on in his head.

Willow Beeman was not singular in his disbelief in both men and his own man-ness. Once he had cast off the memories, to say nothing of the overbearing swaggers, of *Homo sapiens*, it was easy for the animals to take his presence among them for granted. And, excepting Patrox, who had his doubts, they, too, thought of Willow only as a large dog without hair. Willow drank with them at the water holes and licked salt with them at the salt lick. He slept on the ground when he was tired, and he ate crawdads and wild berries when he was hungry. So he had all of the animal comforts and pleasures.

Except one. Willow kept noticing animals copulating.

"What makes them do that?" he wondered aloud one mellow day of a mellow spring.

"There's a story about it," Patrox murmured at his side. "But it's a dirty one, and my mother would spin in her grave if I told it."

Willow frowned, perplexed by the oddness of the words *dirty* and *grave*. His head began to throb from the nibbling. He turned Patrox over onto his shell and left him kicking there for a day or two, just to pay him back.

As the mellow spring passed into a mellower summer, Willow noted that all of the animals who had previously been copulating were now birthing lots of little animals which resembled them somewhat, despite a certain largeness of skull and a marked clumsiness of foot. Willow devoted no small amount of thought to the matter and, by and by, put together a fantastic theory, which he then presented to Patrox.

Patrox listened, nodded sagely, and said, "See, Willow, I told you it was dirty."

"You mean, I'm right?" said Willow, awed by his own hitherto unsuspected brilliance.

"You hit the nail squarely on the head," Patrox affirmed.

Willow winced and rubbed his temples.

A little more time passed, and Willow Beeman forgot all of his newly gained knowledge of reproduction. Or, rather, he placed the information in that portion of his mind which contained all the rest of the useless information he had accumulated about the way the world was. Like how the leaves kept coming off the trees at a certain time of year. Like how that big useless white thing in the night skies sometimes was round and sometimes was only a curved line of light with pointy ends and sometimes was not there at all. But another mellow spring came along eventually, and Willow looked around at the copulating animals, sighed, sat down on Patrox's back, and said,

"I'm lonely. I think."

"You have me, don't you?" said Patrox.

"Well, it occurs to me that this thing the animals do must be a lot of fun, since all of the animals do it at least once a year. And they always seem to be in great spirits afterward."

"How well I remember!" Patrox snorted. There was a note of longing in his snort.

"Really, Patrox? You've done it, too?"

"Yes, but it was a long time ago, when I was young and limber and full of juice, so don't get any ideas. Besides, we're both boys."

"What's *boys*?"

"Never mind, Willow."

Willow ground his teeth in frustration for a few seconds, then: "Patrox, the more I think about it, the more I'd like to have some little animals that look like me. So I'm just going to have to find somebody with whom to do this wonderful copulation thing."

And he did, too.

It took Willow Beeman five weeks to recover completely from the wounds he suffered at the claws of the she-wolverine. He wondered where he had gone wrong.

"As I remember it," Patrox told him, "animals only copulate with other animals of the same kind."

"I'll have to find another big, hairless dog in that case," said Willow. Or, he added to himself, if that doesn't pan out, at least a gorilla.

"I tend to doubt that you'll find another big, hairless dog out here in the woods, Willow."

"Maybe I should go to one of those places that don't look like the woods," and, six days later, Willow pulled into just such a place. It was actually all that was left of a city, but Willow didn't know this. He was rather sore of foot and had begun to ache peculiarly in the groin, which is how it goes when notions about copulation take root in one's brains.

Willow searched through the city looking at disintegrating hulks of automobiles, rust-eaten shards of tin cans, a Lacrosse missile launcher, and the like, though, to Willow, these things were just some sort of strange plant life that couldn't be eaten.

Willow began to lose heart after a while. "This isn't getting me anywhere," he muttered to himself. "I do believe I've been everywhere in this place, and I haven't seen a single dog. Or even any gorillas. Maybe it'd be better if I just went on back to the woods and spent my time crawfishing with my hands in some pool."

It was as he was about to leave the place that he came upon the low stone edifice with its door ajar and the sign that read CRYOGEN, INC. Willow couldn't read the sign, reading being one of the things Patrox had never quite got around to showing him how to do. But the door was half open, and Willow, who was now feeling rather ferocious with frustration, barged in furiously. What happened next you would not believe, even if we told you. Suffice it for explanation that there was still some power running this or that arcane machine when Willow entered.

Willow stayed inside for a long, *long* time. When this or that arcane machine finally did sputter and give up the ghost, thereby releasing Willow from his protracted sleep, the low stone edifice had been worn away to the level of the ground. The door and the sign were gone, too.

Willow sat up, looked around, and immediately saw that the strange inedible plant life had given way to salt marshes and mud flats. There were a few stunted, scraggly trees, several of whom regarded him with baleful equivalents of eyes. Their attitude toward him appeared to be "Hmpf, and what is *this?*"

Willow scratched his skull bemusedly and asked, "Where have all the animals gotten off to?"

"Dead and gone, most of them!" snapped one of the trees. "And good riddance, I say!"

Willow recalled the purpose in his coming to the place. "You haven't seen any big, hairless dogs around here, have you? Or any gorillas?"

"No dogs or gorillas," the tree answered irritably. "Just something that looks very like a Galapagos tortoise."

"That must be Patrox!"

"Yes, I believe he did say his name was Patrox. And, now that I think about it, he spoke of some animal that looks the way you look. He said that he had known this animal a long time ago and had always thought highly of it." The tree peered closely at Willow. "I can't say as I find much in you to think highly of."

Willow was dejectedly surveying the new landscape. "So everything is gone," he muttered.

"What did you expect?" the tree demanded. "I've been listening to your infernal snoring ever since I can remember, and my mother says you were here when she was a sapling. You've been asleep for some time, and things have a natural tendency to change with time. Even people, though they generally resist that change."

"What is people?"

"Why, now that most of the animals are gone, people are the dominant form of life on the Earth today. Look, I can't stand here all day and explain things to you, so why don't you walk around and sort of acclimate yourself to stuff. It stands to reason that you've got some catching up to do."

"What is reason?"

"Never you mind. Now run along."

Willow Beeman ran along, still considerably confounded. The world seemed drabber, uglier. The air tasted funny, frankly. Willow was fairly well put out with it all after he had acclimated himself to only a few square miles of stuff. He parked his fanny on a smooth, green rock and said, "On top of everything else, I still haven't gotten to do what the animals do to make little animals like themselves."

"Eh?" said the rock, who was actually Patrox, who had been taking a nap. "Why, Willow! It's you! Long time, no see."

"I'm mighty glad to see you again," Willow confessed.

"Need help?" Patrox said solicitously.

"What is *help*?"

"What do you want more than anything else right now?"

"I want to copulate," said Willow. "I want to make little animals like myself. I came looking for another big, hairless dog. Or a gorilla, if I couldn't find a dog. I never found either. There must be something with which I can copulate."

"Have you tried it with people?"

"I wouldn't know people if I saw one."

Patrox squinted toward the salt marshes. "People hang around over there. As long as you're determined to do this, you might as well give them a try, Willow."

"Well, if you say so." Frowning deeply, Willow went over to the salt marshes. He returned shortly, and he was frowning more deeply than before. "They're *frogs*, Patrox. I know frogs when I see them."

"They're people now."

"But when I lived in the woods, they used to keep me awake at night going *breedeep breedeep breedeep*. They're frogs."

"They're the best I can offer," Patrox stated flatly. "Take them or leave them."

"Oh, all right." Willow walked back to the salt marsh and tried to get the frogs to copulate with him, but whenever he made a lunge at one of them, it would vanish in a puff of pale blue smoke.

Not like frogs at all, Willow thought disgustedly. He squatted in the muck, feeling very sorry for himself. The ache in his groin was worse now, his stomach was rumbling with hunger, and his throat was raw with thirst. He did not look up when Patrox settled into the mud at his side.

"What now?" Patrox said softly.

"I don't know," admitted Willow. "I was doing just fine in the woods. But now everything's so depressing. Where'd all the grass and ferns go? Where are the birds and deer and wolverines? I miss them. Everything's been a mess ever since I decided to make little animals like myself."

"Well, maybe that's *why* everything got messed up," Patrox said. "Weren't you happy being a big, hairless dog in the woods?"

Willow nodded forlornly.

"You probably could've gone right on being a big, hairless dog if you hadn't gone off looking for someone like yourself. When the time came for all the dogs to go away, you would simply have become something else. An ostrich, maybe. You'd have been an ostrich for as long as you could, then something else, then something else again. That's how you managed to hang on as long as you did back there in the woods, Willow."

"I'm not sure I quite follow you," Willow said, "and, besides, what's this got to do with everything going away?"

"It has everything to do with it," Patrox said. "Willow, I've always been pretty certain that you were a gorilla before you were a dog, even though I didn't know you personally before then. You yourself apparently suspect as much. Before you were a gorilla, who knows? At any rate, the point is that you, being the only one left of your kind, managed to stay alive by not being whatever it is that you really are. And as long as there was only one of you, Mother Nature could pretend not to notice you and go along with the idea of you being a gorilla or a dog or whatever."

"But then," Patrox continued, "Mother Nature got panicky when you decided to try and make little animals like yourself. Don't you see? You were safe in the woods as long as you were content to remain one of a kind, a unique exception to the rules. If you wanted to be a gorilla, fine, Mother Nature let you be a gorilla for as long is there were real gorillas in the world. The same goes for dogs. But there just wasn't—and isn't—a place for more than a single Willow Beeman creature. While you were away, Mother Nature was making everything become extinct. She was looking for you, trying to keep you from upsetting her apple cart, but she couldn't find you. The more she didn't find you, the more panicky she became, and the more things she made become extinct. So now just about everything is gone, except for the trees and the people—and my kind. And you're in terrible danger, Willow. I suggest that you decide, but *fast*, what you intend to become now. You can't stay a dog, because there aren't any dogs left. You're too soft to make a good tree, even if they'd have you. And the people don't seem to care for you at all."

Patrox got to his four feet, turned, and started to amble away. "Be something quickly," he said over his shoulder. Otherwise, Willow, you're extinct."

"But what else is there to be," Willow called after him, if not a tree or a people?"

Patrox paused and shrugged within his shell.

Willow Beeman got up out of the muck and walked over to him. "Say, Patrox, why don't I be whatever you are?"

Patrox laughed. "Now *that* would be interesting. But what would you do for a shell? Your camouflage has to be good if you don't want to die off."

"I—I could make a shell out of dried mud." Willow walked around Patrox several times, examining him closely. "Yes, I think it can be done. I'll be one of your kind. Uh, Patrox? Just what are you anyway. I mean, in case anybody asks."

"Don't you think that I look very like a Galapagos tortoise?" Patrox inquired slyly.

"But what are you *really?*"

Patrox looked around and asked, in a lowered voice, "You promise you won't ever tell anyone?"

"I promise, Patrox," said Willow.

"Tyrannosaurus Rex, at your service, Willow."

Afterword, by Steven Utley

Writers like to make out that the act of writing is comparable, in terms of difficulty and sheer two-fistedness, with wrestling alligators or putting out oil-field fires. Writers want (besides lots of money) all the prestige they can eat. It's for this reason and this reason alone that so much writing about how writing got itself written gets itself written. The truth is, no matter who does it, you, me, or Ernest goddamn Hemingway, writing is a deadly dull spectator sport; watching someone else set words down on paper will make your behind fall right off from boredom. Pay no attention to anyone who tells you differently, not even your own mother; that person is certainly a writer, and writers, like lawyers, will lie like dogs when there is something in it for them, and lie all the rest of the time just to stay in practice. Many young people from good homes have been ruined because they believed writers' lies.

Nevertheless, what follows is the truth: one long-ago, tornado-infested spring day in Grand Prairie, Texas, while our wives (or, more accurately, one wife, one wife-to-be, and two then-wives) held a baby shower next door, Geo. W. Proctor, Buddy Saunders, Howard Waldrop, and I sat around Buddy's living room, waiting for a funnel cloud to carry us off to Oz and passing the time by noodling on

Buddy's typewriter. Someone would write an opening paragraph or page, then someone else would take over. The game is called "Can You Top This?" and it's a party stunt beloved of fledgling writers. We couldn't do it now to save our lives—not so much because Time has slowed us down (ahem, harrumph) as because maturing writers inevitably form systems of work habits that are uniquely their own. Howard thinks his stories out from start to the end before he puts a word on paper, and is discombobulated when asked to make changes in work he regards as finished. I assemble mine like jigsaw puzzles, or Pangaea, or Frankenstein's Monster, hoping all the while that I shall be able to goose it to life, and that the sutures won't be too conspicuous.

But back to that afternoon at Buddy's: I have to rely on Howard's records, which he's kept all these years in the belief that somebody would eventually be interested in learning how what had been written was in fact written. Out of that session came a story by Buddy, Howard, and me, which we sold to *Vertex*; one by George, Howard, and me, which we sold to a men's magazine called *Adam*; one by Howard and me, which we sold to *Eternity SF* (which magazine then went out of business; Howard and I have ever since squabbled over credit for the kill); and, finally, another by Howard and me which Judy-Lynn del Rey used in her *Stellar Science Fiction Stories* anthology. Now, while "Willow Beeman" (which del Rey rechristened "Sic Transit. . . ? A Shaggy Hairless-Dog Story" was certainly the pick of the litter and I like it just fine for what it is, none of these efforts exactly qualified as Literature.

Still, everything considered: not a bad afternoon's work for four fresh-out-of-the-gate writers. Each of us came away from it confident that he had commercial talent. Marketable typing skills, at the very least.

Howard Waldrop is the multiple award winning author of "The Ugly Chickens" and about a hundred other stories, each one a gem. His latest collection is Horse of a Different Color, out from Small Beer Press. Howard has been inspired by Lafferty for several decades and has kept a model streetcar on his writing desk ever since reading "Interurban Queen." He was gracious enough to allow us to reprint "Willow Beeman" in celebration of R. A. Lafferty.

An Interview with R. A. Lafferty

by Tom Jackson

(This piece originally appeared in Lan's Lantern #39, *published by George Lankowski.)*

C.J. Cherryh is Oklahoma's most popular science fiction author, but R. A. Lafferty has the most tenacious cult following. We Lafferty fans have been waiting for years for the literary world outside SF to discover Lafferty and make him wealthy and famous. We're still waiting, but our loyalty has persuaded several small presses to come out with previously unpublished novels and short story collections in recent years despite the fact that Lafferty has virtually ceased writing.

Lafferty was born November 7, 1914, in Neola Iowa, but has lived in Tulsa, Oklahoma, since age four, with the exception of a stint in the South Pacific during World War II. Lafferty published his first story in 1959; his first SF story was published in 1960. His short story "Eurema's Dam" won the Hugo Award in 1973, in a tie with Frederik Pohl's and Cyril Kornbluth's "The Meeting." Lafferty's work is noted for its humor, imagination and originality; much of it seems much more akin to magic realism than traditional science fiction. Many of his stories are set in Tulsa or northeast Oklahoma.

Lafferty tends to be a shy man of few words when interviewed in person; I chose to interview him by sending questions in the mail.

Tom Jackson: What are some of your short stories and novels that you especially like? Are there any which you think have been overlooked?

R. A. Lafferty: Short stories of mine that I particularly like are "Selenium Ghosts of the 1870s," "You Can't Go Back," "Continued on Next Rock," "All Pieces of a River Shore," "Narrow Valley," "Configuration of the North Shore," "Golden Gage," "Old Foot

Forgot," "Rainbird," "Faith Sufficient," "Bird-Master," "One-Eyed Mockingbird," "Great Tom Fool or the Conundrum of the Calais Custom-House Coffers," and "Snuffles."

Novels of mine that I particularly like are *Okla Hannali, The Fall of Rome, Half a Sky, Archipelago* (none of these four are science fiction), *Past Master, Reefs of Earth, Space Chantey, Fourth Mansions, Arrive at Easterwine,* and *The Three Armageddons of Enniscorthy Sweeny.*" The most overlooked of the novels is *The Three Armageddons.* It was published as the second novel of a two-novel book called *Apocalypses,* and it may have been that many readers stopped after the first novel and never got back to the second one. The most neglected of my favorite short stories is "Bird-Master." The reason for this is probably that it was published in a Chris Drumm booklet that maybe reached 500 readers, whereas many of the other stories published in magazines reached one hundred times as many readers.

Tom Jackson: Have some of your novels been inspired by books of theology or philosophy? Haven't some of your novels been inspired by the works of writers such as Thomas Aquinas and St. Teresa of Avila?

R. A. Lafferty: Several of my novels have counterparts to specific works of theology, yes. The book *Aurelia* (Donning-Starblaze Books, 1982) has parallels with the *Summa Theologica* of Thomas Aquinas. The fourteen-year-old girl student Aurelia (in the bottom half of her classes) is completing her tenth form schooling, The last item of her tenth form is "World Government" in which the students must literally go out from their "Golden World cultus" to an inferior world and take control of it and govern it for a period. If a student should fail to master and govern a world, that student would die, of course, and would also fail the course. Aurelia comes down (more by accident than competent navigation) on the world Gaea (sometimes confused with Earth.) There she quickly becomes a cult figure, believed by some to be a girl messiah. She does give striking and reasoned homilies or orations or sermons that make her sound a little like a messiah. In fact, they form a mini-outline of the great

(3011 double column pages in my edition) *Summa* of Aquinas. But it is only a coincidence that the balanced sanity of the "Golden World Cultus" of Aurelia's home world should parallel the *Summa* of the Angelic Doctor. Aurelia was no messiah, but she was a very nice girl, and I regret that my story line required her failure and death.

And then there is the book *Fourth Mansions* (Ace, 1969) which I worked into the context of *Las Morada* ("The Mansions") of Teresa of Avila (the English translation is usually called *The Interior Castle*.) There are seven sets of Mansions or steps to perfection, but the Fourth Mansions is the perilous step, the midpoints where the devil and his principalities counter-attack with all their fury. And that counter-attack, really the scenario of today's world, is the theme of my book.

Tom Jackson: I noticed that the ending of "Old Halloweens on the Guna Slopes" is different in the original magazine version from the reprints in your anthologies. Did you revise it after publication, or did the magazine editor change it? Have you made changes in other stories between first publication and reprinting in your anthologies? Have editors changed your stories very often?

R. A. Lafferty: I revised "Old Halloweens" after the first publication and before its printing in the anthology *Through Elegant Eyes: Austro and the Men Who Knew Everything*. I revised it to give a little more zoom to it, and no editor had anything to do with it. I have made minor changes in other of my stories between first printing and anthology printing, but editors haven't been involved. The only editor who changed many of my stories was Pohl, and none of his changes was fatal. He just had a fetish of leaving his mark on every story he edited.

Tom Jackson: Terry Carr bought several of your early books. What effect did he have on your writing? How much voice did he have in selecting which stories would be published in *Nine Hundred Grandmothers*, your first collection?

R. A. Lafferty: Terry Carr taught me that a story must begin with a bang. As a consequence, the first book of mine he edited and published, *Past Master*, has in its first paragraph:

> *[…] There was a clattering thunder in the street outside […] the clashing thunder of mechanical killers, raving and raging. They shook the building and were on the verge of pulling it down. They required the life and blood of one of the three men […] now […] within the minute.*

Well, maybe all stories don't have to begin with a bang, but all Terry Carr stories had to begin with a bang of some sort. Terry also told me that, 'You can lose a reader, completely and forever, in fifteen seconds. Never leave him even a fifteen-second interval without a hook to jerk him back.' Anything else Terry told me is contained in those two very good pieces of advice.

On *Nine Hundred Grandmothers*, Terry gave me his preferences of the stories to go in the book, and asked me if I wanted to make any changes. They were all good stories, and I didn't make any changes.

Tom Jackson: Who are your favorite editors? Who do you think have been the most perceptive critics of your work?

R. A. Lafferty: My favorite editors were Horace Gold of *Galaxy*, Terry Carr of Ace and of his *Universe* series, and Damon Knight with his *Orbit* series. They are my favorite editors because they bought more of my stories than any other editors did. I guess it's a quirk of my make-up that I remember the least perceptive of my critics (those who panned me) more than the most perceptive of my critics (those who praised me.) The least perceptive of my panners were James Blish, Christopher Priest (in England), Thomas Monteleone and Spider Robinson. I got back at the Spider a tad in an obscure booklet (*True Believers* by United Mythologies Press) with the stanza:

He cannot write nor yet apprize,
He ladles with a rusty ladle,
He's neither talented nor wise.

But spider bites are seldom fadle.

Tom Jackson: What was it like winning the Hugo Award for "Eurema's Dam"? What effect did it have on your career?

R. A. Lafferty: Winning the Hugo Award for "Eurema's Dam" puzzled me completely, and I'm still puzzled by it. It was a pleasant little story, but I had four or five better stories published that year. And moreover it was tied by a story by Fred Pohl, which out of common decency I will not name, which was one of the worst stories ever written by anybody, anywhere. Still, I was glad to have a Hugo. I don't believe it had much effect on my career. I think the effect of Hugos is greatly exaggerated. And I've heard four or five different writers express puzzlement over winning Hugos with stories that were pretty ordinary and being passed over on stories which they really believed were earth-shaking.

Tom Jackson: Chris Drumm's *R. A. Lafferty Checklist* indicates that you published four stories in 1972: "Eurema's Dam," Rang Dang Kaloof," "Dorg" and "A Special Condition in Summit City." Can you clarify which stories you thought were better than "Eurema's Dam"?

R.A Lafferty: My memory was confused about stories published in 1972, and about everything else of 1972, which was probably the worst year of my life. I was sick that year, and I did not write anything at all in 1972. Some good things were published that year (*Okla Hannali*, for instance), but they were written and sold earlier. I had only one short story published for the first time that year, other than those you name. "Once on Aranea," in the book *Strange Doings*, had never been published before. But it and "A Special Condition in Summit City" were my only stories published that year that were better than anything. What I had in mind, I guess, was the spate of really good stories which I had published in 1970 and 1971, the best run of good stories I ever did, that didn't attract any notice at all. Seventeen of them, in that two-year period, were quite a bit better than "Eurema's Dam," and were better than almost anything else around: "Ride a Tin Can," "About a Secret Crocodile," "Been a Long Long Time," "Entire and Perfect Chrysolite," "Continued on Next Rock," "Old Foot Forgot," "All Pieces of a River Shore," "Interurban Queen," "Frog on the Mountain," "The Man Underneath," "Incased in Ancient Rind," "Boomer Flats," "Bubbles When They Burst," "Groaning Hinges of the World," "Ishmael Into the Barrens," "Nor Limestone Islands," and "Sky."

"Eurema's Dam" (which was written in 1964 and bounced around to all the markets) simply wasn't in it with this group, although it was a nice little comic story. I cancelled out on the 1972 Worldcon in Los Angeles, although I had fallen in love with the Worldcons with my first two (St. Louis in 1969, and Boston in 1971), but I wasn't able to travel in 1972. When I began to write again in 1973 I gradually began to write some pretty good stories again: "And Walk Now Gently Through the Fire," "Mud Violet," "The World As Will and Wallpaper," "By the Sea Shore," but I never again put together a consistent string of superior stories as I had done in 1970 and 1971. At the Toronto Worldcon in 1973, which gave the awards on stories published in 1972, I was well again, and felt it ironic that I had won a Hugo for "Eurema's Dam."

Tom Jackson: Do you read much science fiction these days? Did you ever read much? Are there any current SF writers you especially like?

R. A. Lafferty: No, I don't reach much science fiction these days. I never did read very much except for a four month period when I read several hundred of what were supposed to be the best science fiction books ever. This was when I first decided to major in science fiction, as it was selling for me and other things weren't. Well, it was a good crash course, and I was glad that I absorbed it. And I read quite a bit of science fiction during several of the golden ages or "little golden ages." But the present time is not a "little golden age" and I do not read much science fiction.

Of the current SF writers I probably like Gene Wolfe the best. And Gregory Benford, David Brin, Greg Bear (the three busy bees),

John Shirley (I don't like his opinions or the movements he attaches himself to, but he can write), Madeleine L'Engle, Robert Bloch (he's been doing it for more than 50 years, but he's still good), James Hogan (I think of him as a young writer, but he's forty-eight), Michael Bishop, Ed Bryant. And Ray Bradbury who is still at the top of whatever it is that he writes. I have no idea why so many writers on this short list have names beginning with "B." I had nothing to do with naming them.

Tom Jackson: Do you think you should be getting more attention from mainstream book reviewers?

R. A. Lafferty: No, I don't think I should be getting more attention from mainstream book reviewers. I've never written any mainstream books, and I'm always surprised when the mainstreamers notice me at all.

Tom Jackson: What do you think of the artwork publishers have put on your books? Are there any book covers you especially loved or hated?

R. A. Lafferty: The only covers of my books I really hated were those on *Arrive at Easterwine* (Ballantine Books, 1971) and on *East of Laughter* (Morrigan Publishing, 1988). One I especially liked was on *The Devil Is Dead* (Avon Books, 1971).

Tom Jackson: I liked the cover for *The Devil Is Dead* too, but I couldn't tell by looking at the book who the cover artist was. Can you help me?

R. A. Lafferty: No, I don't know who was the artist of the cover of *The Devil Is Dead*. I have wondered, too, but I never found out.

Tom Jackson: Is Bertigrew Bagley in the novel *Fourth Mansions* a self-portrait of yourself?

R. A. Lafferty: No, Bertigrew Bagley, the Patrick of Tulsa, is not a self-portrait, consciously at least. But quite a few people have asked me if he wasn't myself, so I must have some resemblance at least to that shabby old bum.

Tom Jackson: Some of your stories include dream sequences. Would you describe some of your writing as Surrealist?

R. A. Lafferty: I don't regard myself as a Surrealist in the sense of the "Surrealist Manifesto" published by Andre Breton in 1924. To me, that Manifesto is somewhat dated, being a recoil from World War I, and being too heavily Freudian. My own unconscious is more Jungian than Freudian. But if Breton hadn't staked claim to the name, I would probably call myself a Surrealist in the "Remembrance of Things Within" sense, but not in the "world of dream and fantasy joined to the everyday rational world, becoming 'an absolute reality, a surreality'." I suppose that I believe in another sort of a surreality or super-reality, but it would have to be on a wider basis than the encounters of myself and me. As often as not, it is the subconscious that supplies the rational element, and the exterior world that supplies the dream and fantasy feeling.

Tom Jackson: Is it true that you have retired from writing? When a baseball player retires, he is usually asked what his biggest thrill was. What's been your biggest thrill as a writer?

R. A. Lafferty: Yes, it's true that I've been retired from writing, except for a little bit of revision when old and unsold books finally push themselves into the "accepted" category.

Yes, when a baseball player retires he is usually asked what his biggest thrill was. But most of them are uncomfortable with the question, unless they have won the seventh game of a World Series with a homer. And I've never done that. I am reasonably happy with what I have written and with the reception it has had. But I can't think of any work or event that makes it to the "greatest thrill" category. It's a little bit like asking a man who has loved his breakfast eggs for 60 years to name the most thrilling egg he ever ate. He might hesitate a bit and come out with something no better than:

"Oh, there was a really superior egg on June 9 of 1932, and another on Feb. 8 of 1947. And in 1951 (it was either April 4 or April 5) I had two absolutely perfect eggs. But no, it would be presumptuous of me to name the most thrilling egg I ever ate. They were all so good!"

Tom Jackson has worked as a newspaper reporter in Oklahoma and Ohio and currently writes for the Sandusky Register. He is a longtime science fiction fan. He blogs at http://RAWIllumination.net and at the Sandusky Register newspaper's Jackson Street Book Club.

Sodom and Gomorrah, Texas
By R. A. Lafferty

The place called Sodom was bad enough. But right down the road was the other town—and that was even worse!

Manuel shouldn't have been employed as a census taker. He wasn't qualified. He couldn't read a map. He didn't know what a map was. He only grinned when they told him that North was at the top.

He knew better.

But he did write a nice round hand, like a boy's hand. He knew Spanish, and enough English. For the sector that was assigned to him he would not need a map. He knew it better than anyone else, certainly better than any mapmaker. Besides, he was poor and needed the money.

They instructed him and sent him out. Or they thought that they had instructed him. They couldn't be sure.

"Count everyone? All right. Fill in everyone? I need more papers."

"We will give you more if you need more. But there aren't so many in your sector."

"Lots of them. *Lobos, tejones, zorros,* even people."

"Only the *people,* Manuel! Do not take the animals. How would you write up the animals? They have no names."

"Oh, yes. All have names. Might as well take them all."

"Only people, Manuel."

"*Mulos?*"

"No."

"*Conejos?*"

"No, Manuel, no. Only the people."

"No trouble. Might as well take them all."

"Only people—God give me strength!—only people, Manuel."

"How about little people?"

"Children, yes. That has been explained to you."

"*Little* people. Not children, little people."

"If they are people, take them."

"How big they have to be?"

"It doesn't make any difference how big they are. If they are people, take them."

That is where the damage was done.

The official had given a snap judgement, and it led to disaster. It was not his fault. The instructions are not clear. Nowhere in all the verbiage does it say how big they have to be to be counted as people.

Manuel took Mula and went to work. His sector was the Santa Magdalena, a scrap of bald-headed and desolate mountains, steep but not high, and so torrid in the afternoons that it was said that the old lava sometimes began to writhe and flow again from the sun's heat alone.

In the center valley there were five thousand acres of slag and vitrified rock from some forgotten old blast that had melted the hills and destroyed their mantle, reducing all to a terrible flatness. This was called Sodom. It was strewn with low-lying ghosts as of people and objects, formed when the granite bubbled like water.

Away from the dead center the ravines were body-deep in chaparral, and the hillsides stood gray-green with old cactus. The stunted trees were lower than the giant bushes and yucca.

Manuel went with Mula, a round easy man and a sparse gaunt mule. Mula was a mule, but there were other inhabitants of the Santa Magdalena of a genus less certain.

Yet even about Mula there was an oddity in her ancestry. Her paternal grandfather had been a goat. Manuel once told Mr. Marshal about this, but Mr. Marshal had not accepted it.

"She is a mule. Therefore, her father was a jack. Therefore his father was also a jack, a donkey. It could not be any other way."

Manuel often wondered about that, for he had raised the whole strain of animals, and he remembered who had been with whom.

"A donkey! A jack! Two feet tall and with a beard and horns. I always thought that he was a goat."

Manuel and Mula stopped at noon on Lost Soul Creek. There

would be no travel in the hot afternoon. But Manuel had a job to do, and he did it. He took the forms from one of the packs that he had unslung from Mula, and counted out nine of them. He wrote down all the data on nine people. He knew all there was to know about them, their nativities and their antecedents. He knew that there were only nine regular people in the nine hundred square miles of the Santa Magdalena.

But he was systematic, so he checked the list over again and again. There seemed to be somebody missing. Oh, yes, himself. He got another form and filled out all the data on himself.

Now, in one way of looking at it, his part in the census was finished. If only he had looked at it that way, he would have saved worry and trouble for everyone, and also ten thousand lives. But the instructions they had given him were ambiguous, for all that they had tried to make them clear.

So very early the next morning he rose and cooked beans, and said, "Might as well take them all."

He called Mula from the thorn patch where she was grazing, gave her salt and loaded her again. Then they went to take the rest of the census, but in fear. There was a clear duty to get the job done, but there was also a dread of it that his superiors did not understand. There was reason also why Mula was loaded so she could hardly walk with packs of census forms.

Manuel prayed out loud as they climbed the purgatorial scarp above Lost Souls Creek, "*ruega por nosotros pecadores ahora*"—the very gulches stood angry and stark in the early morning—"*y en la hora de neustra muerte.*"

Three days later an incredible dwarf staggered into the outskirts of High Plains, Texas, followed by a dying wolf-sized animal that did not look like a wolf.

A lady called the police to save the pair from rock-throwing kids who might have killed them, and the two as yet unclassified things were taken to the station house.

The dwarf was three foot high, a skeleton stretched over with brown-burnt leather. The other was an un-canine looking dog-sized beast, so full of burrs and thorns that it might have been a porcupine. It was a nightmare replica of a shrunken mule.

The midget was mad. The animal had more presence of mind: she lay down quietly and died, which was the best she could do, considering the state that she was in.

"Who is census chief now?" asked the mad midget. "Is Mr. Marshal's boy the census chief?"

"Mr. Marshal is, yes. Who are you? How do you know Marshal? And what is that which you are pulling out of your pants, if they are pants?"

"Census list. Names of everybody in the Santa Magdalena. I had to steal it."

"It looks like microfilm, the writing is so small. And the roll goes on and on. There must be a million names here."

"Little bit more, little bit more. I get two bits a name."

They got Marshal there. He was very busy, but he came. He had been given a deadline by the mayor and the citizen's group. He had to produce a population of ten thousand people for High Plains, Texas; and this was difficult, for there weren't that many people in the town. He had been working hard on it, though; but he came when the police called him.

"You Marshal's little boy? You look just like your father," said the midget.

"That voice, I should know that voice even if it's cracked to pieces. That has to be Manuel's voice."

"Sure, I'm Manuel. Just like I left, thirty-five years ago."

"You can't be Manuel, shrunk three feet and two hundred pounds and aged a million."

"You look here at my census slip. It says I'm Manuel. And here are nine more of the regular people, and one million of the little people. I couldn't get them on the right forms, though. I had to steal their list."

"You can't be Manuel," said Marshal.

"He can't be Manuel," said the big policemen and the little policeman.

"Maybe not, then," the dwarf conceded. "I thought I was, but

I wasn't sure. Who am I then? Let's look at the other papers and see which one I am."

"No, you can't be any of them either, Manuel. And you surely can't be Manuel."

"Give him a name anyhow and get him counted. We got to get to that ten thousand mark."

"Tell us what happened, Manuel—if you are. Which you aren't. But tell us."

"After I counted the regular people I went to count the little people. I took a spade and spaded off the top of their town to get in. But they put an *encanto* on me, and made me and Mula run a treadmill for thirty-five years."

"Where was this?"

"At the little people town. Nuevo Danae. But after thirty-five years the *encanto* wore off and Mula and I stole the list of names and ran away."

"But where did you really get this list of so many names written so small?"

"Suffering saddle sores, Marshal, don't ask the little bug so many questions. You got a million names in your hand. Certify them! Send them in! There's enough of us here right now. We declare that place annexed forthwith. This will make High Plains the biggest town in the whole state of Texas."

So Marshal certified them and sent them into Washington. This gave High Plains the largest percentage increase of any city in the nation, but it was challenged. There were some soreheads in Houston who said that it wasn't possible. They said High Plains had nowhere near that many people and there must have been a miscount.

And in the days that the argument was going on, they cleaned up and fed Manuel, if it were he, and tried to get from him a cogent story.

"How do you know it was thirty-five years you were on the treadmill, Manuel?"

"Well, it seemed like thirty-five years."

"It could have only been about three days."

"Then how come I'm so old?"

"We don't know that, Manuel, we sure don't know that. How big were these people?"

"Who knows? A finger long, maybe two?"

"And what is their town?"

"It is an old prairie-dog town that they fixed up. You have to dig down with a spade to get to the streets."

"Maybe they were really all prairie dogs, Manuel. Maybe the heat got you and you only dreamed that they were little people."

"Prairie dogs can't write as good as on that list. Prairie dogs can't write hardly at all."

"That's true. The list is hard to explain. And such odd names on it too."

"Where is Mula? I don't see Mula since I came back."

"Mula just lay down and died, Manuel."

"Gave me the slip. Why didn't I think of that? Well, I'll do it too. I'm too worn out for anything else."

"Before you do, Manuel, just a couple of last questions."

"Make them real fast then. I'm on my way."

"Did you know these little people were there before?"

"Oh, sure. There a long time."

"Did anybody else ever see them?"

"Oh, sure. Everybody in the Santa Magdalena see them. Eight, nine people see them."

"And Manuel, how do we get to the place? Can you show us on a map?"

Manuel made a grimace, and died quietly as Mula had done. He didn't understand those maps at all, and took the easy way out.

They buried him, not knowing for sure whether he was Manuel come back, or what he was.

There wasn't much of him to bury.

It was the same night, very late and after he had been asleep, that Marshal was awakened by the ring of an authoritative voice. He was being harangued by a four-inch tall man on his bedside table, a man of dominating presence and acid voice.

"Come out of that cot, you clown! Give me your name and station!"

"I'm Marshal, and I suspect that you are a late pig sandwich, or caused by one. I shouldn't eat so late."

"Say 'sir' when you reply to me. I am no pig sandwich and I do not commonly call on fools. Get on your feet, you clod."

And wonderingly Marshal did.

"I want the list that was stolen. Don't gape! Get it!"

"What list?"

"Don't stall, don't stutter. Get me our tax list that was stolen. It isn't words that I want from you."

"Listen, you cicada, I'll take you and—"

"You will not. You will notice that you are paralyzed from the neck down. I suspect that you were always so from there up. Where is the list?"

"S-sent it to Washington."

"You bug-eyed behemoth! Do you realize what a trip that will be? You grandfather of inanities, it will be a pleasure to destroy you!"

"I don't know what you are, or if you are really. I don't believe that you even belong on the world."

"Not belong on the world! We own the world. We can show written title to the world. Can you?"

"I doubt it. Where did you get the title?"

"None of your business. I'd rather not say. Oh, well, we got it from a promoter of sorts. A con man, really. I'll have to admit that we were taken, but we were in a spot and needed a world. He said that the larger bifurcates were too stupid to be a nuisance. We should have known that the stupider a creature, the more of a nuisance it is."

"I had about decided the same thing about the smaller a creature. We may have to fumigate that old mountain mess."

"Oh, you can't harm us. We're too powerful. But we can obliterate you in an instant."

"Hah!"

"Say 'Hah, *sir*' when you address me. Do you know the place in the mountain that is called Sodom?"

"I know the place. It was caused by a large meteor."

"It was caused by one of these."

What he held up was the size of a grain of sand. Marshal could not see it in detail.

"There was another city of you bug-eyed beasts there," said the small martinet. "You wouldn't know about it. It's been a few hundred years. We decided it was too close. Now I have decided that you are too close."

"A thing that size couldn't crack a walnut."

"You floundering fop, it will blast this town flat!"

"What will happen to you?"

"Nothing. I don't even blink for things like that."

"How do you trigger it off?"

"You gaping goof, I don't have time to explain that to you. I have to get to Washington."

It may be that Marshal did not believe himself quite awake. He certainly did not take the threat seriously enough. For the little man did trigger it off.

When the final count was in, High Plains did not have the highest percentage gain in population in the nation. Actually it showed the sharpest decline, from 7313 to nothing.

They were going to make a forest preserve out of the place, except that it has no trees worthy of the name. Now it is proposed to make it the Sodom and Gomorrah State Park from the two mysterious scenes of desolation there, just seven miles apart.

It is an interesting place, as wild a region as you will ever find, and is recommended for the man who has seen everything.

—R. A. LAFFERTY

Contributors

Editor: Kevin Cheek

Publisher: John Owen

Copyrights and Permissions: Kevin Cheek, John Owen, Daniel Otto Jack Petersen, Rich Persaud

Layout and Design: Noah Wareness, Rich Persaud

Proofreading: Gregorio Montejo, John Owen, Rich Persaud, Daniel Otto Jack Petersen, Noah Wareness

Cover Art and Photography: Lissanne Lake, Keith Purtell, Anthony Rhodes

Historical Documents: Ned Brooks, Nat!

Essays: David Barnett, Clinton R. Claussen, Greg Ketter, Dan Knight, John Ellison, Kenji Matsuzaki, Craig May, Patrick May, Gregorio Montejo, John Owen, Rich Persaud, Daniel Otto Jack Petersen, Anne Lake Prescott, Peter Sijbenga, Sergei Sobolev, Yakov Varganov

Introductions and Afterwords: Robert Whitaker Sirignano, Michael Swanwick, Steven Utley, Howard Waldrop

Reviews: Stephen R. Case, Kevin Cheek, Andrew Ferguson, Martin Heavisides, Keith Purtell, Heywood Reynolds, Darrell Schweitzer, Don Webb

Interviews: Kevin Cheek, Tom Jackson

Music, Artwork and Poetry: Vladimir Anikin, Anonymous, Logan Giannini, Bill Rogers, Peter Sijbenga, Noah Wareness, Natalya Zatulovskaya

Fiction: Stephen Case, R. A. Lafferty, Daniel Otto Jack Petersen, Steven Utley, Howard Waldrop